To Barbara –
Reality's thinking!
Warmly
[signature]

Strategies
That Work

Teaching Comprehension
to Enhance Understanding

Stephanie Harvey • Anne Goudvis
Foreword by Donald Graves

Stenhouse Publishers
Portland, Maine

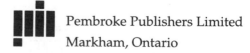

Pembroke Publishers Limited
Markham, Ontario

Stenhouse Publishers
www.stenhouse.com

Credits
Cover: "Floyd's Fury." Copyright © 1999. TIME FOR KIDS (September 24). TIME FOR KIDS is a registered trademark of Time Inc.
  Up North at the Cabin by Marsha Wilson Chall. Copyright © 1992. Lothrop, Lee & Shepard. Shown by permission.
  Permission for all other books generously given by Boyds Mills Press.
Pages 44–45: "This Is Cruising" by Kevin Keating. Copyright © 1998. *Hemispheres Magazine,* March. Reprinted courtesy of *Hemispheres,* the magazine of United Airlines.
Page 133: From *Exploring the Titanic* by Robert Ballard. Copyright © 1988 by The Odyssey Corp. Copyright © 1997 by Scholastic Inc. Reprinted by permission of Scholastic Inc.
Page 138: "Should Cities Sue Gunmakers?" from *Junior Scholastic,* February 8, 1999 issue. Copyright © 1999 by Scholastic Inc. Reprinted by permission of Scholastic, Inc.
Page 148: "In Sickness and in Health." Copyright © 1999. *Kids Discover Magazine,* April.
Pages 160–161: "Moonstruck Scientists Count 63 and Rising" by Robert S. Boyd. Copyright © 1999. *Denver Post.* Reprinted with permission of Knight Ridder/Tribune Information Services.
Pages 293–294: From *My Freedom Trip* by Frances Park and Ginger Park. Copyright © 1998. Boyds Mills Press. Reprinted by permission.

Library of Congress Cataloging-in-Publication Data
Harvey, Stephanie.
    Strategies that work : teaching comprehension to enhance understanding / Stephanie Harvey and Anne Goudvis.
        p.   cm.
    Includes bibliographical references.
    ISBN 1-57110-310-4
    1. Reading comprehension. 2. Reading (Elementary) 3. Thought and thinking—Study and teaching (Elementary) 4. Children—Books and reading. I. Goudvis, Anne. II. Title.
LB1573.7 .H37 2000
372.47—dc21   99-057373

Published in Canada by
Pembroke Publishers Limited
538 Hood Road
Markham, Ontario L3R 3K9

Cover design by Richard Hannus, Hannus Design Associates
Cover photography by Andrew Edgar

Manufactured in the United States of America on acid-free paper
07 06 05 04 03 02   20 19 18 17 16 15 14 13

Contents

List of Strategy Lessons

Making Connections

Questioning

Visualizing

Inferring

Determining Importance

Synthesizing

When I was in elementary school I might have been categorized as a "dreamer reader." I remember reading *T Model Tommy*, by Stephen W. Meader, when I was in sixth grade. As I recall, the book was about a young enterprising boy who parlayed owning a small truck into a growing business enterprise. I immediately wanted to live the life of Tommy and start my own business. I read along, living through the characters, and would soon be lost in a reverie that had little to do with the text at hand.

When I came to my reading group, however, I lacked precision in answering precise questions about the text. For most of my life I've viewed myself as a defective reader. In one sense I was a problem reader, since I couldn't match my meaning with the original text required for discussion. I needed teachers who had read this book by Stephanie Harvey and Anne Goudvis.

Strategies That Work taps into the urge of all children to make sense of the world around them through reading. The authors make complicated theories of comprehension accessible to teachers. They never diverge from their focus of showing what reading is for along with the strategies of how to make connections between texts, lives, learning to read fiction, nonfiction, and all the genres. Each strategy is designed to open up new worlds for the child. In this case, reading is for living, a lifetime of enjoyment, and significant intellectual engagement with a fascinating world through people and books.

This is a book written by readers, for teachers of reading, whose children will become readers. The authors' enthusiasm leaps off the page as they demonstrate their own strategies for reading through actual books and texts. Several of the books they use in the strategy lessons appealed to me, and I started a list of these titles. The list exploded when I reached the wonderful resource section. Be prepared to have pencil and paper handy to jot down titles of must-read books. You're going to need them!

While reading *Strategies* I was struck by how distant most texts about teaching reading are from the act of reading itself. Other texts are steeped in comprehension strategies and skill lessons but rarely show the author in action with specific texts in the classroom. Our authors never get off the subject of showing how they think when they read with real texts so that teachers and children can do the same. Written and spoken examples of student thinking fill this book. This evidence of student thinking informs and guides the instruction in *Strategies That Work*.

We can't tell children how to read; we simply have to show them. We learn with the authors how to show children to make connections, synthesize, and approach new genres. The authors teach reading from the inside out. That is, they are already in the middle of reading a book by sharing the love of the book, how to read it, and how to develop lifetime strategies. I think of David McCulloch's statement that when he was teaching history at Cornell he was not satisfied until each student had fallen in love with history. He soon realized that unless the student was on a quest to discover some aspect of history that meant something to her, she wouldn't fall in love with the subject. Our authors show both teachers and children coming inside the process and developing a love affair with books.

Donald Graves

Acknowledgments

The process of reading is not a half sleep, but in highest sense, an exercise, a gymnast's struggle: that the reader is to do something for him or herself, must be on the alert, must construct indeed the poem, argument, history, metaphysical essay—the text furnishing the hints, the clue, the start, the framework.

Walt Whitman

We wrote this book to grapple with that jungle gym of thoughts, words, and ideas that make up reading. We are insatiably interested in kids' thinking. We love to hear what kids think about their reading—their questions, reactions, interpretations, opinions, inferences, arguments, and celebrations. Much of what we have learned about teaching reading comes from our conversations with children as we read along with them and talk about their reading and their lives. And so we thank them first, all of the children with whom we have worked and from whom we have learned so much. They are our inspiration. Listening to their insightful comments and reading their work has made those all-day Friday revision sessions worthwhile.

For the past dozen years, we have worked as reading and writing staff developers both in private practice and for the Denver-based Public Education and Business Coalition. The PEBC is a nonprofit group dedicated to providing private-sector support to public schools, both urban and suburban, in the metro Denver area. The PEBC staff development model allows us to work alongside teachers and librarians in their rooms and libraries for an extended period of time.

About ten years ago, reading comprehension instruction became a primary focus of our staff development. As we worked with educators in Denver and across the country, many told us that although most of their students could read the words in the texts, they didn't seem to understand what they read. Additionally, they didn't seem to linger in books or spend much time reading. Above all, these teachers wanted their students to love reading, yet reading didn't seem to engage enough of their kids.

Along with our colleagues at the PEBC and many fine teachers, we began to explore the research on reading comprehension. We looked closely at the work of P. David Pearson, Jan Dole, and others for guidance in how to best teach reading comprehension strategies to young readers. In the 1980s reading researchers distilled a group of reading strategies that proficient readers use to build meaning and comprehend text. We thank those many comprehension theorists upon whose shoulders our work rests.

The PEBC developed a reading comprehension project that translated these research findings into educational practice. We owe a debt of gratitude to everyone at the PEBC. Thanks to Ellin Keene, who believed in the power of these comprehension strategies and always reminded us to think about our own process as readers first. Also to Susan Zimmermann, founder of the PEBC, who, with Ellin, wrote a seminal book on reading comprehension called *Mosaic of Thought: Teaching Comprehension in a Reader's Workshop*. To Barb Volpe, the executive director of the PEBC, who has always been there to support our efforts. To our friend and original PEBC staff developer, Liz Stedem, who spent countless hours researching books old and new to include in our lengthy appendixes. To Debbie Miller, a first-grade teacher and PEBC staff developer, who has taken comprehension instruction further than anyone we know. To Cris Tovani, who moved from first grade to high school and courageously teaches reading comprehension to reluctant ninth graders as well as twelfth-grade World Lit students. To Fran Jenner, librarian extraordinaire, who has taught us so much about children's literature. To Jonathan Bender, our technology wizard, who brought a fresh and thoughtful perspective to two women old enough to be his mother. To Chryse Hutchins, who never ceases to amaze us with her ability to inspire teachers to become learners. To Mary Urtz, intermediate teacher and PEBC staff developer, who has taken nonfiction strategy instruction to new heights. To Laura Benson, who long ago shared with us her ideas for implementing strategy instruction. And to the PEBC staff developers with whom we work most closely, Dee Bench, Bobbie Benson, Kathy Haller, Judy Hendricks, Ilana Spiegel, Kristin Venable, and Cheryl Zimmerman. Thanks to all of you for your thoughtful insights.

We each began our teaching careers in the classroom and to this day we are teachers, first and foremost. Steph taught elementary and special education for fifteen years in the Jefferson County Schools in Lakewood, Colorado. Anne taught for ten years in Chicago schools as well as in Montessori schools in both Illinois and Colorado. We honor all teachers. We know how hard they work and we applaud them. We owe a tremendous debt to the teachers and librarians in this book who welcomed us into their rich rooms to study reading comprehension strategy instruction.

These thoughtful educators create rooms that breathe literacy. Books abound. Children choose their own. Comfortable surroundings are the norm. A grateful thanks to Kelly Daggett, first-grade teacher, who artfully crafted the strategy charts in Appendix F. Many thanks to Nell Box, who thoughtfully summarized a number of periodicals and Web sites and provided a list of publications that are of great use for book selection and curricular connections. A huge thank you to Eleanor Wright, who spent months talking with her children about the impact of comprehension instruction on their thinking, including two weeks in the summer after school was out! Many of their responses fill this book. Thank you, also, to Leslie Blauman, Margaret Bobb, Tiffany Boyd, Jane Brunot, Nancy Burton, Angie Carey,

Glenda Clearwater, Debbie Deem, Tim Downing, Anne Ertman, Jeanine Gordon, David Harris, Jacqueline Heibert, Kathy Higgins, Paige Inman, Sharon Ivie, Jennifer Jones, Sue Kempton, Joe Kolodziej, Mary Lawlor, Monica Marucheau, Michelle Meyer, Carla Mosher, Gloria Mundel, Barbara Munizza, Carol Newman, Melissa Oviatt, Susan Prentiss, David Shinkle, Barb Smith, Kristi Sutherland, Paula Windham, and Kim Worsham. We couldn't have written this book without you.

We want to express our thanks to our mentors and colleagues around the country. To Don Graves, who continually challenges us to question our thinking and practice and learn from the kids. To Shelley Harwayne, who always enlightens us whenever we call. To Joanne Hindley and Judy Davis, who welcome us with open arms whenever we come to their classrooms in the most extraordinary of school communities, the Manhattan New School. To Meg Gallagher, our friend and colleague, from whom we've learned so much about instruction. To Kelly Chandler and Brenda Power, whose careful reading and constructive comments on the manuscript always kept us on track.

Many thanks to Stenhouse Publishers. First, to our editor and friend Philippa Stratton, who despite the book's burgeoning word count maintained a sense of humor and provided us with the moxie to go on. Thanks also to Tom Seavey and Martha Drury for their constant attention.

We can't believe we wrote this book while chasing and chauffeuring four teenagers around Denver and Boulder. Anne thanks her husband, David Johnson, for willingly helping with computer snafus at any time, night or day. She couldn't have written this without him. She thanks her children, Kai and Allison, for all of their wonderful distractions. They rose to the occasion by getting off the computer without question whenever she asked and by answering her endless requests to read a book and tell her what they thought of it. Steph once again has her kids, Alex and Jessica, to thank for being the great kids they are and for leaving her alone to write. The truth is, after she finished the last book, they couldn't wait for her to get back at it so she'd quit bugging them all the time. And although her husband, Edward, did not read the drafts this time, he did come down and haul her out of the office for a bite to eat now and then, for which she thanks him immeasurably.

Our collaboration was a source of joy that went off without a hitch. No one would believe it, but we never had a cross word. We high-fived our way through the book and learned that two heads really are better than one.

This book is truly our homage to thinking. Schools need to be havens for thinking, classrooms incubators for deep thought. Thinking thrives when readers connect to books and to each other. We hope kids' thinking shines through here.

To thoughtful kids everywhere, especially our own.

The Foundation of Meaning

Books are the means to immortality. Plato lives forever, as do Dickens, and Dr. Seuss, Soames Forsyte, Jo March, Scrooge, Anna Karenina and Vronsky. Over and over again Heathcliff wanders the moor searching for his Cathy. Over and over again Ahab fights the whale. Through them all we experience other times, other places, other lives. We manage to become much more than our own selves.
Anna Quindlen, *How Reading Changed My Life*

Books offer little without readers. Books need us—to wander with Heathcliff, to grimace with the Grinch, to learn with Scrooge. The chapters in Part I hover in that twilight area between reader and text, that elusive space where meaning takes shape and personal insight takes root.

These chapters attempt to fathom the mystery of reading that allows us to become more than ourselves. When the writer Annie Proulx won the Pulitzer prize for fiction with her novel *The Shipping News,* she stated simply, "The reader writes the story." The aim of the comprehension instruction and practice in this book is to help readers interact more completely with their reading, bringing themselves to the text to engage in a richer, deeper, more thoughtful reading experience.

A local Denver book club once had the pleasure of hosting the writer Sue Miller at a discussion of her novel *For Love.* The readers talked about the book and asked questions of the author. One of the participants had noticed a clothesline that was strung between two houses in the novel. She commented on the clever literary device that seemed to nicely symbolize a repaired relationship in the story. The author looked surprised. She didn't remember the clothesline and had not placed it there with any intent. But she thanked the reader and noted that it was an interesting interpretation that merited consideration. She herself had simply never thought of it.

For years, many English teachers concentrated their instruction on what has come to be called "author's intent." Their lectures focused on what the author meant to symbolize in Melville's great white whale, Frost's snowy woods, or Dickens's Madame LaFarge. Meaning is constructed in that realm where readers meet the words in the text and consider the ideas in terms of their own experience and knowledge. The author's creation stems as much from what readers bring to the text as from the author's own preconceived notions. More than anything, authors intend to capture readers and hold their attention throughout the book and beyond.

Chapters 1 and 2, "Strategic Thinking" and "Strategic Reading," explain how readers make meaning when they read and how they bring their own experience and prior knowledge to the text. These chapters explore the strategies readers use to comprehend the text and how readers monitor their own comprehension when reading. Chapter 3, "Strategy Instruction and Practice," elaborates on a number of instructional approaches and responses that teachers and kids use to better understand what they read. Chapter 4, "Teaching with Short Text," advocates the use of short text, such as picture books, articles, essays, and short stories, to teach reading comprehension. Teachers portrayed in this book use short text to introduce a comprehension strategy and then guide students to transfer the strategy to longer text later. Chapter 5, "Book Selection," describes how teachers choose books for comprehension instruction and how they help kids choose books to practice the strategies on their own. The first five chapters in this book provide the Foundation of Meaning upon which rest the Strategy Lessons in Part II.

Chapter

1 Strategic Thinking

Thirty sixth graders crowd onto a woven area rug in the reading corner. A brass floor lamp casts a warm, amber glow onto their faces. Steph takes a seat in the rocking chair in front of them. "Today, I am going to read you a picture book called *Up North at the Cabin,* by Marsha Wilson Chall. I wish I had written it. I'll tell you why. This book reminds me exactly of my own childhood. It is the story of a young girl about your age who left the city every summer to spend time in a cabin on a lake in Minnesota. Minnesota is called the land of ten thousand lakes. I grew up in the neighboring state of Wisconsin. We had our share of lakes, too," Steph tells them as she points out the location of these two upper-midwestern states on the wall map.

"Writers write best about things they know and care about," Steph says. She reads from the inside flap that the author spent her summers on northern lakes and was inspired by her own experience as a child and later on as a mother when she returned to this cabin with her own children. "I was a kid who loved summer," Steph says while a dozen heads nod in agreement. "Like the young girl in the book, I spent summers on a lake where we fished, swam, water-skied, hiked and canoed." Steph mentions how fortunate she feels that Marsha Chall wrote a book with which she identifies so closely. "Have you ever read a book that reminds you of your own life?" she asks. Hands wave wildly as kids share their favorites.

"*Koala Lou*" [Mem Fox 1988], Shelby blurts out. "I have a whole bunch of brothers and sisters and sometimes I get really jealous of them, just like Koala Lou did."

"*I Hate English*" [Levine 1989], Jen-Li chimes in. "I couldn't understand a word of English when I first came from Korea. School was really hard. I know exactly how that girl felt."

Steph points out that Shelby and Jen-Li have made a connection between books and their lives. "If we connect to a book, we usually can't put it down. Good readers make connections between the texts they read and

3

their own lives. Let's try something. I am going to read you *Up North at the Cabin*. As I read the words, I am going to show you the thinking that is going on in my head. I'll use these sticky notes to jot that thinking down and mark a connection. I'll mark the sticky note with the code T-S for text-to-self connection because it reminds me in some way of my own life and prior experience. Then I'll place the sticky note on the appropriate passage or picture. I'll let it stick out of the book a little, like a bookmark, so I can find it easily if I want to come back to it later on."

Steph reads through the book page by page sharing her thinking about waterskiing, the local bait shop, pruney fingers from too much swimming, and portaging canoes. She marks the text and illustrations with sticky notes coded T-S and jots down a few words such as, "Sometimes we even used peanut butter for bait when we ran out of night crawlers" or "Boy, was I mad when my dad made me carry that canoe."

When she comes to a page that shows the main character in an orange canvas life jacket with two white cotton closures, she laughs and stops to share a brief story. "I can't help but think of my mom when I see this orange life jacket. There were five of us kids, and we lived right on the edge of the water. When we were toddlers, my mom was wracked with worry that one of us might fall into the lake and drown. Her solution: the day we started to walk, she wrapped us in those orange life jackets. We wore them everywhere. We ate our cereal in them. We watched TV in them. Sometimes, we even slept in them. We looked like five little bulldozers!" Two kids in front grab the book to take a closer look at the tell-tale life jacket.

"How embarrassing," Josh murmurs.

"You'd better believe it. But I think my mom was onto something. We learned to swim quicker than any kids around just to get rid of those goofy life jackets!"

When Steph finishes reading out loud, she encourages kids to find a book they connect with and to use sticky notes to mark their text-to-self connections and jot down their thinking. We urge teachers to do the same. Find that book you relate to above all others, your connection book. Unless you are one of Steph's life jacket-bound siblings or a Wisconsin ice fisherman, it may not be *Up North at the Cabin*. Read it to your students, sharing your connections as you read. There is nothing more powerful than a literacy teacher sharing her passion for reading, writing, and thinking. Passion is contagious. Kids will respond.

The Reader Writes the Story

Reading out loud and showing the thinking readers do when they read is central to the instruction we share in this book. When we read, thoughts fill our mind. We might make connections to our own life, as Steph did. We might have a question or an inference. It is not enough to merely think these thoughts. Strategic readers address their thinking in an inner conversation that helps them make sense of what they read. They search for the answers to their questions. They attempt to better understand the text through their connections to the characters, the events, and the issues.

Readers take the written word and construct meaning based on their own thoughts, knowledge, and experiences. The reader *is* part writer. The novelist E. L. Doctorow says, "Any book you pick up, if it's good, is a printed circuit for your own life to flow through—so when you read a book, you are engaged in the events of the mind of the writer. You are bringing your own creative faculties into sync. You're imagining the words, the sounds of the words, and you are thinking of the various characters in terms of people you've known—not in terms of the writer's experience, but your own" (Plimpton 1988).

When readers interact with the texts they read, reading becomes important. Reading shapes and even changes thinking. Getting readers to think when they read, to develop an awareness of their thinking, and to use strategies that help them comprehend are the primary goals of the comprehension instruction outlined in this book.

Reading Is Thinking

When we walk into classrooms, we often begin by asking kids to describe reading for us. "What is reading?" we ask. A variety of answers bursts forth, and we record these on a chart. "Figuring out the words," "spelling the words," "knowing the letters" are common responses. Fourth grader DeCoven answered that "reading is thinking." He went on to explain that "when you read, you have to figure out the words and what they mean. Sometimes it's easy. Sometimes it's hard." DeCoven hit the target. He understood that reading is about more than decoding words.

Reading encompasses both decoding and the making of meaning. The first entry on the word *read* in *Webster's New World Dictionary* (1991) defines reading as "getting the meaning of something written by using the eyes to interpret its characters." We're inclined to add "by using the brain" to that definition. Reading demands a two-pronged attack. It involves cracking the alphabetic code to determine the words and thinking about those words to construct meaning. Of the many books currently in print on the subject, most deal with the decoding aspect of reading. This book focuses primarily on the thinking aspect of reading.

Ask your students to define reading. Keep a chart posted in the room with their responses. The nature of their answers may evolve as your class begins to explore thinking when reading and as you provide explicit instruction in reading strategies that help readers better understand what they read.

Why Teach Comprehension?

Teachers have never been under more pressure. Pressure to perform. Pressure to cover the curriculum. Pressure to ensure high scores on standardized tests. Pressure to meet standards. The political climate surrounding education is more demanding than ever before. Teachers are overwhelmed with state mandates, running records, and rubrics for every task. "I already have to teach kids to decode words, spell them, learn vocabulary, and respond in writing. And now you're asking me to teach one more thing?" is a common refrain.

The truth is, we sympathize. It has never been tougher to be a teacher. But after ten years of study and practice in reading comprehension, we are convinced that comprehension instruction is not just one more thing. In fact, when it comes to reading, it's likely the most important thing. If the purpose for reading is anything other than understanding, why read at all? Researchers Linda Fielding and P. David Pearson (1994) recently described the shift in our thinking about comprehension: "Once thought of as the natural result of decoding plus oral language, comprehension is now viewed as a much more complex process involving knowledge, experience, thinking, and teaching."

Why the shift? In 1979, Dolores Durkin jolted the reading world when she concluded, after hundreds of hours of observation in classrooms, that the questions in basal readers and on worksheets were the primary focus of comprehension instruction in classrooms. Teachers thought they were providing instruction in comprehension through the use of story questions. Durkin suggested that teachers were actually assessing students' literal understanding rather than teaching them specific strategies to better comprehend what they read.

What Strategies Should We Teach?

For many years educators studied struggling readers for clues about the best ways to teach reading. Research in reading comprehension took a different tack in the 1980s when researchers identified and systematically investigated the reading strategies that proficient readers used to understand what they read. Building on this work, researchers then explored ways to teach these strategies to children. Pearson et al. (1992) summarized the strategies that active, thoughtful readers use when constructing meaning from text. They found that proficient readers

◆ Search for connections between what they know and the new information they encounter in the texts they read
◆ Ask questions of themselves, the authors they encounter, and the texts they read
◆ Draw inferences during and after reading
◆ Distinguish important from less important ideas in text

- ◆ Are adept at synthesizing information within and across texts and reading experiences
- ◆ Repair faulty comprehension
- ◆ Monitor the adequacy of their understanding

Later others (e.g., Keene and Zimmermann 1997) added sensory imaging to this list of comprehension strategies. Proficient readers visualize and create images using the different senses to better understand what they read.

Why Teach These Strategies?

Much of our understanding about the relationship between teaching and learning comes from the work of Donald Graves, writing researcher and professor emeritus at the University of New Hampshire. Graves believes that teachers must be the chief learners in the classroom, spending a significant amount of time modeling their own learning and showing students how. When you follow the natural flow of this idea upward, then principals need to be the chief learners in the building and superintendents the chief learners in the district. What a concept!

This notion holds for reading as well. As the custodians of reading instruction, teachers must be readers first. Of all professionals who read, teachers must top the list. Ellin Keene and Susan Zimmermann drive this point home in their book *Mosaic of Thought: Teaching Comprehension in a Reader's Workshop*. They remind us that we need to understand reading comprehension strategies ourselves and notice how they play out in our own reading before we can successfully teach them to children.

Using Comprehension Strategies in Our Own Reading

We became convinced that these comprehension strategies were worthwhile when we began to consciously apply them in our own reading. We can safely say that we are better readers today than we were before we studied comprehension instruction. And this is something, considering we're at that stage in life where we can't remember who we're calling half the time when we pick up the phone!

Thinking about how we use strategies with adult literature provides the best foundation for understanding how to teach comprehension. For instance, when Anne read *Into Thin Air*, by Jon Krakauer, the gripping story of tragedy striking expert and novice mountain climbers alike as they tried to conquer Everest, she found herself trying to visualize what was going on by creating a mental map of who was where on the mountain. This proved a tough task, but visualizing in this way prevented her from becoming hopelessly confused about the different clients, guides, and climbing teams all trying to reach the summit in the face of a raging blizzard. Because of Krakauer's riveting images and considerable skill as a writer, Anne's lack of background knowledge of mountain topography and technical climbing terms wasn't much of a disadvantage. She had little trouble understanding the terrible dilemmas that arose for people when fate, heroism, and hubris combined to cause a tragic loss of life.

Anne found *Into Thin Air* to be one of those books you just can't put down. Krakauer's vivid writing drew Anne into the text to the point that she felt like she was trudging up Mt. Everest herself. When we began to ask children to visualize, make connections, and tell us what they wondered about, we noticed increased interest and engagement on their part. We sensed that using these strategies encouraged children to think more carefully about their reading, just as Anne had done.

As we explored our own process as readers and listened to our students, they taught us the power of these strategies. Their commitment to making meaning soared when they began to understand that their own interpretations and ideas mattered. "Can we please read now?" became the anthem in many classrooms where we worked. Kids couldn't wait to get on with reading once they began to interact with the text.

Constructing Meaning

We believe that constructing meaning is the goal of comprehension. We want students to

◆ Enhance their understanding
◆ Acquire and use their knowledge
◆ Monitor their understanding
◆ Develop insight

When we began our teaching careers, we typically checked children's story comprehension by evaluating their answers to oral or written questions. Dolores Durkin might have completed her comprehension studies in our classrooms! Initially, comprehension for us was about literal understanding of stories and narrative text. And, of course, this remains one goal of reading comprehension instruction. But this is not the only goal. True comprehension goes beyond literal understanding and involves the reader's interaction with text. If students are to become thoughtful, insightful readers, they must extend their thinking beyond a superficial understanding of the text.

As we read the research about reading, we also noticed that reading strategies such as determining importance or synthesizing information helped students as they read for information, particularly in social studies and science content areas. Comprehension came to mean more than merely literal story understanding. A new definition of understanding involves acquiring knowledge as well. Isabel Beck et al. (1997) define a constructivist view of understanding as "being able to explain information, connect it to previous knowledge, and use information."

Comprehension means that readers think not only about what they are reading but what they are learning. When readers construct meaning, they are building their store of knowledge. But along with knowledge must come understanding. Howard Gardner, the preeminent Harvard psychologist, states simply, "The purpose of education is to enhance understanding" (1991).

By enhancing understanding, we mean that readers go beyond the literal meaning of a story or text. A reader who understands may glean the message in a folk tale, form a new opinion from an editorial, develop a deeper understanding of issues when reading a feature article. Acquiring information allows us to gain knowledge about the world and ourselves in relation to it. We build up our store of knowledge not so much for its own sake but in order to develop insight. With insight, we think more deeply and critically. We question, interpret, and evaluate what we read. In this way, reading can change thinking (Harvey 1998).

Content or Process: Why Not Both?

In light of our view of reading, we believe that the national content/process debate, still raging at present, is a smokescreen. Why argue that teaching content (what students learn) is more important than teaching process (how students learn), or vice versa? You can't think about nothing. We believe that we must teach our students to access content when they read as well as teach them the strategies they need to better understand text and become more thoughtful readers.

When we use the term *constructing meaning*, we refer to building knowledge and promoting understanding. We all remember times when we've had to work hard to gain meaning or when a startling piece of information or outrageous opinion has jolted our thinking. Meaning doesn't arrive fully dressed on a platter. *Readers* make meaning. But they can't do it alone. Our students need to be transformed by great literature (Harwayne 1992) as well as be given opportunities to explore their passions, interests, and questions to bring the world into focus (Harvey 1998).

In Mary Urtz's fourth-grade classroom, student responses to a Colorado history lesson illustrate how acquiring knowledge and enhancing understanding go hand in hand. While reading a nonfiction trade book called *It Happened in Colorado* (Crutchfield 1993), Jonathan conveys a sense of astonishment and wonder when he responds to a gripping vignette on ancient buffalo hunting (see Figure 1.1). His classmate Amanda reveals both knowledge and understanding in her response to the same piece (see Figure 1.2). Amanda imagines herself "in the hunt" and responds in a very personal way. Both she and Jonathan acquire factual information as they read. Amanda uses the strategy of visualizing to better understand what she is reading, while Jonathan can't resist asking piercing questions and making inferences about the entire scenario. More than anything else, Jonathan and Amanda are constructing meaning.

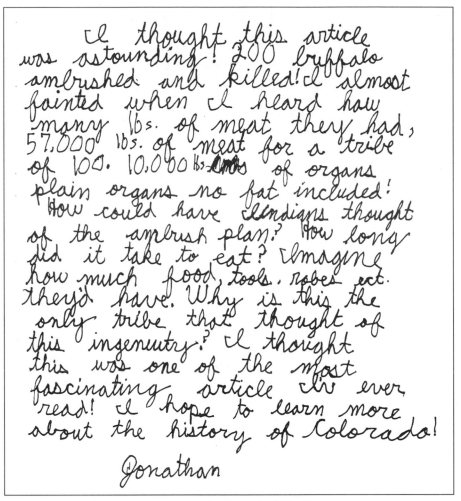

Figure 1.1 Jonathan's Response to "The Great Buffalo Hunt"

Like Amanda and Jonathan, during reading our thinking is peppered with connections, questions, inferences, important ideas, mind pictures, syntheses, and fix-up strategies. Let's look a little more closely at the strategies proficient readers use.

Strategies Used by Proficient Readers

Making connections between prior knowledge and the text Readers pay more attention when they relate to the text, as Steph showed in the vignette that begins this chapter. Readers naturally bring their prior knowledge and experience to reading, but they comprehend better when they think about the connections they make between the text, their lives, and the larger world.

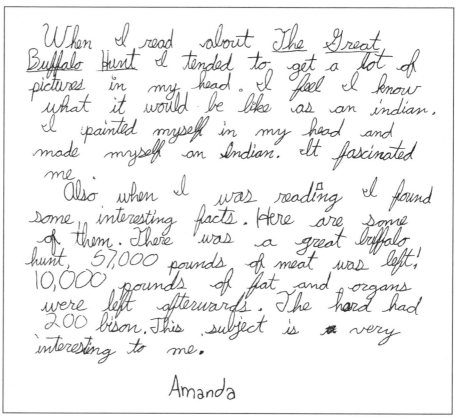

When I read about The Great Buffalo Hunt I tended to get a lot of pictures in my head. I feel I know what it would be like as an indian. I painted myself in my head and made myself an Indian. It fascinated me.

Also when I was reading I found some interesting facts. Here are some of them. There was a great buffalo hunt, 57,000 pounds of meat was left, 10,000 pounds of fat and organs were left afterwards. The hard had 200 bison. This subject is very interesting to me.

Amanda

Figure 1.2 Amanda's Response to "The Great Buffalo Hunt"

Asking questions Questioning is the strategy that keeps readers engaged. When readers ask questions, they clarify understanding and forge ahead to make meaning. Asking questions is at the heart of thoughtful reading.

Visualizing Active readers create visual images in their minds based on the words they read in the text. The pictures they create enhance their understanding.

Drawing inferences Inferring is at the intersection of taking what is known, garnering clues from the text, and thinking ahead to make a judgment, discern a theme, or speculate about what is to come.

Determining important ideas Thoughtful readers grasp essential ideas and important information when reading. Readers must differentiate between less important ideas and key ideas that are central to the meaning of the text.

Synthesizing information Synthesizing involves combining new information with existing knowledge to form an original idea or interpretation.

Reviewing, sorting and sifting important information can lead to new insights that change the way readers think.

Repairing understanding If confusion disrupts meaning, readers need to stop and clarify their understanding. Readers may use a variety of strategies to "fix up" comprehension when meaning goes awry.

A word of caution: Although we tend to introduce these strategies independently of one another, we recognize that readers rarely infer, determine importance, or synthesize in isolation. These thoughts interact and intersect to help readers make meaning and often occur simultaneously during reading. We stress the interrelationship of these strategies so that with practice our students will come to expect their interactive nature.

What's the Best Way to Teach Comprehension Strategies?

Showing Kids How vs. Telling Them What to Do

For too many years in education we have been telling students what to do without showing them how. In our work, we make a distinction between what might be called mentioning and explicit instruction. Durkin's classroom observations (1979) found that teachers were most likely to say just enough about an assignment so that students understood the formal requirements, but they stopped short of demonstrating how to solve the task cognitively. From our perspective, mentioning is similar to the education we received in the 1950s; the teacher stood at the head of the class, read a lengthy set of directions, and assigned a variety of tasks. Questions were more likely to be used to clarify procedures than to enhance understanding. In many classrooms, assigning was the norm; teaching was conspicuously absent. We advocate more teaching, less assigning.

Much of our responsibility when teaching reading is to make what is implicit, explicit. Explicit reading instruction means that we show learners how we think when we read, as Steph did when reading *Up North at the Cabin*. We explicitly teach reading comprehension strategies so that readers can use them to construct meaning. We are likely to teach a strategy by modeling the strategy for the class, guiding students in its practice in small groups and pairs, and providing large blocks of time for students to read independently and practice using and applying the strategy.

Eventually, the goal is for readers to use these strategies automatically and seamlessly. No one envisions readers lying in bed with a great book and having to get up, find a pencil, and jot a question on a sticky note. That's why we frame our instruction in what Pearson and Gallagher (1983) call "the gradual release of responsibility approach." We encourage this approach because independence is our ultimate goal. All of our instruction is geared toward children's using these strategies independently, applying them if and when they need them.

The Gradual Release of Responsibility

We encourage teachers to deliver instruction using the gradual release of responsibility approach. Staff developer Laura Benson visualizes gradual release in terms of learning to ride a bike. First, the child watches the adult ride a bike, which parallels the teacher's doing the activity alone while the students watch. Next, the child rides the bike with training wheels, a metaphor for guided practice in pairs or small groups. Finally, the happy five-year-old sheds the training wheels and cruises down the street, illustrating how children perform the task independently and apply it in new situations (Harvey 1998).

Fielding and Pearson (1994) identify four components of comprehension strategy instruction that follow the gradual release of responsibility approach, which we elaborate on here.

Teacher Modeling

- The teacher explains the strategy.
- The teacher demonstrates how to apply the strategy successfully.
- The teacher thinks aloud to model the mental processes she uses when she reads.

Guided Practice

- After explicitly modeling, the teacher gradually gives the student more responsibility for task completion.
- The teacher and students practice the strategy together.
- The teacher scaffolds the students' attempts and supports student thinking, giving feedback during conferring and classroom discussions.
- Students share their thinking processes with each other during paired reading and small- and large-group discussions.

Independent Practice

- After working with the teacher and with other students, the students try to apply the strategy on their own.
- The students receive regular feedback from the teacher and other students.

Application of the Strategy in Real Reading Situations

- Students apply a clearly understood strategy to a new genre or format.
- Students demonstrate the effective use of a strategy in more difficult text.

To get an idea of when readers are effectively applying a strategy to construct meaning, we look closely at their writing and listen carefully to their conversations. When Amanda wrote about using visualizing to get a better feeling for the life of a Native American buffalo hunter, her teacher, Mary Urtz, had evidence that Amanda understood how to use a strategy to better comprehend text.

Listening into student conversations and scrutinizing student written responses inform us about our students' developing facility with a certain strategy. We move on to another strategy focus when we find repeated evidence that our students are using the strategy to help them understand what they read.

Like writing, reading is an act of composition. When we write, we compose thoughts on paper. When we read, we compose meaning in our minds. Thoughtful, active readers use the text to stimulate their own thinking and to engage with the mind of the writer.

In an interview with George Plimpton (1988), E. L. Doctorow said,

I really started to think of myself as a writer when I was about nine. Whenever I read anything I seemed to identify as much with the act of composition as with the story. I seemed to have two minds: I would love the story and want to know what happened next, but at the same time I would somehow be aware of what was being done on the page. I identified myself as a kind of younger brother to the writer. I was on hand to help him figure things out. So you see, I didn't actually have to write a thing, because the act of reading was my writing. I thought of myself as a writer for years, before I got around to writing anything. It's to blur the distinction between reader and writer. As a child, I somehow drifted into this region where you are both reader and writer: I declared to myself that I was a writer. I wrote a lot of good books. I wrote *Captain Blood* by Rafael Sabatini. That was one of my better efforts.

Wouldn't you be thrilled if your students saw reading in this light? The comprehension strategies that we describe in this book, along with the powerful literature we recommend, serve to help readers construct their own meaning and interact with the text to enhance understanding and acquire and use knowledge.

Chapter
2

Strategic Reading

S teph slid her chair up next to Alverro to confer with him. A second grader, he was reading Diana Short Yurkovic's *Meet Me at the Water Hole,* a nonfiction emergent-reading book filled with captivating photographs and interesting cutouts to stimulate thinking. He turned to a picture of a baby giraffe drinking at the water hole and began to read the one sentence of text that constituted the entire page: "When a baby giraffe is born, it is already six feet tall." Stunning information, to say the least!

Alverro read easily through the first clause and then stumbled on the word *already.* He tried a number of decoding strategies to figure it out, including parsing the word, going back and rereading, and reading ahead. After several tries, he got it. He read *already.* His teacher beamed, deservedly so. She had dedicated considerable time to teaching Alverro those very decoding strategies. And now here he was, using them to crack the code independently without teacher intervention.

When Alverro reached the end of the sentence, however, he went right on to the next page without taking even a moment to ponder the remarkable fact about giraffe birth size.

"Whoa! Not so fast," Steph said. "What did you just read?"

He scrunched his nose and looked at her quizzically. "*Already*?" he asked.

"Besides that."

But he couldn't answer. He had no clue. He had committed himself single-mindedly to decoding the word *already* and had lost all track of meaning in the process. Worse, so pleased was he with his decoding triumph that he didn't realize that he had missed the meaning. Steph suggested he read the sentence again and think about what the words meant. As he did, his face lit up. He pointed to the life-size cut-out of Michael Jordan in the corner of the room and made an authentic connection. "Wow, baby giraffes are almost as tall as Michael Jordan on the day they are born! That's incredible!" And he was right, of course, that is incredible.

Steph and Alverro talked about what had happened in his first reading of the sentence. Together they decided that from now on when he reached the bottom of the page, he would stop and think about what he had just read. The end of a page became a sort of red light for Alverro to remind him to think about what he was reading, before forging on through the text. Stopping to digest and synthesize information periodically helps readers construct meaning.

Alverro had successfully activated strategies to decode text but had difficulty figuring out the words and gaining meaning simultaneously. When readers focus solely on decoding, meaning takes a back seat. While Alverro struggled to figure out the word *already*, he simply couldn't pay attention to the overall meaning of the text. Readers have to learn that reading is an interactive process involving decoding words *and* constructing meaning. Teachers need to teach students like Alverro to become more active, strategic readers as well as proficient decoders.

A Closer Look at Strategic Reading

Before describing in detail each comprehension strategy, let's take a closer look at what we mean by strategic reading and some related terms, such as *metacognitive knowledge* and *comprehension monitoring*.

The term *strategic reading* refers to thinking about reading in ways that enhance learning and understanding. Researchers who explicitly taught students strategies for determining important ideas (Gallagher 1986), drawing inferences (Hansen 1981), and asking questions (Gavelek and Raphael 1985) found that teaching these thinking/reading strategies improved students' overall comprehension of text. Research by Palincsar and Brown (1984) and Paris, Lipson, and Wixon (1983), however, suggests that it isn't enough for students to simply understand a given strategy. They must know when, why, and how to use it.

Metacognitive Knowledge

Proficient readers, then, adapt strategies to their purposes for reading. But matching strategies to one's purpose requires metacognitive knowledge— an awareness and understanding of how one thinks and uses strategies during reading. For instance, when Amanda read and responded to the buffalo hunt passage, she purposefully created visual images in her mind to better understand what happened during the hunt (see Figure 1.2 in Chapter 1). According to Amanda, "I feel I know what it would be like as an Indian. I painted myself in my head and made myself an Indian." This strategy worked for Amanda. Not only did she begin to get a sense of what it might have been like to have been there; she remembered amazing facts as well. Jonathan's strategy of choice was questioning. He asked questions to clarify and reinforce what was to him incredible information (see Figure 1.1 in Chapter 1).

The real question is how Jonathan and Amanda knew which strategies would enhance their understanding. For us, what Jonathan and Amanda were able to do is what metacognitive knowledge is all about. They were aware and ready as readers to use the strategy knowledge they had to understand unfamiliar information. They successfully linked that knowledge with their purpose for reading. Once we've taught students a variety of strategies, it's important to keep track of how well they are using and applying them. Perkins and Swartz (Perkins 1992) define four levels of metacognitive knowledge that are helpful for understanding how learners and readers adapt strategies to their reading purposes. These four levels illustrate how learners move from less to more sophisticated ways of monitoring their own thinking. Perkins and Swartz identify four kinds of learners/readers:

◆ *Tacit learners/readers.* These are readers who lack awareness of how they think when they read.
◆ *Aware learners/readers.* These are readers who realize when meaning has broken down or confusion has set in but who may not have sufficient strategies for fixing the problem.
◆ *Strategic learners/readers.* These are readers who use the thinking and comprehension strategies we describe in this book to enhance understanding and acquire knowledge. They are able to monitor and repair meaning when it is disrupted.
◆ *Reflective learners/readers.* These are the readers who are strategic about their thinking and are able to apply strategies flexibly depending on their goals or purposes for reading. According to Perkins and Swartz, they also "reflect on their thinking and ponder and revise their use of strategies."

Based on these descriptions, we can see that Amanda and Jonathan, who were able to use visualizing and questioning to enhance their understanding of content, are well on their way to becoming strategic if not reflective learners/readers. Alverro, a second grader still learning to decode print, is an example of a tacit learner/reader, one who is not aware of his thinking while reading. When Steph intervened to help Alverro think about the content, she nudged him toward becoming an aware reader, one who knows when meaning breaks down.

A clear knowledge of comprehension strategies combined with an awareness of when and how to use them can provide Alverro and others like him with an arsenal of tactics to ensure that they construct meaning as they read. Our goal in teaching comprehension strategies is to move readers like Alverro from the tacit level of understanding to a greater awareness of how to think while reading. And we need to challenge readers like Amanda and Jonathan to apply their strategy knowledge in progressively more difficult text and different genres. The next section discusses some ways in which we scaffold students' thinking to help them become aware of and monitor their comprehension.

Monitoring Comprehension

Both of us read before turning in for the night. We mark the chapter and turn off the light. Or we wake up with lights blazing at 2:00 A.M., our glasses cocked, our books sprawled across our chests. But whichever the case, we've each had the same experience of picking up the book the next night, opening to the marked page, and having no clue what the last page or so was about. We know we read it, but we don't know what we read. We flip back a few pages and slowly begin to reconstruct meaning. The fact is that all readers space out when they read. Kids need to know this, or they risk feeling inadequate when it happens to them. We share these stories of our attention lapses with our students. When they learn that adult readers space out, too, they are less likely to brand themselves poor readers at such times.

Proficient readers know how to compensate for lapses in attention. Once they are made aware of this tendency, they catch themselves quicker the next time. We need to teach less experienced readers how to stay on top of their reading. When readers pay attention, they are able to use the strategies we describe to gain meaning. Readers take a giant leap toward independence when they develop the ability to monitor or keep track of how well they are understanding what they read. This means readers need explicit instruction to

◆ Become aware of their thinking as they read
◆ Detect obstacles and confusions that derail understanding
◆ Understand how strategies can help them repair meaning when it breaks down

As Perkins and Swartz suggest, becoming aware of ourselves as readers is the first step in learning to monitor and repair comprehension that has gone awry. Proficient readers—adults and children alike—proceed on automatic pilot most of the time, until something doesn't make sense or a problem arises and understanding screeches to a halt. At that point, experienced readers slow down and reread, clarifying confusions before they continue. Less proficient readers like Alverro may be so focused on decoding that they can't give adequate attention to making meaning when they run into trouble. Just as Steph taught Alverro to stop and think about meaning, students need to be reminded to stop periodically in order to keep track of their understanding. Awareness and monitoring go hand in hand, enabling an active reader to constantly check for understanding.

Monitoring by itself, however, isn't enough. Just because a reader realizes there's a problem with comprehension doesn't mean he can solve it. A reflective, strategic reader knows which strategies to activate when meaning is lost. The ability to repair comprehension means that a reader can access different strategies—asking questions, visualizing, or inferring—to construct meaning in the face of problems. A reader's repertoire of fix-up strategies needs to be flexible enough to solve comprehension problems with words, sentences, or overall meaning.

Tracking Thinking: Teaching Students to Monitor and Repair Comprehension

The Wisconsin that Steph described in Chapter 1 is Wisconsin in the heart of the summer. Wisconsin in the dead of winter is a different animal. One of Steph's annual winter childhood games will give you an idea; it involved counting the string of subzero highs each January in hopes of breaking the established record. But what northern Wisconsin lacked in Fahrenheit each winter, it made up for in beauty. The roof-top icicles, the frosty pines, and the drifting snow lent winter a luster one never forgets. Each morning after a fresh snow, northern Wisconsin kids would scan their backyards for critter tracks. They knew whose pawprints were whose, and they leapt out of bed at the crack of dawn to see who had trespassed during the night.

We tell kids these stories about fresh tracks in the snow, or in the sand for those who live near water. We explain that fresh tracks let us know who's been there, even after they've gone. In the same way as animals leave tracks of their presence, we want readers to "leave tracks of their thinking." It is impossible to know what a reader is thinking when she reads unless she tells us through conversation or written response. The reading comprehension instruction described in this book encourages students to mark and code text with thoughts and questions, to "leave tracks" so they can remember later what they were thinking as they read. Kids love the idea of making tracks in the margins, tracks on sticky notes, tracks in their journals. These written tracks help the reader monitor comprehension and enhance understanding. They also provide clues to the teacher about a reader's thinking, evidence that is difficult to ascertain without some form of oral or written response.

Keeping track of thinking while reading helps students make meaning as they go. But meaning breaks down for multiple reasons and in myriad ways. One reader may have insufficient background knowledge to understand unfamiliar concepts or ideas. Another may focus on details rather than on important ideas and information. Younger readers are particularly susceptible to maintaining misconceptions in the face of more accurate information. And some readers simply lose track of meaning by spacing out, as noted earlier. We need to be explicit about teaching kids to be aware, to constantly check for understanding, and to dip into their reservoir of reading comprehension strategies to make meaning. When we teach students to monitor and repair their understanding, we explicitly teach them to

- ◆ Track their thinking through coding, writing, or discussion
- ◆ Notice when they lose focus
- ◆ Stop and go back to clarify thinking
- ◆ Reread to enhance understanding

- ◆ Read ahead to clarify meaning
- ◆ Identify and articulate what's confusing or puzzling about the text
- ◆ Recognize that all of their questions have value. There is no such thing as a stupid question.
- ◆ Develop the disposition to question the text or author
- ◆ Think critically about the text and be willing to disagree with its information or logic
- ◆ Match the problem with the strategy that will best solve it

In this book, comprehension monitoring means that kids learn to match strategies to their purposes for reading. When we ask kids to share their thinking during read-alouds and mini-lessons, we are providing an opportunity for them to clarify confusions and misconceptions. Discussing ideas and interpretations and tracking thinking by coding the text and jotting written responses during independent reading allow kids to continually build understanding and stay on top of meaning. If we monitor thinking as we go, we are unlikely to come to the end of a chapter without a clue as to what we have read. It is much easier to be proactive and construct meaning as we go than to have to go back, reread, and salvage what little meaning we can. The more we practice this together, the better each student will be able to do it alone.

Strategies That Work

Over the past few years, we have become completely committed to the effectiveness of these strategies to help readers understand and enjoy reading. Time and time again, stories from kids, teachers, and parents convey how using these strategies has changed them as readers. One father of a third grader, who had participated in a parent-child book club, commented that none of his high school friends would believe that he belonged to a book club where he read books with his daughter. "I dropped out of high school, reading was such a chore for me. I wish I'd learned to read like this in school. I might have graduated," he told us. His experience poignantly captures the power of these strategies to engage readers in reading and thinking.

We introduce these strategies one at a time by modeling our own use of each one. Then we give students time to practice each strategy. We are aware, however, that these strategies do not occur in isolation. Strategic readers are connecting, inferring, questioning, visualizing, and synthesizing continually as they read. Certain strategies emerge to help readers better understand a specific aspect of text. We want readers to keep track of their thinking as they read and to become flexible enough with strategy use to choose the strategy best suited to their needs at the time. But all of these strategies work together to help readers construct meaning. A detailed description of each strategy follows.

Making Connections: A Bridge from the New to the Known

In the 1980s cognitive psychologists devised the term *schema theory* to explain how our previous experiences, knowledge, emotions, and understandings have a major effect on what and how we learn (Anderson and Pearson 1984). Our schema—the sum total of our background knowledge and experience—is what each of us brings to our reading. Applied to reading, we can activate and use schema theory as we guide students to make connections between books and their own lives.

When students have had an experience similar to that of a character in a story, they are more likely to understand the character's motives, thoughts, and feelings. And when readers have an abundance of background knowledge about a specific content area, they understand more completely the new information they read. Additionally, when readers have a general understanding of the nature of text and literature itself, they comprehend more completely.

Having students access and use their prior knowledge and experiences to better understand what they read is often our launching point for strategy instruction because every student has experiences, knowledge, opinions, or emotions to draw upon. Several years ago, the children in Colleen Buddy's classroom described three kinds of connections they made to their reading. It made a lot of sense to distinguish between connections that are

◆ Text-to-self—connections that readers make between the text and their past experiences or background knowledge
◆ Text-to-text—connections that readers make between the text they are reading and another text, including books, poems, scripts, songs, or anything that is written
◆ Text-to-world—connections that readers make between the text and the bigger issues, events, or concerns of society and the world at large

Some connections cross these boundaries. But it is helpful to teach them independently over time, beginning with text-to-self connections, then introducing text-to-text connections, and finally bringing up text-to-world connections. Discriminating between different types of connections encourages kids to look in several directions when activating prior knowledge.

Text-to-self, text-to-text, and text-to-world connections arise from the content readers come across in text. Readers also make connections to the nature of different texts and build schema for that, too. As readers are exposed to a wider variety of genres, forms, and structures, they become increasingly aware of literary and style characteristics. They soon come to expect certain features in different texts. This, too, enhances their understanding when reading.

Questioning: The Strategy That Propels Readers Forward

Very young children brim with questions. If we didn't delight so in their youthful enthusiasm, they might drive us crazy with the sheer number that burst forth. Primary teachers know this. Kindergartners blurt out questions fast and furiously, often without raising a hand. Why is the moon out during the day? How do birds fly? Do animals talk to each other? Where did the cowboys go? Sadly, by fifth grade, kids' questions practically disappear. Schools do not foster questions. Schools demand answers—answers to teachers' questions, answers to literal questions in basal readers, and answers to math operations many kids can do but can't explain. For too many years, schools have focused on answers to the exclusion of questions.

Questions are at the heart of teaching and learning. Human beings are driven to make sense of their world. Questions open the doors to understanding. We need to celebrate kids' questions and help facilitate their answers.

Questioning is the strategy that propels readers forward. When readers have questions, they are less likely to abandon the text. Proficient readers ask questions before, during, and after reading. They question the content, the author, the events, the issues, and the ideas in the text. Readers ask questions to

◆ Construct meaning
◆ Enhance understanding
◆ Find answers
◆ Solve problems
◆ Find specific information
◆ Acquire a body of information
◆ Discover new information
◆ Propel research efforts
◆ Clarify confusion

Visualizing: Becoming Wordstruck

In his book *Wordstruck,* Robert MacNeil remembers being overwhelmed with the images and feelings—the sights, sounds, touches, and tastes—that words conjured up in his mind. On a cold night in Nova Scotia, Robert Louis Stevenson's poem "Windy Nights" brought images to MacNeil's young mind of his father, a Canadian naval officer, at sea in a gale.

If only all of our students could be as riveted by the printed word. Visualizing is the reading world's term for describing what Robert MacNeil does as a reader. Like E. L. Doctorow (quoted in Chapter 1), MacNeil's love for and understanding of language allow him to paint a picture of the story in his mind. It is almost as if he produces the text as a full-blown theatrical experience.

Visualizing, according to Keene and Zimmermann (1997), is a comprehension strategy that enables readers to make the words on a page real and concrete. Teachers sometimes explain visualizing as creating a movie of the text in your head. We've found that when students create scenarios and pictures in their minds while reading, their level of engagement increases and their attention doesn't flag. Younger children seem particularly able to become involved in stories, often "living through or living in" the stories they read (Miller and Goudvis 1999).

Creating mental images for other genres is equally important. Photographs, diagrams, charts, and maps in nonfiction books support our ability to understand what the text is attempting to convey. When one is slogging through a written description of photosynthesis, a picture is worth a thousand words. Teaching children to construct their own mental images when reading helps them stop, think about, and visualize text content. Visualizing

◆ Allows readers to create mental images from words in the text
◆ Enhances meaning with mental imagery
◆ Links past experience to the words and ideas in the text
◆ Enables readers to place themselves in the story
◆ Strengthens a reader's relationship to the text
◆ Stimulates imaginative thinking
◆ Heightens engagement with text
◆ Brings joy to reading

Making Inferences: Reading Between the Lines

Writers don't spill their thoughts onto the page, they leak them slowly, one idea at a time, until the reader can make an educated guess or an appropriate inference about an underlying theme in the text or a prediction about what is to come. Inferring relates to the notion of reading between the lines. According to the writer Susan Hall (1990), "Inferring allows readers to make their own discoveries without the direct comment of the author."

Inferential thinking occurs when text clues merge with the reader's prior knowledge and questions to point toward a conclusion about an underlying theme or idea in the text. Proficient readers infer implicit notions from the text and create meaning based on those notions. If readers don't infer, they will not grasp the deeper essence of texts they read. Readers' questions are often only answered through an inference. The more information readers acquire, the more likely they will make an inference that hits the target.

Human beings infer in many realms. We make inferences about expressions, body language, and tone as well as text. Inferential thinking serves people well in all walks of life. Certain genres, such as mystery, deliberately attempt to mislead readers and trick them into making incorrect inferences. Background knowledge for a specific genre helps readers overcome this hurdle. When readers infer, they

◆ Draw conclusions based on clues in the text
◆ Make predictions before and during reading
◆ Surface underlying themes
◆ Use implicit information from the text to create meaning during and after reading
◆ Use the pictures to help gain meaning

Determining Importance: Distilling the Essence of Text

We'd like to think that the days of underlining or checking off the main idea are over. Unfortunately, comprehension exercises and test questions still require students to choose one main idea. Indeed, in artificially constructed paragraphs such as those we see on standardized tests, often there is only one main idea. However, determining essential ideas in authentic text such as a piece of historical fiction, a newspaper editorial, or a nonfiction trade book may not be so easy.

In narrative text, characters' actions, motives, problems, and personalities all contribute to the overall themes. The main idea often depends on who the main reader is. If the reader has had experiences similar to those of the main character, the reader is likely to enjoy a richer, more fulfilling reading experience. Poems, with figurative language, metaphor, and imagery, require that we dig deep for meaning. In poetry meaning is not always what it may appear on the surface. Nonfiction presents its own problems. What's important may relate to a combination of interesting details and information essential to a basic understanding of a topic (Harvey 1998). One good reason to determine important ideas is that they are the ones we want to remember. And don't we need to know a little about a topic before we can discern what is most important about it?

Regardless of genre, what we determine to be important in text depends on our purpose for reading it. When we model determining importance for our students, we need to ask whether our purpose is to

◆ Remember important information
◆ Learn new information and build background knowledge
◆ Distinguish what's important from what's interesting
◆ Discern a theme, opinion, or perspective
◆ Answer a specific question
◆ Determine if the author's message is to inform, persuade, or entertain

The ability to determine importance in text often requires us to use related comprehension strategies such as drawing inferences and summarizing information. We may have to infer the lesson or moral in a folk tale. We may have to summarize the information in a science textbook to extract the essence. When reading an editorial, we can weigh the evidence for and against the author's opinion after sorting through the information to make our own determination about the author's conclusion.

Synthesizing Information: The Evolution of Thought

Synthesizing information involves combining new information with existing knowledge to form an original idea, a new line of thinking, or a new creation. Synthesis is the opposite of analysis in the classical sense of those terms. Analysis is breaking down something whole into its parts, while synthesizing is putting together separate parts into a new whole. Synthesizing is a process akin to working a jigsaw puzzle. In the same way that we manipulate hundreds of puzzle pieces to form a new picture, students must arrange multiple fragments of information until they see a new pattern emerge (McKenzie 1996). The strategy of synthesizing has become increasingly important. Our information-rich society requires us to sift though ever-increasing amounts of data to make sense of them and act. We couldn't possibly remember all the information that appears on our radar screen each day. Synthesizing allows us to make sense of important information and move on.

As readers move through text, their thinking evolves. They add new information to what they already know and construct meaning as they go. Synthesizing requires readers to sift and sort through large amounts of information to extract essential ideas and combine these to form an overall picture of what has been read, to get the gist. As readers distill text into a few important ideas or larger concepts, they might form a particular perspective that leads to new insight. Synthesizing is the strategy that allows readers to change their thinking.

The need to sift important ideas from interesting details is one challenge that trade literature presents to readers. It is often so well written that rich, less important details carry readers away from the essential ideas. In order to synthesize what they read, readers need to stop every now and then, think about what they have read, and take stock of meaning before continuing on through the text. When readers synthesize, they

◆ Stop and collect their thoughts before reading on
◆ Sift important ideas from less important details
◆ Summarize the information by briefly identifying the main points
◆ Combine these main points into a larger concept or bigger idea
◆ Make generalizations about the information they read
◆ Make judgments about the information they read
◆ Personalize their reading by integrating new information with existing knowledge to form a new idea, opinion, or perspective

A Common Language About Strategic Reading

It can only be helpful for readers if we settle on a common language for teaching and talking about reading comprehension across grade levels in schools. It makes sense to develop clear explanations for each strategy that remain consistent from one grade level to another. When children come into the classroom knowing how to make connections, visualize, or determine important ideas, teachers don't have to reinvent the wheel each year.

We encourage teachers to work together to become conversant with each strategy and decide as a group on the language that makes the most sense for their kids. For example, the terms *background knowledge, prior knowledge* and *schema* actually represent three different ways of referring to a similar concept, the knowledge and experience that readers bring to the text. Go ahead and teach these various terms for the purpose of exposure, but encourage your team and others in the school to choose one and use it consistently. We confound kids with our ever-changing jargon.

The cumulative effect of teaching comprehension strategies from kindergarten through high school is powerful. When kindergartners who have learned to visualize hit first grade, they are more likely to activate that strategy when they hear the word again, see their teacher doing it, and try it themselves. Fifth-grade teachers in schools that begin teaching comprehension strategies in kindergarten report that most of their kids walk in on the first day already able to ask questions, visualize, and make connections. This allows them to dedicate more time to teaching more sophisticated strategies such as inferring, determining importance, and synthesizing.

One caution, however. P. David Pearson, reading researcher and professor of education at Michigan State University, reminds us that "just because readers say they are using a strategy to better understand what they read doesn't necessarily mean that they are. And conversely, just because students do not articulate the thinking behind the strategy doesn't mean they aren't using it to better understand what they read" (1995). In schools where we work, it is not unusual to hear one first grader turn to another and say, "I inferred that...." Our initial inclination is to pat ourselves on the back for all the wonderful teaching we have done. But we hold our exuberance and check with that child to see if she really did make an inference. Or is she just playing with the new language or trying to impress the teacher? We determine whether readers are using strategies to better comprehend by having conversations with them, reading their written responses, and observing them closely.

Great books are central to teaching comprehension. The next three chapters show the instructional approaches we use to teach comprehension strategies, give our rationale for using short text to teach comprehension, and provide some suggestions for how we choose books and how we help kids choose books for comprehension strategy instruction.

Chapter

3   Strategy Instruction and Practice

Anne closed Allan Baillie's *Rebel* after reading the last page out loud to a group of eighth graders. This clever picture book, about the courageous response of a group of rural Burmese peasants to a dictatorial military strongman, was one of her favorites. She glanced up at the clock and noticed the time slipping away. She really wanted to confer with the kids, and she couldn't wait to read their responses to this compelling story. Feeling pressed for time, she asked the kids to divide a sheet in half and mark one column What the Text Is About and the next column What the Text Makes Me Think About. She had found this form useful in the past to get at children's deeper thinking. Although she had never introduced the form to this group of kids, it appeared to be self-explanatory.

As the kids returned to their tables to respond on this form, Anne sat down at one table and began to confer with Jasmine. Others at the table soon joined in and a lively book discussion ensued. The kids brimmed with questions and comments. With Anne present, they talked about what really went on in the story, where it took place, who these people were, and why they were fighting.

As she began to construct meaning from the discussion, Jasmine wrote the following in the first column: "This was about some people in Burma who used to be free and now were under the control of a bad government and an even worse general. The people rebelled in a surprising way." "Great thinking," Anne commented to Jasmine. In the second column, Jasmine wrote that the book reminded her of stories her grandfather had told about Vietnam. Anne felt pleased with Jasmine's summary and viable connection. She left the table with Jasmine writing about her grandfather's Vietnam experience and her table group writing about all kinds of things.

The bell rang and Anne collected the forms as kids filed out the door. Her heart sank as she paged through them. With the exception of the kids at Jasmine's table and a few very prolific writers who always filled entire pages regardless of the instruction, most of the forms stared blankly at her, hardly a word written in either column. She knew the form couldn't be at fault; it had worked effectively in the past. As Anne pondered the disappointing results of her instruction, she realized that she had once again made a familiar mistake.

Almost every time she reflected on why a certain lesson had been ineffective, she concluded that it was because of a lack of explicit instruction. She either hadn't modeled explicitly enough what she was trying to do or she hadn't given her students enough time to practice what she had shown them. If she had modeled how to use this form on the overhead projector rather than giving a series of directions, she suspected, things would have gone quite differently.

The next time Anne saw Steph, she described the debacle. Steph could only smile knowingly. She herself had repeatedly told her own kids that it was okay to make a mistake as long as they didn't make the same mistake over and over. But when it came to delivering instruction, she, too, continued to make the same mistake over and over. Like Anne, whenever Steph cut corners on modeling, her instruction suffered.

Don't surrender to the clock. It takes time to show kids how, but it is time well spent. When it comes to instruction, it is nearly impossible to be too explicit. So much for making the same mistake over and over.

Effective Strategy Instruction

Teaching kids to read strategically means we show them how to construct meaning when they read. Comprehension strategy instruction is most effective when teachers

◆ Model their own use of the strategy repeatedly over time
◆ Show students their thinking when reading, and articulate how that thinking helps them better understand what they read
◆ Discuss how the strategy helps readers make meaning
◆ Make connections between the new strategy and what the reader already knows
◆ Respond in writing by coding the text according to a particular strategy
◆ Gradually release responsibility for the use of the strategy to the students
◆ Build in large amounts of time for actual text reading by the students
◆ Provide opportunities for guided practice in strategy application
◆ Show students how the strategy applies to other texts, genres, formats, disciplines, and contexts
◆ Help students notice how these strategies intersect and work in conjunction with one another
◆ Take time to observe and confer directly with students about their strategy learning, and keep records of those observations and conferences

◆ Remind students that the purpose for using the strategy is to better comprehend text

Teaching Comprehension in a Reading Workshop

Strategic reading takes hold in classrooms that value student thinking. In our work in classrooms, we've noticed that the classroom context makes all the difference for effective strategy instruction. The comprehension instruction described in this book is best taught through the reading workshop model. The reading workshop promotes thinking when reading. In the reading workshop, the teacher models a whole-group strategy lesson and then gives students large blocks of time to read and to practice the strategy in small groups, pairs, or independently. During this time, the teacher moves about the room, slides her chair up next to readers (as Anne did with Jasmine), and confers with them about their reading and about how they use a strategy to better comprehend text. Sometimes the teacher meets with small, flexible groups to provide instruction in a particular strategy. Much of the time kids read independently in books of their choice. Regular strategy practice combined with teacher and peer response is central to reading improvement.

The reading workshop model emphasizes choice in book selection. Researcher Donald Graves recommends that readers self select about 80 percent of the texts they read. We know that readers get better at reading when they choose books they can and want to read. We need to fill our rooms with terrific books at every level, on every conceivable topic, to ensure that kids get their hands on books they want to read. In Chapter 5 we describe how we choose books for strategy instruction and how we help students choose their own books to read independently when practicing various comprehension strategies.

For a more in-depth discussion of reading workshops, see Nancie Atwell's *In the Middle*, Pat Hagerty's *Reader's Workshop: Real Reading*, Joanne Hindley's *In the Company of Children*, and Janet Allen and Kyle Gonzalez's *There's Room for Me Here*. Each of these books describes the necessary components of a successful reading workshop where student ideas and thoughts carry weight.

Building a Literate Community

Successful comprehension instruction requires that we create an environment that builds a community of thinkers and learners, a community where kids and teachers care and wonder about each other's interests and ideas and take time to talk about them, think about them, and explore them. Some components that help foster a learning community that promotes thinking include the following.

Immersion in print of every genre Surround your students with text of every conceivable genre, style, form, and topic. Read and discuss them all out loud, sharing your thinking as you go. Don't forget to include poetry and nonfiction, both of which seem to get short shrift in schools. And remember to share magazines and newspapers as well. If we don't share these different forms, we minimize their importance. Reading is contagious. When rooms are filled to bursting with a vast array of print, kids pick it up.

Large blocks of time for extended reading and writing We get better at reading by reading. Richard Allington (1994) notes that American students spend less than 10 percent of the school day engaged in actual text reading. If we want students to think when they read, we need to give them time. Opportunities to respond in writing allow students to think again about their reading, this time on paper.

Explicit instruction in reading strategies Showing our thinking and the mental processes we go through when we read gives students an idea of what thoughtful readers do. We explicitly teach reading comprehension strategies by demonstrating them for students before turning the task over to them.

Opportunities for readers to read and practice strategies in self-selected text that they are able to read If we only went to a piano lesson on Monday and never sat down to practice the rest of the week, we wouldn't get better at piano. Steph and Anne can both attest to that! We need to build in time for readers to practice specific strategies in texts they choose. Much of the reading done outside of school is self-selected. We need to provide a wide variety of accessible text so that all kids can find a book they are able to and care to read.

Continuing opportunities for teacher and peer response Readers need to talk with their teachers in conferences to clarify their understanding and share important thoughts, ideas, and questions. The conference is the crux of the reading workshop, the place where teachers can address the individual needs of readers. Opportunities for peer discussion and response build community and enhance understanding for all kids in the class. And when kids talk about books and ideas, they learn what matters to other kids in their class.

Accessible resources Books aren't the only resource in classrooms that promote thinking. Overhead projectors and oversized charts are indispensable equipment in rooms where teachers practice explicit instruction. Transparencies and transparency pens can't be overlooked. Clipboards with pencils attached are a must so kids can sit close to the teacher and respond in writing while she models instruction. Pads of sticky notes top the supply lists of classrooms that value student thinking. Notebooks and journals for written responses fill student cubbies and desks. Book baskets at the center of each student table categorize text by genre, strategy, author, or theme and bring dusty books out into the open where kids can easily find that book to die for. In classrooms that value thinking and promote a community of learners, resources that support literacy are easily accessible.

Teachers may sigh at this extensive list of resources. In an era of ever-dwindling funds for education, many teachers are lucky just to have books and paper. These days of diminishing financial support require a creative response to resource acquisition. Use your budget for whatever you can, and use your brain to get the rest. Head first to the school or local library and check out as many books as they will part with. Wander around garage sales, used book sales, and bargain sections of bookstores. Introduce yourself to local businesses. Business-school partnerships are increasingly common and productive. And don't forget about grants. You may just have to add "grant writer" to your list of responsibilities. But it can pay off, big time!

Any further discussion of building a literate community is probably beyond the scope of this book. We have learned much about community from a number of teacher-writers, however, and we would highly recommend Don Graves's *Build a Literate Classroom*, Shelley Harwayne's *Going Public: Priorities and Practices at the Manhattan New School*, and Linda Rief's *Seeking Diversity* for a further look at how to create a literate, thinking community in your classroom and school.

Best Practice Instruction: Showing Kids How

For too long, we have been telling kids what to do—as Anne did in the *Rebel* fiasco—rather than showing them how. The way we deliver effective instruction always involves modeling in one form or another. We may use charts or overheads, or show our thinking when reading out loud. We use the gradual release of responsibility approach and work hard not to release our students too soon or, conversely, keep them immersed in our instruction to the point of boredom. This involves a delicate balance.

The beating heart provides a good visual metaphor for instructional delivery in classrooms, where the balance between modeling instruction and guided practice pulses evenly back and forth. Gathering kids in front for instruction, releasing them to practice, and then bringing them back to share their thinking represents the steady flow that is at the heart of effective teaching and learning.

When we take the time to show kids how, we reap big rewards. The following approaches represent instructional practices that show students how we activate strategies to better comprehend what we read. Each of the strategy lessons in Part II of this book includes at least one of these instructional approaches:

◆ Reading aloud
◆ Thinking aloud and coding the text
◆ Lifting text
◆ Reasoning through the text
◆ Providing anchor experiences
◆ Rereading for deeper meaning
◆ Sharing our own literacy by modeling with adult literature

Reading Aloud

Jim Trelease, author of *The New Read Aloud Handbook* (1989), says that the purpose of literature is to provide meaning in our lives. He believes that literature is the most important medium, more important than television, film, and even art, because it "brings us closest to the human heart." He states that reading aloud serves to "reassure, entertain, inform, explain, arouse curiosity and inspire our kids."

We wholeheartedly agree. Some of our best moments have come from reading aloud or being read to. Steph first encountered Dr. Seuss in kindergarten when Miss Buehler read *The 500 Hats of Bartholomew Cubbins.* Anne remembers reading E. B. White's *Charlotte's Web* to her five-year-old daughter, Allison, and finding herself unable to continue through the tears when Charlotte died. The recent proliferation of books on tape illustrates our love affair with oral reading. Suddenly, we endure traffic jams with a smile, as we listen to authors like Toni Morrison and Frank McCourt regale us with compelling stories.

Thoughtful teachers everywhere dedicate time each day to read out loud to their students in all genres and content areas. Much of the strategy instruction described in this book involves reading out loud. We read aloud to immerse students in terrific literature as well as to teach reading comprehension strategies. Occasionally, we worry that efforts to design reading strategy lessons around trade literature might ruin a great picture book. We know the last thing kids need is a monotonous litany of comprehension lessons every time their teachers pick up a great book to read to them. We need to remember to share books for the sheer joy of reading as well as for strategy instruction.

Thinking Aloud and Coding the Text

It is through the read-aloud that teachers show students their thinking process when reading. We call these instructional demonstrations think-alouds (Davey 1983). Think-alouds are central to comprehension instruction.

It is nearly impossible to make reading concrete. Even the most involved math problem can be demonstrated in a concrete fashion, although it could take a football field of blackboards to write it out. The primary way we have found to make reading concrete is to show students our thinking as we read aloud and then record it in writing by coding the text. We need students to get an idea of what we are thinking when we read so that they might take a crack at it themselves. The think-aloud gives them an opportunity to see our thinking when we read, the connections we make, the questions we ask, our inferences and predictions.

Steph demonstrated a think-aloud in her *Up North at the Cabin* prior knowledge mini-lesson. She simply showed students what she was thinking as she read, coded the text with T-S on a sticky note, and wrote a comment or two related to the code. Much of the strategy instruction in this book occurs through thinking aloud and text coding with a wide variety of short text. We use codes for different strategies and then write a few words in the margin or on a sticky note that express our thinking. For instance, we might use ? to note a question, * to signal an important idea or theme, or Huh? or C to indicate confusion and signify that meaning has broken down. And we usually jot a few words on the note to hold our thinking. See Part III, Appendix F, for a listing of response options for each strategy.

When we walk into a classroom that emphasizes strategic reading, we know it. The books of kids and teachers who read deeply and monitor their comprehension burst with sticky notes. After seeing the teacher model text coding, kids practice it themselves in groups, pairs, and finally, independently. These written codes and responses record thinking, which helps readers remember what was going on in their minds for later discussion and application.

Teachers often ask us what kids should do with these ubiquitous sticky notes once they finish the book. Most of the time, we recommend that they place them in their reading notebooks. They might sort them, noting questions they can answer or questions that linger. Often these brief notes give students ideas for longer written responses. Personal narrative pieces emerge from text-to-self connections the kids have made in their reading. In addition, as a record of student thinking, sticky notes are useful to teachers for assessment and planning purposes. When we read aloud to our students, we might ask them to use sticky notes to keep track of their thinking about the text. Their sticky notes become a time line of their thinking and a record of their evolution of thought.

A word of caution here. Occasionally students will mention that coding text while reading interferes with their train of thought. We address this in a conference and suggest that the student read through the text first and then take a few moments to record thoughts and questions on sticky notes. The purpose of text coding is to enhance our students' understanding, not break their concentration and disrupt meaning.

Lifting Text

We frequently use the overhead projector to model instruction through close readings of short text. We lift a piece of text, make a transparency of it, and distribute a copy to each student in the class. We might lift the first page of a chapter from a social studies textbook and spend a few minutes showing students how we figure out unfamiliar words and terms. Or we might copy a newspaper article, read through it, and show how we sift out important information. We invite kids to bring their clipboards up near the overhead projector and crowd around. If there's no carpet or they resist sitting on the floor, we encourage them to pull up a chair. We need our students to be up close and personal during our mini-lesson as we read through the text, stop to point out how we activate a specific strategy, and invite them up to the overhead transparency to add their own responses. We are frequently amazed at how hard it is to understand text that appears easy on a cursory first reading.

The overhead projector is the supreme ally of explicit instruction. We like this user-friendly piece of equipment so much that we occasionally use two of them at once when we lift text. That way we can place the transparency of the text on one projector, where it remains undisturbed, and write our responses, comments, and notes on a transparency on the second overhead projector. This serves to minimize distractions that arise when we constantly move transparencies back and forth. When you know you are planning a mini-lesson that involves text lifting, you might simply borrow an extra overhead projector from a colleague.

Charts and Big Books are also favored friends of teachers who model instruction. We lift text and copy it onto charts to give kids a shared reading experience through the use of enlarged text. We might use such a chart when we teach inferring in poetry to young children, rewriting a poem on large chart paper and then encouraging kids to come up and code this giant version of the text. They can write their inferences in markers right next to the words that prompted their thinking. Or students might place a sticky note on the text and illustrations of a Big Book to share their questions, inferences, or connections. In this way, children's thinking is visible for all to see, providing an explicit and permanent example.

Reasoning Through the Text

When Anne models her own thinking in front of kids, she has difficulty restraining the children's participation. She knows it is necessary to show her thinking first and give children clear, explicit language for talking about their reading before they join in (Keene and Zimmermann 1997). But ignoring dozens of waving hands is nearly impossible for her. Furthermore, the insights and ideas that children bring to the discussion strengthen her teaching and their learning. After Anne has launched a lesson by thinking aloud, she invites the kids to join her in the discussion. This invitation seldom goes unanswered, since most of them are dying to jump in. Active participation in the discussion is essential if students are to construct meaning.

When we engage students in conversation about the text, we are reasoning through the text (Anderson et al. 1992). We listen very carefully to one another. We ask questions. We clarify ideas. We restate children's responses. We clear up misconceptions. We help children monitor their understanding by stopping to think when the text no longer makes sense. We draw inferences and encourage our students to synthesize the information as they go on to collectively build an understanding of the text.

During this type of conversation, the teacher becomes a facilitator who leads the discussion. We think this is guided practice at its best. We introduce a strategy or concept through modeling and thinking aloud, but we can't drone on forever. If we are going to keep children engaged, we need to involve them. When children have opportunities to share their thinking with peers, kids pay attention. This joint thinking allows our students to learn from each other and enhances meaning for the whole group. In many of the strategy lessons described in this book, children, alongside the teacher, acquire knowledge and enhance understanding by thinking through the text together. Once we've introduced a strategy, much of our instructional time is devoted to this sort of class discussion. This, more than any other approach, leads our students to a common understanding of the text.

Providing Anchor Experiences

We try to provide students with anchor experiences when we deliver instruction in reading comprehension strategies. We identify and choose our most effective mini-lessons as anchors for students to remember a specific strategy and better understand it. After Steph read *Up North at the Cabin,* the sixth graders searched for books they connected with. When they found that special book with which they identified closely, they coded their own text-to-self connections. The next time Steph talked about connection making with that group of kids, she referred back to that lesson and reminded them, "Remember when I read that book about the girl in the cabin in Minnesota, which reminded me so much of my own life, and then you chose books of special importance to you and marked your own connections? Try to find some places in today's reading where you connect to the text like that." Steph's reading *Up North at the Cabin* became an anchor lesson for kids to return to and activate their prior knowledge independently at a later date.

We recognize that most of the comprehension strategies described in this book are difficult to make concrete. So we scaffold them. Sometimes we do this in surprising ways. For example, when introducing inferring, we might take a group of unfamiliar related items, such as kitchen utensils, to share with kids. We explain that inferring is about taking information we already know, our background knowledge, and combining it with clues or facts to draw a reasonable conclusion about the information at hand.

When we show a kitchen item, we ask those kids who know what it is to hold their thoughts for a minute and let the others try to make an inference. We might show an apple corer. After they've scrutinized and handled it to no avail, we might add an apple. When kids see the apple in juxtaposition, they are likely to infer the purpose of the apple corer. This replicates how inferring works in reading. The more information we have, the more likely we are to make an inference that hits the mark.

The next time we read out loud, we point out when we are making an inference, and we show kids how we relate inferring in the text to the inferential thinking we did about the apple corer. When they head off to read independently, we might say, "Remember when we used the kitchen utensils to introduce inferring? If you need some help remembering what readers do when they infer, think about what you did to figure out what the apple corer was." In place of kitchen utensils, we've seen teachers bring in unusual items related to medicine, carpentry, archaeology, and even golf.

Some anchor lessons relate directly to a think-aloud we did with a book when we introduced a strategy. Others reflect more offbeat ways to scaffold our understanding of a particular strategy, like the kitchen utensil inferring lesson. But whichever we choose, these anchor experiences serve as lifesavers for kids as they develop their understanding of the nature of a specific strategy and recall it for the purpose of using the strategy independently.

Rereading for Deeper Meaning

Oscar Wilde once said, "If one cannot enjoy reading a book over and over again, there is no use in reading it at all" (Charlton 1991). Too often, we mistakenly think that once children have listened to a book one time, we're done with it. In truth, the more children hear or read a story, the better they comprehend it and the more they love it. Yet we don't remember our teachers ever reading the same book to us more than once.

First-grade teacher Debbie Miller, more than any teacher we know, reads books aloud multiple times to help children gain meaning. Debbie, the author of a forthcoming Stenhouse book on primary reading comprehension, points out that kids get little if any meaning from hearing a book only once. When Debbie first read Linda Altman's *Amelia's Road,* the story of the migrant farm life and one little girl's longing for a sense of place, her students asked dozens of questions. They couldn't conceive of a child who had to constantly move from place to place. In fact, they understood very little about what was going on. Without a second or third reading, a basic understanding of the text would have eluded many of them. On subsequent readings, they began to answer their questions and infer deeper meaning.

After reading a book like *Amelia's Road* once to students, some teachers might assume that it is too difficult for first graders to understand, and they might not think to read it again. Our intent in teaching with thought-provoking picture books is to present important topics that may not be within children's experience. They need more rather than less time with books like these to understand them. Rereading enhances understanding and leads to shared insights.

Sharing Our Own Literacy by Modeling with Adult Literature

When Steph's son, Alex, was in the first grade, he received reading support from Laura Benson, the school reading specialist. Alex, it seemed, was far more interested in discussing ideas and thinking than he was in learning to decode words. A thoughtful teacher, Laura understood the role that interest plays in reading, and she conceived ways to hook Alex on the written as well as the spoken word. Nineteen now and a voracious reader, Alex credits the day in first grade when Laura brought in an excerpt from Pat Conroy's *Prince of Tides* as the day reading became important to him. No one had ever shared adult text with him before, and he's never forgotten it.

For many years, Don Graves has said that those of us who teach reading must be readers ourselves. As readers, we experience the hoops and hurdles as well as the joys and insights that come with reading, and we can share the struggles as well as the victories with our students. When teachers model their own reading process using their own reading material, kids take note. See Part III, Appendix C, for lists of some of our favorite adult science, history, and literacy titles.

Fifth-grade teacher Glenda Clearwater frequently brings in her own reading material to teach comprehension strategies. Glenda knows that the books and articles she reads may not be completely appropriate for fifth graders, but she also knows that every book or piece of text has words and ideas that can be appreciated by readers of every age.

One day we watched as Glenda shared an excerpt from Michael Ondaatje's novel *The English Patient* to teach the concept of inferring to her fifth graders. Glenda asked her students to pay close attention to the words as she read them and to raise their hands when they reached the point in the text where they understood what was going on. The excerpt from midway into the first chapter follows:

> She moves backwards a few feet and with a piece of white chalk draws a rectangle onto the wood floor. Then continues backwards, drawing more rectangles, so there is a pyramid of them, single then double then single, her left hand braced flat on the floor, her head down, serious...
>
> She drops the chalk into the pocket of her dress. She stands and pulls up the looseness of her skirt and ties it around her waist. She pulls from another pocket a piece of metal and flings it out in front of her so it falls just beyond the farthest square.
>
> She leaps forward, her legs smashing down, her shadow behind her curling into the depth of the hall. She is very quick, her tennis shoes skidding on the numbers she has drawn into each rectangle, one foot landing, then two feet, then one again until she reaches the last square.

The first hand went up after Glenda read "single then double." Hands continued to shoot up intermittently throughout the excerpt. By the final sentence, all but three kids' hands were raised. When she finished reading, Glenda asked what happened in the excerpt. Kristin answered that the character was playing hopscotch. Glenda noted that the writer never mentioned the word *hopscotch*, and she asked how and when they had figured that out. Their responses varied. Most of the kids needed a few paragraphs to garner enough clues to infer that the passage was about the game of hopscotch. Several mentioned that they relied primarily on visualizing to get a picture of what the character was doing. Three of the kids never figured it out because of their limited background knowledge about hopscotch. Glenda explained that she had to infer, visualize, and activate prior knowledge to conclude that the girl was playing hopscotch. She explained that she uses comprehension strategies in her own reading in the same way the kids do.

Because she is a reader, Glenda knows what it means to think when she reads, and she sees merit in using her own literacy to give her students a model of strategy practice as well as a view of her life-long commitment to reading.

Beyond Dioramas: Responding to Reading

Lucy Calkins, professor and Teachers College writing project director, notes that when she finishes a book late at night in bed, she doesn't grab her husband by the arm and say, "Oh, I just can't wait to get downstairs and make a diorama." We understand. For too many years, kids in classrooms all over the United States have been asked to do a laundry list of activities when they finish reading books. You know the ones—dioramas, shadow boxes, word jumbles, word searches, and so on. Reading response is more than these. Authentic response tells us what's really going on in kids' heads.

In one way or another, every lesson described in this book focuses on student response. Be they oral or written, simple or sophisticated, responses tell us what children are thinking and learning. They let us know if our kids are engaged with reading or are tuning out from boredom. Once students respond to a text, we have some evidence to go on. We have an inkling about whether their understanding is in the ballpark or off the mark. And usually we know a whole lot more. Kids who have experienced some strategy instruction are only too happy to share their thoughts and opinions about their reading.

Although volumes have been written on literary response theory, our notion of responding to literature is quite simple. We believe that the best reason to ask students to respond to literature is that crafting a response enhances understanding for the respondent. When we ask students to respond, we are asking them to go deeper, ask critical questions, argue with the author, or make connections to their own lives.

The responses described in this book tap into how kids are using reading comprehension strategies. The two most common forms of response are oral and written, and many of the responses in this book fall into those two categories. We caution, however, not to neglect other less obvious forms, such as artistic or musical response, that reveal kids' strategy use. The strategy of visualizing, for instance, lends itself to artistic response. There's nothing like sketching to draw in a less verbal, artistic child. Inferring lends itself to some more offbeat responses, such as the kitchen utensil inferring discussion described earlier in this chapter. But these responses are more than mere activities; they show us how kids are using strategies to better understand what they read.

Diverse, open-ended responses tell us the most about what children understand or don't understand when they read. The response options listed in Part III, Appendix F, represent the following categories.

Oral Responses

Oral responses include both individual responses and group discussion responses. Some employ specific words that relate to a certain strategy. For instance, when a student says, "Oh, that reminds me of...," the teacher knows that the student is making a connection. Group responses include

Whole-class discussions The teachers portrayed in this book engage their students in whole-group discussions that encourage kids to reason through and think out loud about the text.

Pair shares After the teacher models a strategy, pairs are encouraged to go back and work through text, talk about it, and respond together.

Small informal discussion groups Similar to pair shares. Three to five kids discuss and reason through a piece of text together.

Compass group four-way shares Some kids talk all the time, others rarely open their mouths. Compass group sharing and responding is a formal technique that helps teachers manage classroom talk and gives equal access to everyone. Four kids sit either on the floor or at tables at the points of a compass, one in the north position, one in east, one in south, and one in west. With groups bunched throughout the room, the teacher announces north's turn. After about five minutes, the teacher suggests that north conclude, and in one minute she announces east's turn, and so on. After about twenty-five minutes, each child will have had a turn to share and respond for about five to seven minutes. The teacher can wander and eavesdrop, comfortable in the knowledge that this process guarantees even the most reticent talkers a chance to respond (Harvey 1998).

Book clubs or literature circles In these groups, students read like-kind text and meet to discuss and respond to it together, much the same way that adults meet in monthly book clubs to talk about a book they have read. Students ask questions, make connections, and talk about themes. Harvey Daniels's book *Literature Circles* describes this process in depth and offers practical suggestions to implement book groups in classrooms.

Informational study groups In these groups, students work together to build knowledge about a common topic of interest. These topics may emerge from a facet of the curriculum or simply from student interest. Participants often begin by asking questions that propel research efforts. The many different types of texts that address the topic allow readers of differing proficiency to participate because they can search for text they are able to read. These groups lend themselves to nonfiction reading because much of nonfiction text is informational.

Written Responses

Students in classrooms where we work use several response options in written form, including

- Coding the text with sticky notes
- Making notes in the margins
- Circling, highlighting, framing, bracketing, and underlining the text
- Using two- and three-column note forms to explore thinking
- Writing and responding in notebooks
- Writing letters to teachers, classmates, others in the school community, and people outside the school

Other Responses

Artistic, dramatic, musical, numeric, scientific, historic, economic. You get the idea. If we only stick to oral and written responses, that future Georgia O'Keeffe or Laurence Olivier may never emerge. As we think about a broader notion of response to draw in the many different kids we have, we work with them to develop the broadest spectrum of meaningful responses.

Where do our ideas for different response options come from? Mostly from the kids. For instance, as we teach a lesson on questioning to first graders, we often notice they have many more questions than we can reasonably record on a class chart. We may decide then and there to turn the kids loose to record their questions in their own notebooks. For us, one measure of classroom success relates to diversity in work product. Kids differ. Their work should, too. Careful observation of children, their interests, and their needs as learners is the best guide to developing different response options. And the purpose of responding to reading remains steadfast: to enhance understanding.

Moving on to a New Strategy Focus

We have found that there is no fixed time when we leave one strategy to focus on a new one. We do have some thoughts to guide our practice, however. To help young readers get a handle on a strategy, we have found it supportive to introduce and practice a specific strategy over time. An introductory focus lesson on prior knowledge on Monday followed by three or four days of guided practice does not mean the class is ready for questioning the following Monday. We are tempted to introduce a new strategy when we observe kids applying the strategy across different genres and in different situations, or when we notice boredom setting in.

To get an idea of when a strategy is sinking in, we travel around the room with clipboards and make notes of indications that kids are using the strategy to solve problems and make meaning in text. In one fourth-grade classroom, when Naomi and Lauren were reading about Colorado mountain men (Schmidt 1984), they came to the following sentence:

> In the early 1800s, no fashionable gentleman in America or Europe considered himself fully dressed without a tall hat made from the glossy fur of the beaver. This fashion craze made beaver pelts very valuable and led scores of tough young men to make the difficult journey across the plains and into the Rockies.

"Why would these men wear such silly hats?" Naomi questioned. Steph noted her question on the clipboard, pleased that Naomi was stopping to think and ask a question. "Because everyone was doing it," Lauren said.

Good, Lauren, Steph thought.

"Oh I get it. I've got a connection. It's kind of like the Furby this Christmas holiday," Naomi said. "It's a pretty ridiculous looking little toy, but kids want it because everybody else has one."

"What a great connection!" Steph told Naomi, confident that Naomi was grasping the connection strategy. "Good thinking, Lauren." Steph patted Lauren on the shoulder as she continued on to the next few readers.

Listening into student conversations while they are reading can be very revealing. We also find evidence of strategy effectiveness in our students' written responses. Carefully reading their written responses tells us how well students understand the strategies. When we notice that students are using a particular strategy effectively, it might be time to introduce a new one. We remind students to think about all of the strategies they've learned so they can use them when needed.

One important point: If the class seems to be getting bored with a particular strategy focus, it's time to move on. You know the telling signs. "Oh no, not this again" or "How much longer 'til recess?" As with all curriculum, when kids seem bored, change the content or, better yet, just let them read. Strategy instruction is no exception.

Chapter

4 Teaching with Short Text

"R ead widely and wildly," suggests Shelley Harwayne, literacy educator and founding principal of the Manhattan New School. The mini-lessons in this book incorporate a wide range of genres, including realistic fiction, historical fiction, nonfiction, and poetry, to teach comprehension strategies. Kids love to read these genres. Not surprisingly, though, we have yet to run into a kid who can't put down his social studies textbook. It's the compelling text in Jim Murphy's *The Great Fire*, the true story of the Chicago fire; the realistic fiction of a changing era in the South in Libba Moore Gray's picture book *Dear Willie Rudd*; and the beautiful poetry inspired by Walker Evans's Depression-era photographs in Cynthia Rylant's *Something Permanent* that hook our kids.

The teachers portrayed in this book present many different genres to lure kids into strategic reading. Increasingly, we find ourselves teaching students a variety of reading comprehension strategies using what we've come to call short text. We have discovered that when students have practiced comprehension strategies in short text of varying genres, they are far better prepared to construct meaning from longer chapter books later.

Comprehension Instruction with Short Text

We often ask teachers to write down the different types of reading they've done over the past few weeks. Usually, they mention newspapers, magazines, letters, manuals, cookbooks, brochures, reports, newsletters, and so on. Many also have a novel or a long nonfiction trade book going, but about 80 percent of the reading they report is of the short-text variety. This is true of adults in general. Yet this is typically reversed in schools, where about 80 percent of the reading kids do is long text. We are convinced that school reading should more closely reflect the reading done outside of school. Since much of the reading our students will do as adults will be short, we advocate more short-text instruction in school. As an added bonus, we have found short text to be the most effective type for teaching comprehension.

Short text is, in a word, short! The length of short text makes it more accessible than full-length novels or textbooks. This term *short text* can refer to a picture book. But it can also describe a favorite poem used for teaching inferring, an essay for modeling how to determine an opinion or perspective, or a short story such as Sandra Cisneros's "Eleven," which brings forth a barrage of students' memories of their own embarrassing moments. Most kids we know love Jean Little's *Hey World, Here I Am!*, a collection of short poems and prose that traces the thoughts and feelings of preadolescent Kate Bloomfield. Short text, in general, gives kids an opportunity to read a piece quickly and to practice comprehension strategies.

Magazines and newspapers are full of short text, but sometimes we forget to share them in school. *National Geographic, Smithsonian, Kids Discover, Time for Kids,* and *Sports Illustrated for Kids,* for instance, all feature well-crafted short text, pictures, and interesting content (see Part III, Appendix D). Trade magazines like these lend themselves to teaching comprehension in both the science and social studies content areas. They rarely fail as sources of information and strong models for writing. The many features of magazines and newspapers, including essays, editorials, feature articles, current events, sports stories, and business updates, give kids in the class the widest range of possibilities for finding and reading interesting text. We need to pack classrooms with magazines and newspapers as well as with picture books.

Choosing Short Text for Comprehension Instruction

We are constantly on the lookout for short text that is surprising, well written, and interesting. Articles from *Ranger Rick, National Geographic World,* and *Wild Outdoor World* have helped us model how to ask questions as we begin animal research. *Cobblestone: The History Magazine for Young People; Faces: People, Places, and Cultures;* and *Muse* are particularly good magazines for addressing social studies content. *Tomorrow's Morning,* a weekly newspaper aimed at grades 4–6, engages kids with age-appropriate articles as well as the news of the world. Kathy Wollard's nonfiction trade book *How Come?* answers many science questions such as How come stars don't fall? Internet articles give the most current information. All of these examples make strong candidates for short-text mini-lessons on the overhead projector, where teachers help students reason through difficult text in preparation for the students doing it alone later.

We are likely to choose short text when we explicitly teach reading comprehension strategies for the following reasons:

◆ It is easily read out loud, which gives everyone in the room a common literary experience.

- ◆ It is often well crafted, with vivid language and striking illustrations or photographs.
- ◆ It provides an intense focus on issues of critical importance to readers of all ages.
- ◆ It is authentic and prepares children for the reading they will encounter outside of school.
- ◆ It is self-contained and provides a complete set of thoughts, ideas, and information for the entire group to mull over.
- ◆ It is easily reread to clarify confusion and better construct meaning.
- ◆ It is accessible to readers of many different learning styles and ages.
- ◆ It allows even very young children to engage in critical and interpretive thinking regardless of their decoding capability. Ideas about the reading are easily shared and discussed.
- ◆ It provides ample opportunities for modeling and thinking aloud.
- ◆ Teachers can provide students with anchor experiences through short-text reading that students can call upon later to help comprehend longer or more difficult text.
- ◆ Picture books and many short-text forms cover an extraordinary range of topics, ideas, and issues.

Short texts often rescue us from turning a mini-lesson into what we sheepishly call a maxi-lesson. When we use just a little bit of text for a demonstration, students can get the point, teachers can stick to the point, and they can all get on with what's most important: students reading and practicing the strategies on their own.

Collecting Short Text Pieces of Every Size and Shape

Although Steph completely understands and agrees with the airlines' recent crackdown on oversized carry-on luggage, she used to lug a bag the size of a small Buick onto every flight. One day last spring, she reached the gate and was asked to check her bag. She did so quickly and without regret, until she sat down in the plane and realized that she had inadvertently checked all of her reading material. Four hours without print! For someone who reads at red lights, this was just short of disastrous.

After several minutes of watching the oxygen mask demonstration, memorizing the emergency exits, listening to the cockpit on the headset, and clicking her tongue, she reached into the seat pocket in front of her and pulled out *Hemispheres Magazine,* the United Airlines in-flight magazine. Although she flew regularly, she had never opened one before, and her expectations were less than sky high. She turned to an article on cruising, which began as follows:

When I was young and slippery as a sea squirt, I spent a sun-splashed summer polishing brass for the glory of waterborne commerce. In those long glorious sea days, we glided into tropical ports—dead slow—in the early morning, the sea like melted glass, the ship causing barely a ripple. You could feel the faint beat of the engines and hear the steady wash of creaming water alongside. The anchor chain went out, the bridge telegraphed "finished with engines" and we looked wonder of wonders on a foreign land. My old cargo line called at dusty little coffee ports, but they were Paris, London and Rome to me. I thought then that traveling by ship was the best way to see the world. I still do. (Keating 1998)

They say necessity is the mother of invention. If Steph hadn't mistakenly checked her reading material, she would have missed this stunning text. So pore over newspapers, magazines, travel books, brochures, and other printed matter to collect interesting short text for instruction.

Short text pieces are chosen for the following.

Content We search for articles that support and build background knowledge of the content we are teaching. These articles are likely to be more current than the texts in our room. We also look for articles that stress themes we have explored in class.

Strategy practice We search for short pieces that push our thinking, perhaps demanding that the reader ask questions, infer meaning, or synthesize information to understand.

Features We look for pieces containing features that signify importance, such as headings, bold print, italics, and captions, so that we can show authentic examples of these conventions and discover their purpose.

Form We select a wide variety of different writing forms, including essays, letters, feature articles, and columns to expose our students to the different characteristics of each form.

Genre We choose a variety of genres in short-text form, including poetry, short stories, and nonfiction informational articles, and we notice how they compare.

Text structure We clip different short-text forms to examine different cue words and text structures. For instance, when a sentence begins with the word *but,* we teach our students to be ready for a change to come. We find articles that are framed around a specific text structure, such as compare and contrast, and look at them closely to better recognize and understand the structure the next time we meet it.

Writing quality We look for vivid writing like that in the cruising article from *Hemispheres Magazine.* A recent *Denver Post* article described a phantom snowstorm as follows: "The forecast for Friday promised much of Colorado a full-fledged affair with the snow, but all the storm could muster was a cheap kiss on the cheek. An overnight snowstorm that swirled its way into the state barely flirted with the metro area but dumped up to 10 inches in parts of southeast Colorado" (Esquibel 1999). A charming metaphor!

Perspective We choose articles that might spark differences in opinion to enhance classroom discussions.

Surprising information We recently read a *Denver Post* headline that said "Misunderstood Sharks, Not Just Feeding Machines" (Broad 1997). We couldn't resist reading and clipping the article because we had always read that sharks were merely instinctive feeding machines, and now this promised a surprising new twist. Kids love surprising information.

Teaching with short text helps us design instruction that serves our goals of acquiring knowledge and enhancing understanding. Wonderful short text is everywhere. We need to live in a way that lets us find it. We read magazines and newspapers differently than we did before. Now, when we come across a great piece of writing or some interesting content, we check it against the previous criteria. We think about how we can use it for comprehension instruction and then we clip it, laminate it, and file it in strategic or thematic text sets.

The next time you read a piece of short text that really grabs you, think about why. Don't just toss it away. Save it, even if you don't know exactly how you will use it. In all likelihood, you will find a place for it in your comprehension instruction sooner or later.

Using Picture Books to Teach Comprehension

Although we encourage students to read a wide range of short-text genres, picture books offer certain unique advantages when we deliver instruction. Of all literature that lends itself to reading comprehension strategy instruction, picture books top the list. Why?

We believe that interest is essential to comprehension. If we read material that doesn't engage us, we probably won't remember much. Engagement leads to remembering what is read, acquiring knowledge, and enhancing understanding. Picture books, both fiction and nonfiction, are more likely to hold our attention and engage us than dry, formulaic text. There's nothing like the beautiful oil paintings of the writer/artist Thomas Locker in *The Mare on the Hill* or a striking photograph of the flukes of a killer whale jutting out from a sky blue sea to capture a reader's interest. Readers are more likely to comprehend material that interests them and that is written in a compelling way.

Picture books have been a prominent feature of elementary classrooms for decades. Elementary teachers the world over share compelling picture books with kids. But elementary kids can't have all the fun! There is a picture book for every reader and a reader for every picture book. The wide range of themes, issues, words, and ideas reach out into classrooms like tentacles drawing in each member, regardless of the different learning styles, ages, reading levels, or prior experiences. We need to think about *all* the students who can benefit from picture books. The teachers portrayed in this book use picture books with the broadest spectrum of students.

Using Picture Books with Older Kids

High school teacher Cris Tovani surprised a group of visiting teachers when she read aloud a picture book to her college-bound, twelfth-grade world literature students. The book, *Rose Blanche* by Roberto Innocenti, set during World War II, recounts the story of a young German girl who passes a concentration camp on the way to school each day. Her daily journey leads her from curiosity to sympathy to action. "I haven't read picture books to my students since I left elementary education," one teacher whispered to another. "Nor I," her teammate said, nodding in agreement.

Cris's students were mesmerized. Several dried their eyes as she read. The power of well-written picture books cannot be overestimated. Traditionally viewed as a genre reserved solely for younger children, picture books lend themselves to comprehension strategy instruction at every grade level. Older kids may balk when you first share picture books with them. Comments such as "Why are you reading those baby books?" will dissipate, however, when you share powerful picture books that are filled with sophisticated content best suited to older students.

Using Picture Books with Very Young Children

Don't readers need to be able to decode before they can comprehend? is a question we are frequently asked. We have found that we can begin teaching comprehension in preschool and kindergarten even though we recognize that young children are mostly nonreaders at this age. But teaching reading comprehension is mostly about teaching thinking. We can teach readers strategies for thinking through listening as well as through reading.

Books written with emergent readers in mind focus primarily on the decoding aspect of reading. Short words, repeated phrases, and patterns are great for decoding and enjoying the sound of language but offer little to prompt thinking. How deep can readers take *Mrs. Wishy Washy* (Cowley 1980), for example? When we read out loud to kids, we expose them to more sophisticated text that requires them to think. We eliminate the barriers that face young readers who can't decode text yet. Steph has read *Up North at the Cabin* to kindergartners as well as to eighth graders.

Retired kindergarten teacher and staff developer Kathy Haller is convinced that teaching strategies for comprehending text to emergent readers gives young readers a distinct advantage when they become more proficient decoders. Kathy thinks out loud to teach comprehension strategies to emergent readers and then gives them opportunities to talk about *their* thinking.

We are always surprised at how well young readers understand sophisticated topics and ideas when decoding no longer stands in their way. For this reason, the teachers portrayed in this book actively teach thinking about text to emergent readers as well as to older students.

Using Picture Books with Reluctant Readers

There are no better print materials to use with reluctant readers than picture books. The pictures complement the text to help less proficient readers access meaning. The topics, ideas, and issues are often sophisticated and prompt stimulating discussion. Readers can choose from many different levels and genres on a single topic. The shorter form is less intimidating than longer chapter books.

Nonfiction picture books, in particular, convey fascinating information through the use of vivid photographs, illustrations, and features such as bold print, italics, captions, and diagrams that support reluctant readers in their quest to gain information and understand the text. We can teach the meaning of these features and help readers use them to better understand. One distinct advantage of nonfiction literature is that it doesn't have to be read sequentially to get needed information. We can teach reluctant readers to use the table of contents to search for the content that is most interesting to them or the section that will best serve their purpose.

In Stephen Kramer's *Avalanche,* for instance, several chapters that focus on avalanche types and causes precede a chapter entitled "Avalanche Safety." Steph, a back-country skier, showed a group of readers how she searched the table of contents for that very chapter before she headed out on a back-country ski trip. Although she was somewhat interested in generic avalanche information, what she really needed was more information on how to stay safe in conditions that were ripe for avalanches. Reluctant readers become easily overwhelmed at massive amounts of information. Nonfiction helps them focus their search and read only what they need to answer their questions or to find specific information.

But sometimes struggling intermediate and middle school readers are more reluctant to choose picture books than their proficient reader counterparts. They believe that reading picture books will further identify them as unsuccessful readers. We need to promote picture books by reading them out loud, both fiction and nonfiction. Book choice is contagious. If we read picture books and share our passion for them, kids will choose them, too. In classrooms where proficient readers and their teachers choose compelling picture books, reluctant readers climb aboard.

Using Picture Books with Second Language Learners

At Denver's Horace Mann Middle School, many of the kids come from Mexico. They arrive daily and begin to make their way in a new world of English, strange food, unfamiliar teachers, and fat textbooks. Using picture books with ESL students can ease life in this new world, particularly if the books relate to their past experiences.

Kristi Sutherland, an enthusiastic first-year teacher, had reported an extreme lack of interest in reading on the part of many of the kids in her seventh-grade room. She understood how difficult it is to live here if you can't read English, and she was worried. She knew that to engage her students in reading, they must connect the text to their lives and activate their prior knowledge. She also knew that many of them had rich lives back in Mexico, but they were reluctant to share their past experiences for a variety of cultural, personal, and practical reasons. Kristi felt that their rich experiences were undervalued in this new American culture. She invited Steph to come in to help the kids see reading in a more positive light.

Steph and Kristi looked long and hard before discovering Eve Bunting's *Going Home,* a book that told the story of a family living in Los Angeles who returned to their hometown in Mexico at Christmastime. They drove for four days and four nights, and when they arrived on Christmas Eve, the entire town celebrated their return. As Steph read, previously bored, even surly, faces lit up. A quiet buzz filled the room; so many of these children had lived this. "Oh, they always comment on my Nikes," Geraldo said of the kids back in Mexico. "And whenever I go back, they always ask me to say something in English," Blanca added. Heads nodded in agreement.

When Steph finished reading *Going Home,* these middle schoolers swarmed around the book like bees to honey in an effort to be the first to hold and reread it. Kristi commented that kids who had never responded to a book seemed to be overjoyed with this one. Kristi recognized and valued all of her kids' prior experiences, both in Mexico and in Denver. And she knew that building on their past experiences would enhance their understanding of the text.

Teachers often tell us that they understand the need to activate children's prior knowledge and experience when they teach, but that some of their kids, particularly those from more impoverished neighborhoods, "don't have any prior knowledge" to activate. It's true that some kids come to school with more experience with books than others. But all kids bring a wealth of experience that we can build on to enhance understanding, even though much of that prior knowledge may lie outside the realm of books.

Kristi and the seventh graders at Horace Mann teach us one of the most important lessons. Classrooms where children's personal histories are valued serve as learning communities that respect differences. Before teachers can create a climate of mutual respect, they must help kids understand and value their differences. Sharing books that kids connect with sparks their interest in reading and builds community.

Don't forget picture books when you plan your next comprehension lesson. Everyone deserves an opportunity to hear, read, and enjoy a compelling picture book.

Now that we've explored a variety of instructional practices when using picture books and other short-text forms for teaching reading comprehension, we can think about how we might choose the best possible texts for instruction and how we help students select short pieces to read for strategy practice. If we aren't choosing great texts, we might as well give up the idea of teaching with literature. Book selection for teachers and students is discussed in Chapter 5.

Chapter
5 Book Selection

W inston Churchill once said, "If you cannot read all of your books, at any rate handle, or as it were fondle them—peer into them, let them fall open where they will, read from the first sentence that arrests the eye, set them back on the shelves with your own hands, arrange them on your own plan so that you at least know where they are. Let them be your friends; let them at any rate be your acquaintance" (Gilbar 1990). We know from whence Mr. Churchill spoke. At last count, between the two of us, we had nearly two dozen books on our nightstands of which we had not read a word. But we have held them, flipped through them, and introduced ourselves to them. The pile, however, just seems to grow. So we hold Churchill's words dear, and dream of when we might have time to read them all. This is true for our children's book reading as well.

Each year, increasingly large numbers of children's books roll off the presses. The sheer number boggles the mind: over 6,000 new books for young people in 1998 alone (Cruise 1999); at that rate, approximately 60,000 to come in the next decade. According to an article in *Time Magazine* entitled "What Johnny Can't Read" (Edwards 1998), teachers are sometimes unfamiliar with the wide range of high-quality contemporary literature available for the kids in their classrooms. It's no wonder; there are so many books out there! As problems go, however, this is a good one. We wrote this book, in part, to ease the job of choosing from among so many books (see Part III, Appendixes A and B).

How do we get to know more books and get them into the hands of kids? We can't possibly read every new publication that hits the shelf. Share those books you love with your colleagues. Spend some time each week talking about books. Your repertoire of picture books will grow with each conversation. Get up close and personal with the library. School librarians and children's librarians in public libraries have the most in-depth knowledge of children's literature of anyone we know.

Chances are that school librarians, in particular, have worked with different curricular topics and are aware of both current titles and classics that have stood the test of time. They regularly read and review publications such as *Horn Book Magazine, Book Links,* and *The New Advocate,* which all include extensive reviews of books that connect to a number of curricular topics. In Part III, Appendix E, we have provided a list of publications that offer thoughtful, critical reviews of trade books and articles on teaching themes, author studies, and a variety of genres with picture books. Teachers have never been more pressed for time. We hope this book will alleviate that time crunch.

Teacher's Choices: Choosing Text for Comprehension Instruction

We're frequently asked, How can I find the best book to launch questioning in my classroom? or What are some great picture books for building students' background knowledge about the Civil War? Teachers comment "I'd love to use more picture books as part of my reading instruction, but where do I begin?"

We've come to relish the search for books that support our teaching of reading comprehension strategies. With the many fiction and nonfiction trade books now available, it's possible to use picture books to study everything from marine biology to colonial America. We evaluate books for their effective, accurate, and interesting content as well as for their stories and themes.

How, then, do we find text that supports strategy instruction in the classroom? We keep the following in mind.

Purpose Our purpose is central to how we choose books for comprehension instruction. When we create instruction around picture books and other short text, we need to be clear about what we want children to learn from the particular experience. Do we want to model a specific strategy or build background knowledge on a particular topic? Sometimes a thoughtful picture book may be the best way to launch a discussion about a pressing issue like racism or an unfamiliar topic like the Great Depression. The clearer we are about our instructional focus, the easier it is to match books with our teaching goals.

Audience The interests, ages, and learning needs of our students are paramount in choosing texts for teaching. Children and adults of all ages and with many interests read and enjoy picture books. Awareness of our students' backgrounds and experiences is essential if we are to select books for our students that, as librarian Fran Jenner says, "touch their souls." Hmong children listening to the story *The Whispering Cloth* by Pegi Deitz Shea were pleased and surprised to see aspects of their traditional culture written about in a book. First-grade students in a Denver classroom read, debated, and loved Mary Hoffman's *Amazing Grace* until the book fell apart. A replacement copy was a small price to pay for these children's strong and personal connections to the book. The sky is the limit on thinking and learning when readers are compelled by the text.

Genre Teachers in literature-based classrooms have always focused on genre studies in folk tales, fairy tales, realistic fiction, historical fiction, and so on, as a mainstay of their reading programs. The recent explosion in nonfiction trade book publishing has made it possible to teach almost any genre or topic with picture books and other nonfiction text. Intermediate and middle school teachers collect curriculum-related text sets of picture books with up-to-date information, an interesting and accessible writing style, and useful photographs and illustrations. Trade books haven't yet replaced textbooks as a staple in classrooms, but many teachers are realizing the appeal of high-quality picture books for instruction.

Writing quality When choosing books or articles, we need to be thoughtful consumers of fiction and nonfiction. We might ask, Is the writing well crafted? Does a story strike our imagination, allow for interpretation, and make us think? Is a nonfiction text logically organized and easy to understand? Is the language clear and vivid? Does the author's choice of information and presentation pique our interest in a subject? Although judgments about quality merge with issues of personal taste, our annotations of selected picture books in Part III, Appendixes A and B, highlight some of the qualities that make picture books and other short texts both appealing to students and useful for comprehension instruction.

Choosing Picture Books to Teach Strategies

When we choose a book for the purpose of teaching a comprehension strategy, we carefully scrutinize it before selecting it for instruction. We check out the cover, flip through the pages, and notice what sort of thinking the text spurs in us. Some books lend themselves to questioning, others to making connections, still others to inferential thinking. Some books are written in a particularly vivid way, which stimulates mental images for visualizing.

Certain genres lend themselves to teaching certain strategies. Realistic fiction and memoirs often spur connections and questions in readers. Poetry is likely to stimulate visualizing and inferential thinking. We frequently choose nonfiction pieces to teach determining importance and synthesizing information when we read. Certain authors, too, cause us to activate one strategy above others. For us, Cynthia Rylant's work spurs the most natural of connections. Eve Bunting's picture books often leave us asking questions. We primarily rely on inferring when we read a book by Chris Van Allsburg such as *The Stranger,* the mysterious story of a wanderer who may, in fact, be Jack Frost. We recognize that all books and genres spawn a wide range of thinking, but we find that some books lend themselves to a particular strategy for the purpose of instruction. We are likely to choose such a book when we launch instruction in a specific strategy.

When we pick up an unfamiliar book, we have no idea which strategies might come into play to help us better understand the text. We have to read it first. Anne used a variety of strategies to comprehend the story when reading Jon Krakauer's *Into Thin Air.* Some of these same strategies proved useful with the children's picture book *Storm Boy* by Paul Owen Lewis. It tells the story of a Northwest Coast Native American boy whose boat capsizes in the rough sea.

As Anne read the first few pages, she found herself asking lots of questions about the text. The book began, "A chief's son went fishing alone, and a terrible storm arose. He soon found himself washed ashore under a strange sky he had never seen before." The illustrations that accompanied the first page of text show the boy plunging deep into olive green water. In the next picture, he's lying on a rocky shore, but the "strange sky" mentioned in the text is olive-green. Anne asked herself, "Where is he? How was he suddenly washed up on shore after falling deep into the sea? Why is that sky so olive-green?"

As she flipped back to reread the previous page, she noticed that the strange olive-green sky was, in fact, the same color as the deep sea. He might still be under the sea, she reasoned, but the words "washed ashore" led her to a different interpretation: he was in a strange land. Her original inference that he might still have been under the sea was confirmed only when, near the end of the story, she saw a picture of the boy being carried to the ocean surface on the back of a killer whale.

Anne realized that she had relied primarily on questioning and inferring to understand *Storm Boy.* As she planned a lesson for second graders who had already been introduced to questioning as a strategy, Anne decided to focus on just one strategy—questioning—with the second graders. Eliciting children's questions about *Storm Boy* as they listened to the story would allow the students to practice this strategy. As teacher Jane Brunot and Anne recorded the children's questions on a chart, many were strikingly similar to Anne's. Children noticed the odd green sky, and one child wondered "if the boy was still under the sea." At the end of the story, the children, realizing the boy had indeed visited the land of the killer whales, returned to their chart to try to answer their initial questions.

When the children begged to listen to the story a second time, Jane read it without interruption. Afterwards, some children raised their hands to share even more questions. They wondered, "Why didn't the boy drown if he was under the sea all that time? Did the killer whale save him from drowning? Was this a lesson to teach him not to go out in his boat in a storm?"

"You know," Ryan pointed out, "sometimes you just can't answer all your questions."

As they debriefed the lesson together, Jane and Anne concluded that the children had successfully used questioning to better understand *Storm Boy*. The kids were beginning to discern the difference between questions that could be answered and those that couldn't be answered, a distinction Anne and Jane would return to in subsequent mini-lessons. Although Anne and Jane hadn't planned it this way, *Storm Boy*, along with the chart of the students' questions and responses, became an anchor lesson for the students to refer back to when they thought about questioning in other texts that they read.

Choosing Picture Books to Build Background Knowledge and Teach Content

It's no secret that trade books are extraordinarily effective for teaching content. In many of the schools we know, teachers and librarians find picture books like Faith Ringgold's *Aunt Harriet and the Underground Railroad in the Sky*, Ann Turner's *Nettie's Trip South,* and Jeanette Winter's *Follow the Drinking Gourd* essential for beginning a study of the Civil War. Nonfiction books like Virginia Wright-Frierson's *A Desert Scrapbook* and Alexandra Wright's *Will We Miss Them?* encourage us to read and write about animals in new and interesting ways. Thoughtful picture books about ecological topics, such as Mary Ann Fraser's *Sanctuary* or Jane Yolen's *Letting Swift River Go*, are ideal for launching a study of environmental concerns. Building text sets in a particular topic or genre is a good start, but focusing on content alone isn't enough.

As we teach content with picture books, we have found that instruction in reading comprehension strategies allows students to access that content. Teaching students to read text strategically sharpens and enhances their understanding of the content. At the same time, we can bring up issues, problems, and concerns without deluging students with facts and information. Unlike longer nonfiction or reference materials, picture books and other short texts focus our attention on one issue or topic at a time. Curricular stalwarts such as history and geography benefit from an ever-growing collection of picture books covering every conceivable time period and culture. Using picture books, children can investigate topics as diverse as the predatory patterns of great white sharks and the contemporary settlement at Dharmsala, the refuge in India where Tibetans strive to preserve their culture. And science trade books provide ample opportunity for children to ask and answer many of the questions they have about the natural world.

Choosing Picture Books That Engage Readers

We remember the words of the writer C. S. Lewis when we choose books for reading and instruction: "No book is really worth reading at the age of ten which is not equally (and often far more) worth reading at the age of fifty"

(Cullinan 1981). When we find a book that inspires our teaching, we can hardly wait to see how children will respond to it. We are hopeful that it will engage them. If, however, they demonstrate a ho-hum attitude, we need to reconsider our choice.

When we think about audience, we have one thought in mind: keep readers engaged and thinking. As mentioned in Chapter 4, Kristi and Steph realized that if they were to be successful in teaching Horace Mann seventh graders how to link their personal experiences and background knowledge to their reading, they had to find a book—like Eve Bunting's *Going Home*—that would elicit personal connections. The kids were anything but ho-hum about it.

That's why books with problems, characters in the midst of dilemmas, or endings that leave the reader wondering have greater potential for strategy instruction than stories that are overly predictable or without problems and resolutions. Debbie Miller introduces comprehension instruction with books that elicit strong responses from her first graders. Children identify with the characters in books like Tomie de Paola's *Oliver Button Is a Sissy* or Mary Hoffman's *Amazing Grace.* Debbie's students become quite involved with the dilemmas these characters face and how each overcomes adversity. Debbie accomplishes her goal of teaching young children to make personal connections because as they listen to picture books they live through the narratives and stories of others.

Picture books may more readily engage children in topics, themes, and big ideas than bland or difficult expository selections. Picture books with varied reading levels and lengths can be used by readers of differing abilities and sophistication. One intermediate class, through a study of picture books, decided that themes like "leaving," "becoming a refugee," "learning a new language," and "will they ever go back?" were important to keep in mind as they continued to learn about immigration. Although the children had little personal experience with immigration, picture books helped them develop empathy for the obstacles and problems encountered by characters in these narratives.

Choosing Challenging Picture Books

Just as we read difficult books ourselves, it's important to share books that are a stretch for children. Fortunately, as mentioned in Chapter 4, decoding usually isn't an issue during strategy lessons because we read literature aloud to students or read through poems and short text together. We usually find that if a book is clearly and engagingly written, even young children can follow intricate plot lines and understand complex characterization. In fact, books with more ambiguity and mystery about them are more likely to hold our students' attention and prompt questions and inferences. We've noticed that stories and narratives set in strange cultures or unfamiliar historical periods result in more rather than less interest. Stories in familiar circumstances with straightforward characters and obvious plots merit little effort and require less of students in the strategic thinking department.

Nonfiction books are often challenging to read and filled with sophisticated information that students love. We know many students who would rather read nonfiction than a riveting mystery or adventure story. Students are fascinated by books on unusual and even wacky topics, such as Sara Bisel's *The Secrets of Vesuvius,* Charlotte Foltz Jones's *Mistakes That Worked,* Walter Wick's *A Drop of Water,* and Aliki's *The King's Day.* The lesson here is never underestimate what a student can read when motivated to do so.

Choosing Picture Books Just Because We Love Them

The best reason of all to read a picture book to a group of students is simply because you love it. Anne and her colleague Nancy Burton made frequent trips to a local bookstore to purchase books for their classroom library. One day they became so engrossed in choosing books that they never noticed when an over-efficient bookstore employee unloaded the mountain of books they had stacked in their cart. Thinking no one in their right mind would buy that many books, she had quietly reshelved each one of them. So, unless you live next door to the public library, beware. Children's books can be habit-forming.

Enthusiasm for books is contagious. Sometimes we become so focused on a theme or curricular topic that we put off sharing our favorites. Big mistake! Steph still reads Margaret Wise Brown's *The Sailor Dog* to nearly every class she meets regardless of their age or content area of study. It was the first book she ever really *read,* and she can't not share it with kids because it means so much to her. Kids pick up on this. Invariably, the moment she closes the book, they leap up and grab for it en masse, even eighth graders. We also choose books we have always wanted to read but have never gotten around to. Anne has a list of several dozen. Once in a while, she picks one up and reads it to the kids. In this way, they learn about the book together, which gives everyone a fresh, authentic experience.

Sharing our thoughts about why we love a book allows students to get to know us better and shows them how discerning we are about what we read. Children in classrooms where everyone talks about books, teachers included, aren't afraid to venture their thoughts about a book. There's no better way to encourage readers than to ask them to contribute their favorites to a classroom text set. And students can't resist becoming engaged when we consistently ask them to voice their honest opinions.

Children's Choices: Helping Students Choose Text

Readers must be reading texts they can and want to read if they are to successfully practice a strategy independently and get better at reading. The reading workshop model described in Chapter 3 includes large uninterrupted blocks of time for readers to engage in text reading. During these reading blocks, students read independently and activate strategies to comprehend text. The teachers portrayed in this book understand that kids are more likely to become engaged in reading if they choose their own books. This is easier said than done. Many readers abandon books they can't read or find boring. Sometimes a very compelling book is too difficult.

Teachers can suggest ways to support students in book choice, and they can explicitly teach students how to choose books they want to read as well as books they can read. Teachers recognize that the reader faces a number of considerations when deciding what to read.

Readability: Easy, Just Right, and Challenge Books

Many teachers encourage readers to choose a book according to how hard or easy it is to read. Readability is an important factor when readers choose books if our goal is to get better at reading. We encourage young readers to think about the level of a book. We talk to them about three kinds of books according to readability: easy, just right, and challenge books (Hagerty 1992). We model each of these categories by showing young readers how we choose books ourselves from a readability standpoint. Our kids often don't realize that adults can't read everything. They seem to believe that grownups have already learned all there is to know in reading. We are here to fill them in on that closely guarded secret: Adults continue to learn to read throughout their lives, and even sophisticated adult readers encounter text that challenges them.

To model this, we bring in three books that we consider easy, just right, and challenging. Steph shares Dave Barry's *Best Travel Guide Ever* as an easy book she reads over and over. She loves his sense of humor and connects much of what he writes to her own zany household. She explains that for her the book practically reads itself. She can read all of the words, and she understands all of the ideas. Next, we share a book that we find extremely challenging. For Steph, it might be a book about physics such as Stephen Hawking's *A Brief History of Time*. She explains that she has always been interested in physics and physicists, although she's never taken a course in physics and wasn't particularly good at math. She has started this book several times, but she doesn't understand quite a few of the words and many of the ideas, probably because of her lack of prior knowledge.

For Anne, it's directions. Rather than read directions, she persuades any available family member to program the VCR or change a flat tire. Her new laptop remained a glorified typewriter until she made up her mind to tackle the extensive and complicated manual. The same can be true for our students. If they are motivated, they will work to comprehend even the most challenging text. Sometimes we postpone reading challenging text until we have the necessary skills to do so. Other times we take a crack at it because we are so motivated to read it.

And then there is the just right book. Just like baby bear's chair, this book fits like a glove. We can read most of the words and understand most of the ideas, but not every one necessarily. For Steph and Anne, it is the novel they keep on their nightstand, their favorite new professional book, a nonfiction trade book in a content area of interest, or the Sunday *New York Times Magazine.* A just right book challenges us to think but doesn't frustrate us when we read it.

We let kids know that reading is a bit like eating. If we only eat ice cream, we won't stay healthy, and if we only choose easy books we won't get better at reading. Yet everyone needs a little ice cream now and then, and everyone needs a respite from difficult text, a moment to enjoy a good laugh from the comics or a Dave Barry column.

Similarly, if we only choose books that are too hard, we are likely to abandon them out of boredom or frustration. Some books are emotionally more rugged than others. Justin, a fourth grader, was reading *Bridge to Terabithia* (Paterson 1977) in his book club. He was completely captured by the book but nevertheless suggested to the group, "Since we are reading such a sad book in November, we'd better read a funny one in December." A constant diet of sad books can be a downer for kids. We have to vary our diets both in eating and reading. Just as we generally try to choose healthy balanced meals, we can strive to choose just right books most of the time.

As our demonstration nears an end, we reiterate that if we only choose easy or challenging books, we won't get better at reading. We close this mini-lesson by creating a chart together with the kids and then posting it in the room for all to see. The one that follows ends with a quote from Sam, a Denver fifth grader.

- ◆ *Easy books.* An easy book is a book in which you can read every word and understand every idea.
- ◆ *Challenge books.* A challenging book is a book where there are many words you can't read and many ideas you can't understand.
- ◆ *Just right books.* A just right book is a book where you can read most of the words, but not all, and you can understand most of the ideas, but not all.

"It is fine to read easy books sometimes and challenging books sometimes, but most of the time we try to choose books that are just right for us. That way we'll get better at reading."

One thing we share with our students is an exciting outcome of classifying books into these three categories: as we grow as readers, books that were once challenging suddenly seem just right and eventually even become easy. These easy, just right, and challenging designations can help readers recognize reading improvement.

Choosing Books for Purpose and Interest

Readability is only one factor in book choice. Teachers need to think beyond readability alone when helping students consider book choice. The subject, the author, the content, and the reasons to read all come into play when choosing books.

Teacher and staff developer Cris Tovani, author of a forthcoming Stenhouse book on teaching reading comprehension to middle and high school students, believes that we must explicitly show our students how to choose a book based on three criteria. She asks her students to consider the following when they select a book:

◆ Purpose
◆ Interest
◆ Readability

Cris demonstrates this by asking young readers to list some different purposes they have for reading, and she records their responses on a chart. Their purposes include

◆ School assignments
◆ To find out information
◆ Entertainment
◆ To read instructions
◆ To cook something
◆ Just for fun

Cris emphasizes that these are but a few of the many purposes for reading and that purpose affects our book selection. She encourages the students to add more purposes to the chart whenever they arise.

Joaquin, a seventh grader at Horace Mann Middle School in Denver, noted that one of his purposes for reading was to put his little sister to sleep at night. Cris asked him if he chose easy or hard books to do that. He said easy books, so his five-year-old sister could understand them. And as for interest, he said he might choose *Cinderella* because princesses were a big deal to his sister. In other words, his primary purpose in this instance was reading to his little sister. Help your students think of the many purposes for reading. Hopefully, they won't forget enjoyment. If they neglect to mention it, add it, or any other purpose you deem worthy, to the list.

Of course, we read out of interest. Nothing compels readers more than their personal interest in a piece of text. We have noticed that readers can read more difficult books if they are interested in the material. It is why text-books are so tough for students to read. They are frequently written in a dull, dry, uninteresting way, making reading more challenging.

Interest is central to book choice for readers of every age. Text that addresses a reader's interest promotes engaged reading. Julia was so engaged in reading *Mistakes That Worked,* Charlotte Foltz Jones's book about inventions like Post-it Notes that came about serendipitously, that she simply couldn't put it down. Her enthusiasm burst forth in a letter to Mary Urtz, her fourth-grade teacher, in which she mentioned that she would soon get back to a science book titled *Ocean Life* but not until she finished *Mistakes That Worked* (see Figure 5.1). For personal reading, we primarily choose books based on our interests. Why expect kids to be any different?

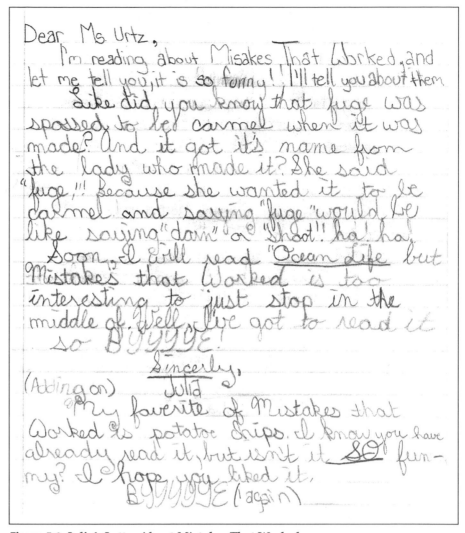

Figure 5.1 Julia's Letter About *Mistakes That Worked*

Helping Kids Select Books to Read

To scaffold book selection, we ask kids how they choose a book. What exactly do they do when they reach for a book on the shelf? We record their responses on a chart in hopes that some of these suggestions will be contagious. The kids in Leslie Blaumann's fourth-grade class compiled the following list for how they choose books:

◆ Reading the back
◆ Reading the flap

- ◆ Reading the first page—an interesting lead can reel them in
- ◆ Reading the first few pages
- ◆ Reading the table of contents
- ◆ The title
- ◆ The length
- ◆ The level
- ◆ Flipping through the pages
- ◆ Reading the last page
- ◆ The pictures
- ◆ The cover
- ◆ The author
- ◆ The subject
- ◆ The series
- ◆ The genre
- ◆ Recommendation

All of these are helpful suggestions, but Leslie understands that if she merely copied this list each year and posted it, the kids in her class would likely ignore it. This list makes sense to them because they create it based on their own needs and practices.

Don't be afraid to weigh in here, however. You, too, are a member of the learning community in your classroom. Leslie recognized that she generally chose a book based on the recommendation of someone close to her. Recommendation never made the original list. So Leslie added it to the list. She wanted her students to know that in her experience the books she enjoyed most were those recommended by her friends and family, who know her and tend to suggest books they know would capture her interest.

Kids need to keep you apprised of their interests so that you can fill the room with books they will read. Post a chart where kids can record their interests and, more specifically, some books they would like to see in the classroom. That way, when teachers order books or head off to libraries, garage sales, and bookstores, they can look for those special books that kids in their classrooms yearn for.

Distinguished author and Newbery winner Katherine Paterson suggests, "It is not enough to simply teach children to read; we have to give them something worth reading. Something that will stretch their imaginations—something that will help them make sense of their own lives and encourage them to reach out toward people whose lives are quite different from their own" (Paterson 1995). We hope the suggestions on book selection in this chapter will help get such books into the hands of kids, where they belong.

Strategy Lessons and More

We read for many reasons. We read to connect the text to our lives, to let our imagination carry us away, to hear the sound of narrative language, to explore age-old themes, to glean information, and to acquire knowledge. Throughout this book, we have emphasized reading purpose. We choose books for different purposes. We choose authors for different purposes. We choose genres for different purposes. And we choose strategy lessons for different purposes. Part II of this book focuses on strategy lessons, practice, and assessment.

We introduce most strategy instruction with think-alouds similar to the *Up North at the Cabin* mini-lesson in Chapter 1. When we introduce the questioning strategy, we are also likely to begin by reading and thinking aloud, this time about a piece of short text that spurs questions in the reader. When we first teach inferring, we choose to read aloud texts that hint at much of the content rather than reveal it up front, and we think aloud about how we draw inferences. After thinking aloud to introduce a strategy, we move on to instruction that features text lifting, rereading, discussing, and reasoning through the text, as described in Chapter 3. These types of lessons are featured in Part II of this book.

We begin with Chapter 6, "Making Connections," and Chapter 7, "Questioning," the two most accessible strategies. These two strategies provide the concrete foundation of meaning construction. Readers of all ages tend to connect text to their experiences. They also brim with questions when they read, which keeps them reading and searching for answers. Beginning strategy instruction supports readers to become aware of their connections and questions and articulate them clearly. We invariably teach making connections first, followed closely by instruction in the questioning strategy, because these are the strategies young readers are most likely to grasp first.

In Chapter 8 we describe the strategies of visualizing and inferring. Both of these strategies involve interpretation of text, pictures, and notions that go unwritten. Readers activate these strategies to get at the deeper meaning of text and further enhance their understanding. Visualizing, more than any other strategy we know of, brings reading to life. We usually introduce these strategies after we have provided instruction in making connections and asking questions, because inferential thinking surfaces once readers make connections and ask questions.

The lessons in Chapter 9, "Determining Importance in Text," illustrate the strategy of identifying essential ideas and important information in text. Most of these lessons occur in the realm of nonfiction because readers usually seek information in this genre.

Chapter 10 presents lessons that show readers how to synthesize information. Synthesizing requires a prior facility with most other strategies and occurs at the intersection of several. In order to synthesize, readers must make connections, ask questions, draw inferences, and determine important ideas. Synthesizing is the most complex of the strategies we describe; it is the strategy that allows readers to change thinking and achieve insight.

Chapter 11, "Strategy Instruction in Context," presents portraits of three classroom teachers providing instruction in reading comprehension and practicing a strategy in context over time. Finally, Chapter 12 explains assessment—how we determine whether kids are effectively using a strategy to better understand what they read.

The lessons in these chapters move from less to more sophisticated. For instance, in Chapter 8, we begin with a lesson on inferring that encourages students to interpret pictures. A later, more sophisticated lesson on inferential thinking involves the interplay between questions and inferences to discern themes and bigger ideas. Most of the early strategy lessons in each chapter are introductory. Those that follow build on the foundation of the earlier lessons.

We want to stress that the upcoming lessons describe some of the many possibilities for teaching reading comprehension strategies. These lessons are generic. We use sticky notes to code our thinking about any strategy and any text. We use two- and three-column note forms for inferring, connecting, asking questions, or any other strategy. We also adapt most of these lessons to different age groups. Just because we feature the lesson with a sixth-grade group doesn't mean that it wouldn't be equally effective if adapted for a group of second graders.

The same goes for book choice. We have chosen text that has worked for us when teaching and practicing a particular strategy, but don't limit yourself to our suggestions. Your personal favorites are likely to work just as well if not better. Help yourself to the books we've described, but feel free to choose your own. All text demands that readers think carefully and use these strategies to make meaning.

The strategy lessons that we describe have worked well for our purposes and for the students we teach. When we plan comprehension strategy instruction with teachers and librarians, we consider the following:

◆ Strategy to be taught
◆ Content of the lesson
◆ Outcome for children's learning
◆ Best instructional approach
◆ Quality and relevance of the materials
◆ Children's interests
◆ Children's prior experience with comprehension instruction
◆ Children's prior knowledge of the content
◆ Children's reading level
◆ Our own interest and enthusiasm for a piece of text
◆ How our lesson teaches children to use the strategy independently

Chapter
6   Making Connections
A Bridge from the New to the Known

A group of second graders swarmed around Anne as she read William Steig's delightful picture book *Amos and Boris*, the story of a friendship between a whale and a mouse, and the predicament they face when the whale becomes stranded on the beach. William Steig is one of Anne's favorite authors, and *Amos and Boris* was one in a long line of Steig books that Anne had read out loud to these kids. With each new book by William Steig, the kids added more information to their store of background knowledge about his books, and they began to see a variety of connections. Rashid noticed that most of the characters were animals that could talk. Julianna observed that all the characters seemed to encounter difficult problems over the course of the story. The more these second graders read William Steig's books, the more they came to expect certain themes, humor, and ideas to emerge.

As serendipity would have it, the night after Anne read *Amos and Boris* she heard a remarkable story on National Public Radio of a whale marooned on a Texas beach. The local citizens of the town had turned out in shifts over a twenty-four-hour period to spray the whale with water in an attempt to keep it wet and alive till a helicopter could rescue it. Having once gone on a whale-watching expedition off the coast of California, Anne was drawn to the NPR story. When she woke up the next morning, all she could think about was that unfortunate whale, and she wondered if it had survived the night. The minute she arrived at school, she rushed off to the library to search the Internet for a news update. Much to her delight, the whale was still alive, so she took copies of the news bulletin to the classroom.

As the children listened to the unfolding news story, the discussion turned to the similarities between the stranded whale and the predicament of Boris, the whale in *Amos and Boris*. Several students coded the news transcripts with connections they noticed between Boris and the stranded Texas whale, and later that day a small group found the sad news online that the whale had died. Two children wrote the following brief news account noting the difference in the two endings: "Boris lived, but the Texas whale died. Sometimes stories have a happy ending. Sometimes real stories don't." Some students were so interested in this event that they continued to seek and find information about the plight of stranded whales and why whales beach themselves in the first place.

The possibilities for making connections are many. We connect to the content as well as the nature of text. Connections enhance our understanding. The kids connected Boris to the Texas whale to better understand his plight, and they connected William Steig to a humorous writing style, coming to expect laughter when they pulled his books off the shelf. Our prior experience and background knowledge fuel the connections we make. The books we read, the authors we choose, the discussions we have, our past experiences, the newspaper, the evening news, the weekly magazines, the Internet, and nightly dinner table conversations all forge connections that lead to new insight. We teach kids to think about their connections and read in ways that let them discover these threads.

Making Connections to Build Understanding

When we begin strategy instruction with children, stories close to their own lives and experiences are helpful for introducing new ways of thinking about reading. Readers naturally make connections between books and their own lives. Once they have heard a wealth of stories and narratives, they begin to connect themes, characters, and issues from one book to another. When children understand how to connect the texts they read to their lives, they begin to make connections between what they read and the larger world. This nudges them into thinking about bigger, more expansive issues beyond their universe of home, school, and neighborhood.

Our suggestions for strategy lessons move from close to home to more global issues or cultures and places further removed from most children's lives. Although some lessons emphasize understanding literature and others focus on building background knowledge in a particular topic or literary form, all have a common purpose: to use our personal and collective experience to enhance understanding.

STRATEGY
LESSONS

Making Connections

Beginning to Make Connections: It Reminds Me of...

Purpose: Thinking aloud to introduce connection making

Resource: The story "Slower Than the Rest" in *Every Living Thing,* a collection of short stories by Cynthia Rylant

Responses: Coding the text R for remind; listing connections on a large chart and a two-
column form headed What the Story Is About/What It Reminds Me Of

"Slower Than the Rest," a short story about a boy who rescues a turtle that
subsequently becomes his constant companion, is one of our favorites for
teaching readers to think about the connections they make as they read to
their own lives as well as to the larger world. The story draws comparisons
between the slow turtle and the little boy, Leo, who attends special education classes at school and frequently feels "slower than the rest" himself.
Leo's self-esteem soars when he shares his knowledge about and love for his
turtle at school, much to the delight and acclaim of his teachers and peers.

When we begin teaching connection making in reading, we often share
realistic fiction or a memoir, because these genres are likely to bring up
thoughts and ideas that are close to the reader's own experience. "It
reminds me of…" is a common refrain from even very young children in
classrooms that feature literature that is close to kids' lives. "Slower Than
the Rest" is a good example of a story most kids can relate to.

At first, we design very simple codes to describe our thinking. For
example, whenever we read parts that remind us of our own lives, thoughts,
or experiences, we stop, think out loud, and code the text R for reminds me
of…. Then we write a few words on the sticky note that explain the incident,
thought, or feeling. Of all connection-making codes, this is the simplest. The
word *remind* makes sense to most kids, and they understand the notion of
being reminded of something when they read.

As students join in and share their own connections, we might list them
on a large chart. This chart sometimes evolves into a list of topics for writing
personal narrative pieces, in which students expand on their individual connections to write stories from their personal experience. As we continue
exploring the notion of connecting the story to our own lives, we may model
a simple two-column form. What the Story Is About/What It Reminds Me Of
encourages students to summarize the story in the first column and respond
to a memory, some prior knowledge, or a past experience in the second.

With "Slower Than the Rest," the connections run the gamut from "I
have a pet iguana" and "I had a turtle once, too" to the more sophisticated,
poignant connection that Randall, a reticent fourth grader, shared: "It
reminds me of how I feel just like Leo sometimes, especially when Mrs.
Steadly [the special education teacher] comes to get me." He went on to say
that he always wondered what the rest of the class was doing while he was
out of the room. This brave and honest boy changed the tenor of the discussion that day. A lively conversation ensued that enhanced the understanding of the rest of the students, who became more aware of what it felt like to
be just a little different.

As our students practice coding R for remind, becoming familiar with
the notion of connection making, we go on to more sophisticated codes. We
introduce text-to-self (T-S) connections next because kids quite naturally
relate their reading to their own lives. We follow with text-to-text (T-T) con-

nections, which readers make between different texts, and then with text-to-world (T-W) connections, which readers make between the text and the bigger issues, events, or concerns of the world at large. In addition, we remember to point out the different aspects of genre, structure, and style so that our students build background knowledge of the nature of different literary forms, too.

Making Connections Between Snippets and Real Life

Purpose: Making connections in writing

Resource: The picture book *Snippets,* by Charlotte Zolotow

Response: Choosing a snippet and writing a personal response to it

Snippets, a picture book described by its author, Charlotte Zolotow, as a collection of "pictures, poems, and possibilities," provides a wonderful model for encouraging children to make connections in their writing. Zolotow's *Snippets* contains little, short pieces on just about anything from aardvarks to zithers. To avoid long, drawn-out stories, we teach our kids about snippets. We explain that snippets are tiny pieces of their lives that they can write about. The teacher chooses a snippet from the book and models how it connects to her life, to another text, or to a bigger issue in the world. Then she responds by writing a short snippet of her own. The kids then choose a snippet to respond to. Phillip, a first grader, was interested in the snippet on lightning.

After reading this eight-line poem that describes a bolt of lightning streaking through the sky, Phillip wrote about his own experience with lightning following Charlotte Zolotow's example of using very short lines (see Figure 6.1). These kinds of prompts are particularly useful for helping kids make connections to their lives. In fact, we haven't found a better book to inspire kids to make connections than *Snippets.*

Text–to–Self Connections: Relating the Characters to Ourselves

Purpose: Linking the text to our life

Resources: Picture books by Kevin Henkes, including *Owen, Chrysanthemum,* and *Julius, the Baby of the World*

Response: Coding the text T-S for text-to-self connections

When Boulder first-grade teachers Kelly Daggett and Melissa Oviatt introduced a Kevin Henkes author study at the beginning of the year, children found it easy to make text-to-self connections with these books, whose char-

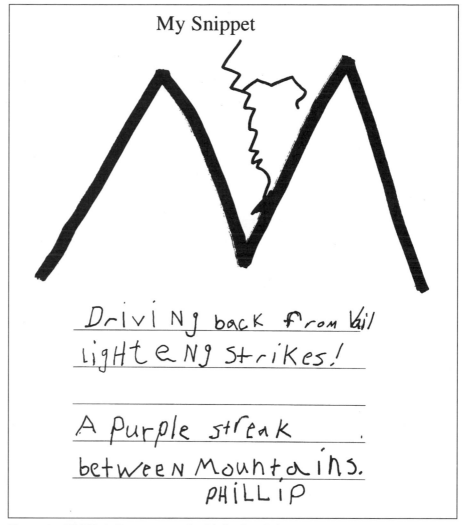

My Snippet

Driving back from Vail
lighteng strikes!

A purple streak.
between Mountains.
PHILLIP

Figure 6.1 Phillip's Response to the Lightning Snippet

acters were about the same age as they were and had similar problems and experiences. They were drawn to characters like Owen, who won't give up his ragged, old blanket, or Chrysanthemum, whose mouthful of a name is problematic for a kindergartner. Melissa and Kelly chose these narratives because they suspected their first graders would relate to them.

Just as Steph did in her *Up North at the Cabin* think-aloud, Kelly and Melissa modeled their own text-to-self connections for the kids as they read the Kevin Henkes's stories aloud, coding the text T-S and writing a few words about their own connections to their past experiences. As they modeled text-to-self coding for these first graders, Gerald waved his hand wildly in the air and asked, "What is text?" Kelly and Melissa thanked Gerald for his right-on question and explained that text is any print that is written down—a book, a newspaper, a poem, a magazine article, and so on. These first graders had to understand the meaning of the word *text* before they could begin to comprehend the term *text-to-self connection*. Once again, we are reminded that we can't be too explicit!

As the children listened to a variety of Henkes stories, they began to make text-to-text connections as well. They noted similarities between characters and their predicaments in Henkes's books. One wise first grader noted that Lily in *Julius, the Baby of the World* was every bit as stubborn about accepting the new baby in the family as Owen was about giving up his blanket. Melissa quickly labeled that comment a text-to-text connection for all other first graders to plainly hear.

Having made strong connections between the characters in the stories and their own lives, and having learned some language for connection making, these first graders had a greater understanding of Henkes's narratives. In fact, the more connections they made, the better they seemed to understand the stories.

Text-to-Text Connections: Finding Common Themes in Author Studies

Purpose: Connecting big ideas and themes across texts

Resources: Picture books by Eve Bunting, including *Smoky Night, The Wall, A Day's Work, Fly Away Home*

Response: Coding the text T-T for text-to-text connections

Denver teacher Anne Ertmann's third graders were engaged in a study of Eve Bunting's picture books. As they pored over books such as *Smoky Night,* an account of the Los Angeles riots; *The Wall,* a book about the Vietnam Veterans Memorial; and *A Day's Work,* a story about a boy and his Mexican immigrant grandfather who were day laborers, the kids realized that Bunting writes about serious topics.

That wasn't all they noticed. Anne Ertmann and her students were avid writers who were currently studying leads in writing and experimenting with different ways to begin their own personal narratives. One day, while meeting with his Eve Bunting book club group, Gregory suggested that the group look at how Eve Bunting begins her stories and list some of the leads. As the children discussed what they had found, Lauren flipped to the end of *Fly Away Home,* Bunting's book about a father and child who are homeless and take shelter in an airport. "Wait a minute," she exclaimed. "Eve Bunting doesn't really tell us what happens at the end of this book, to the boy and his dad."

"Yeah," Josh chimed in. "At the end of *Fly Away Home* I still had a lot of questions about what would happen."

"She leaves us up in the air a lot," ventured Sara. "Sometimes there isn't really an ending."

No one orchestrated their responses or told these kids what to think about Eve Bunting. They came up with their own ways of understanding and interpreting the text. They moved from studying leads to delving into endings in the most natural way. Their teacher had prepared them to think beyond the obvious by teaching them to "read like writers." Another group of children might well have come up with equally thoughtful but quite different observations about Eve Bunting's books.

Generally, kids start by making text-to-text connections to more obvious elements of stories, such as characters or problems. Some text-to-text connections, in order of increasing sophistication, might include

◆ Comparing characters, their personalities, and actions
◆ Comparing story events and plot lines
◆ Comparing lessons, themes, or messages in stories
◆ Finding common themes, writing style, or perspectives in the work of a single author
◆ Comparing the treatment of common themes by different authors
◆ Comparing different versions of familiar stories

Building Background Knowledge to Teach Specific Content

Purpose: Collecting information and listing prior knowledge to build a store of knowledge about a content area

Resources: Assorted books on Africa, including Gray and Dupasquier's *A Country Far Away*

Responses: Large chart and fact sheet

At Sabin Elementary in Denver, kindergarten teacher Paige Inman's goal was to explore the continent of Africa with her students. Asking children what they already knew about Africa allowed Paige to discover that, in fact, they knew very little. With librarian Jeanine Gordon, Paige found and read lots of books about Africa to the children to build their background knowledge. They discussed pictures and photographs, and asked questions. These five-year-olds were amazed at some of the information they unearthed. As the children asked questions, Paige wrote each on a sticky note and placed them on a chart for all to see. As the number of questions grew, she helped the children sort their questions into categories like food, homes, wildlife, games, and customs.

After much discussion, Paige asked her students to write what they knew. Using an African fact sheet, the children used their knowledge of letter-sound relationships and invented spelling to write what was memorable. Tiffany shares her new information about African butterflies on her fact sheet (see Figure 6.2). The children's enthusiasm for their work illustrated what Paige had most encouraged in these beginning researchers: a sense of curiosity and a willingness to investigate life in another culture.

An African Fact

by Tiffany

ButtREl Lv IN The LNGL.

Figure 6.2 Tiffany's Response to the Africa Fact Sheet

At the conclusion of this project, Paige had learned a lot from her kindergartners. She now viewed them as veritable sponges soaking up information about Africa. They continued to wonder out loud about a culture quite different from their own. And once her kids heard a fact, they seldom forgot it. It's not often we start from scratch to build background knowledge about a topic. But when we do, sharing information and encouraging student questions is the simplest route to teaching content.

Building Background Knowledge Based on Personal and Text-to-World Connections

Purpose: Sharing connections to build historical understanding

Resource: Sherry Garland's picture book *The Lotus Seed*

Responses: Coding the text T-W for text-to-world connections; listing student connections on a large chart

As we introduce new topics or issues, we observe students struggling to understand unfamiliar ideas and information. Students who have background knowledge about a topic have a real advantage because they can connect the new information they encounter to what they already know. Our responsibility is to help build students' background knowledge so that they can read independently to gain new information. Encouraging students to make text-to-world connections supports our efforts to teach students about social studies and science concepts and topics.

Intermediate teacher Tim Downing introduced his fourth and fifth graders to Sherry Garland's picture book *The Lotus Seed,* the story of a refugee family fleeing their homeland during the Vietnam War. Tim believed that this story of a young woman who took a lotus seed with her as she journeyed to a new life in the United States would provide information about this particular historical time period. He encouraged the students to focus on text-to-self and text-to-world connections as they read. As the students shared copies of the book, jotting down their thoughts on sticky notes, Anne wondered whether they would have many connections. Most elementary students she'd worked with had little knowledge about, let alone personal connections to, the Vietnam War. However, as she conferred with pairs during reading time, she noticed the response on Jimmy's sticky note: "My uncle fought in Vietnam and he told me all about it."

When the students shared their connections later, Jimmy elaborated on his T-S connection, telling his classmates that his uncle had fought in Vietnam. Sylvia looked puzzled. As she studied a *Lotus Seed* illustration of bombs falling on a rice paddy, she asked incredulously, "You mean, we were the ones bombing Vietnam?" Jimmy explained that probably the people in the picture were North Vietnamese and that U.S. planes may have been doing the bombing. At that point, Rory chimed in with his text-to-world connection and his summary of the war, saying "the North Vietnamese were fighting for communism and the South Vietnamese were fighting for freedom."

Jimmy's personal connections and Rory's knowledge about the Vietnam War added to their classmates' background knowledge of this event and time period. Later, Anne charted the students' responses to display the thinking that supported their connections. In this lesson, not all of the students were able to make connections like Jimmy and Rory. The chart served as a continuing reminder to the children of ways to link text to their own lives and the larger world.

Building Background Knowledge for Literary Elements

Poetry has its white space, fiction its characters, and nonfiction its bold print. In fact, every literary genre or form has certain features that define it. When we explore fiction, we teach our students about character, setting, problem, and solution. When we investigate nonfiction, we share expository text structures such as "compare and contrast" and "cause and effect." We teach these features so that students will have the background knowledge to better comprehend a specific genre or form when they read and write.

Text-to-self, text-to-text, and text-to-world connections are content-based connections. Readers also make connections to the nature of text and the literary features. Once they become aware of these features, readers know what to expect when they read a novel, pick up the newspaper, follow a manual, or glance at an advertisement. We design instruction around the following features so that readers will see the connections and better comprehend what they read.

Genre Nonfiction, fiction, poetry, and so on vary. With exposure, readers become familiar with the special characteristics and conventions of each genre.

Format Readers learn the differences among picture books, novels, nonfiction trade books, and so on. They rely on these differences to better understand what they read.

Form Readers learn to distinguish among essays, editorials, manuals, feature articles, and so on. This awareness heightens their understanding when they read different forms.

Author Readers learn that certain authors carry similar themes, issues, and topics throughout their writing. Readers come to expect these.

Text structure Readers recognize the differences between narrative and expository text and other structures, and learn the characteristics of each to better comprehend.

Cue words Readers learn to identify cue words that alert them about what's to come. For example, *but* suggests a coming change, *in other words* is followed by a definition, and *most important* means exactly that. (See Part III, Appendix F, for Text Cues chart.)

Writing style Readers notice the various writing styles of different authors, develop an appreciation of them, and begin to make connections between them.

Literary features Readers learn to search for themes, identify problems, and recognize settings when they read. They develop background knowledge for these features of text. When readers think about connections they make to the features or nature of text, they might code them LC for literary connection. For instance, when they recognize the white space in a poem from having seen the same feature before, they might code it LC to help them think about the purpose of white space in poetry. They could do the same with boldface print or italics in nonfiction. The more they understand about the nature of text, the better they will comprehend it.

Pitfalls When Making Connections

Once children understand the concept of connections, there seems to be no stopping them. They link books, experiences, and ideas in delightful ways. In classrooms where teachers teach connection making and build in time to practice strategy application, kids fill their pages with sticky notes coded R, T-S, T-T, and T-W. We've encountered certain pitfalls on the connections path, however.

Tangential Connections

Students may need to be shown how to make meaningful rather than tangential connections. For instance, some kids might make a connection between the fact that there is a grandfather in Bunting's *A Day's Work* and that they have one, too. A more meaningful connection would involve the relationship between the grandfather and the grandson. The story delves into that relationship and describes the boy's embarrassment at disappointing his grandfather by telling a lie. A more sophisticated connection might be to a lie once told or to an embarrassing moment. We need to read student work carefully and listen well to conversations to see that kids are making meaningful connections. The student-teacher conference offers the perfect venue for nudging students to make meaningful connections rather than more tangential ones.

Will Any Connection Do?

We can watch for authentic connections that support understanding. Kids are terrific teacher-pleasers and may think that any connection is better than no connection at all. Sometimes, particularly when kids are new to the practice, text coding runs rampant and authentic connections get left in the dust. Younger kids often get so excited about writing on sticky notes that they write down just about anything that comes to their mind. "It reminds me of when I went down on a sinking ship," third grader Jake wrote while reading Robert Ballard's *Exploring the Titanic*. His teacher guessed that Jake was getting carried away with connection making. When she quizzed him privately about this connection, he sheepishly admitted that he had never really been on a sinking ship.

After the untimely death of a class pet, Michelle Meyer read her first-grade class *The Tenth Good Thing About Barney*, Judith Viorst's picture book about the death of a beloved pet and the family's attempt to gain closure after the incident. After reading the story, Michelle encouraged the kids to write down their connections in their notebooks. Katie was clearly moved by the story and wrote prolifically about her similar past experience (see Figure 6.3). And although Daniel wrote less, a smile crept across Michelle's face as his honesty burst through (see Figure 6.4). Sharing Daniel's connection with the class as well as Katie's shows how Michelle values authentic, honest connections.

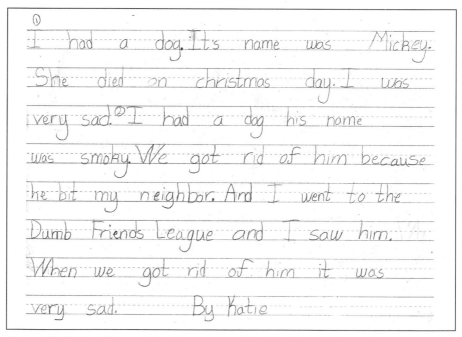

Figure 6.3 Katie's Connection Response to *The Tenth Good Thing About Barney*

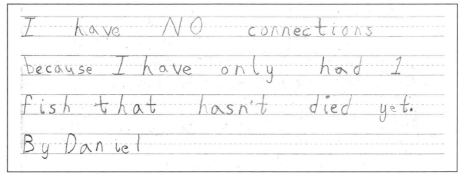

I have NO connections because I have only had 1 fish that hasn't died yet. By Daniel

Figure 6.4 Daniel's Connection Response to *The Tenth Good Thing About Barney*

Which Connection Is It?

Alexandra, a fifth grader, was reading *When Jessie Came Across the Sea* (Hest 1997), the story of a young Jewish girl at the turn of the century who was chosen by the local rabbi to emigrate to America from Eastern Europe but was forced to leave her beloved grandmother behind. When Alexandra came to a passage that said, "The ship docked at Ellis Island. Wait on line. Inspections. Wait on line. Papers. Wait on line. Questions. Wait on line." she stopped, coded the passage T-S, and wrote "I've been to Ellis Island," referring to a trip she'd made with her parents the previous summer.

But she had trouble moving on from there because she also began to think about the history of Ellis Island and the difficulty some people faced while waiting in line, how the lucky ones got through, and how the less fortunate were turned back. She knew that even today immigrants sometimes have a tough time at the border and some are denied entry. Connecting immigration today with immigration during the heyday of Ellis Island caused her to recode the passage T-W to note a text-to-world connection that said, "Life is very hard for immigrants."

Either code works. Connections overlap. As Alexandra reread the passage, her contemplation about Ellis Island drove her to a deeper, more meaningful connection. But we don't want kids, or teachers for that matter, to get hung up on which code belongs where. The purpose of coding the text is to monitor comprehension, think about meaning, and enhance understanding. Alexandra was definitely doing those things.

How Does That Connection Help You Understand?

One day Steph conferred with Allison, a seventh grader reading *Mirette on the High Wire* (McCully 1992), the story of a brave little girl who helps an aging tightrope walker overcome his fear. She noticed Allison's sticky note coded R that said, "I get really scared in high places just like Bellini does."

"Tell me about that," Steph nudged.

"Oh, I don't know. I just get scared looking down from tall buildings or standing on the edge of a cliff," Allison explained.

"That's interesting. So how does that connection help you understand the story?" Steph asked.

"I don't know," Allison replied. She hadn't even thought about it because she was so busy reading and writing down her connections.

"It seems to me that you have a leg up on understanding the character of Bellini because you, too, have a fear of heights. You bring your own experience to the character and you know better how that character feels and even how he might react. Better than me, for instance, because although I have plenty of fears, height isn't one of them," Steph said.

Steph and Allison agreed that the next time Allison made a connection, she would stop and ask herself how the connection helped her understand the story.

Although children may initially have trouble articulating more significant connections, with teacher and peer modeling and plenty of time they gradually begin to refine and limit their connections to those that deepen their understanding. Readers make connections to better understand their reading. Reminding our students of this fact keeps them on track with strategy practice. As we focus on the strategy of making connections, we can't forget that increasing understanding, not a plethora of tangential or inconsequential connections, is the goal of activating background knowledge and prior experience to make connections.

We almost always move onto the strategy of questioning after having studied and practiced connection making. As soon as kids start to make connections when they read, questioning is rarely far behind. It's a given. The more we know, the more we wonder. Chapter 7 follows this natural progression and shows how our connections and background knowledge spawn meaningful questions that propel us further down the road to insight.

Chapter

7

Questioning
The Strategy That Propels Readers Forward

A lbert Einstein once said "I have no special talents, I am only passion-
ately curious" (Calaprice 1996). Although some might argue with his
talent assessment, Einstein meant it. As teachers, we can't overlook
the fact that his curiosity prompted him to solve one of the greatest mysteries of our physical universe. We must strive to create classrooms that celebrate passionate curiosity.

Curiosity spawns questions. Questions are the master key to understanding. Questions clarify confusion. Questions stimulate research efforts.
Questions propel us forward and take us deeper into reading. Human
beings are driven to find answers and make sense of the world. The Nobel
prize–winning physicist Richard Feynman referred to this need as his "puzzle drive" (Feynman 1985). He couldn't not search for answers to those
things that confounded him, those things he didn't understand.

Teachers portrayed in this book encourage this same "puzzle drive" in
their students. Matt, a space lover, began writing what he knew and was
learning about his favorite topic. But his curiosity got the better of him, and
halfway into a letter to his teacher his questions burst forth and hijacked his
response (see Figure 7.1). Matt reminds us that good questions spring from
background knowledge. Matt knew about and loved space; hence he could
ask terrific questions. It's tough to ask a substantive question about something we know or care nothing about.

As adult readers, we question all the time, often without even thinking
about it. When we first began to pay attention to our thinking as we read,
we were stunned at the number of questions we had, many of which were
inspired by relatively small amounts of text. Kids don't grow up knowing
that good readers ask questions. In fact, schools often appear more interested in answers than in questions.

Our students need to know that their questions matter. They need to see
us asking questions as well as answering them. Asking questions engages us

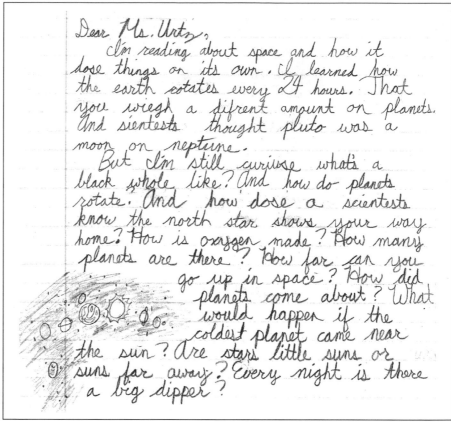

Dear Ms. Urtz,

I'm reading about space and how it dose things on its own. I learned how the earth rotates every 24 hours. That you wiegh a difrent amount on planets. And sientests thought pluto was a moon on neptune.

But I'm still curiuse whats a black whole like? And how do planets rotate. And how dose a sientests know the north star shows your way home? How is oxygen made? How many planets are there? How far can you go up in space? How did planets come about? What would happen if the coldest planet came near the sun? Are stars little suns or suns far away? Every night is there a big dipper?

Figure 7.1 Matt's Response, Full of Questions

and keeps us reading. A reader with no questions might just as well abandon the book. When our students ask questions and search for answers, we know that they are monitoring comprehension and interacting with the text to construct meaning, which is exactly what we hope for in developing readers.

STRATEGY
LESSONS

Questioning

Share Your Questions About Your Own Reading

Purpose: Using adult text to show the questions we have when we read

Resource: The novel *The God of Small Things*, by Arundhati Roy

Responses: Sticky notes coded with ?; follow-up group discussion

The next time you read a piece of adult text, pay close attention to the questions that surface and share those questions with your kids. Let them know that all readers—even adults—have questions. When introducing questioning to a group of sixth graders, Steph shared an excerpt from the novel *The God of Small Things* by Arundhati Roy, a book she loved despite her many questions and frequent confusion about it.

She gathered the kids in front of her and talked about how the text raised questions for her. She wrote her questions on sticky notes, placed them next to the passages that spurred them, and coded them with ?. She pointed out that some of her questions were answered in the text and others were not. She explained that her sticky note marked with "I love the title, but why is it called *The God of Small Things*?" was not addressed until quite late in the book. Her question "What is a paravan?" was answered several paragraphs further on: it is a member of the untouchable caste in India. When she read the answer, she moved her sticky note to the spot where the question was answered, wrote the answer on the sticky note, and recoded it A for answered.

Sometimes she was mired in confusion. In those cases, she coded a sticky note Huh? to note that meaning had broken down for her. This code signaled her to reread or read a few sentences ahead to try to make sense of the text before going on.

At the conclusion of this mini-lesson, Steph invited the kids to talk about questioning in reading. Robbie commented that he never knew a teacher could have so many questions about her reading. He seemed to be saying, "If she can have questions, so can I."

Some Questions Are Answered, Others Are Not

Purpose: Beginning questioning; listing and categorizing questions to promote understanding

Resource: The picture book *Charlie Anderson*, by Barbara Abercrombie

Responses: Chart with list of kids' questions; codes for categories of questions, including A for answered, BK for background knowledge, I for inferred, D for discussion, RS for research, C or Huh? for confused

When we begin teaching the strategy of questioning, we simply share the questions we have before, during, and after reading, and talk about them. All written text gives rise to questions, but sometimes we find a book that spurs questions from start to finish. Barbara Abercrombie's *Charlie Anderson* is just such a book. It tells the story of a cat who moves surreptitiously between two homes, living with one family by day and another by night, unbeknownst to the two separate owners. This story line parallels the lives of the two young characters, Sarah and her sister, Elizabeth, who move between their divorced parents' homes, as many kids do. This is a terrific book for kids who share this lifestyle. In fact, we have noticed that kids who spend their time in two different homes are more likely to pick up on the parallel theme. Alternatively, many young kids never even notice the divorce angle but seem to enjoy the simple story of a mysterious cat who disappears each night and returns home each morning.

Listing Questions

For all kids, however, we have found this to be a useful book to teach questioning, since they brim with questions when they read it. Ponderosa Elementary second-grade teacher Mary Lawlor read *Charlie Anderson* to her class. The text is sparse, with fewer than five or six sentences per page. When she reached the end of each page, she solicited kids' questions. A parent volunteer recorded their questions on a piece of chart paper as Mary read. Their numerous questions emerged from the cover illustration and the prereading discussion as well as from the text and pictures during the reading. At the end of the story, the chart included the following list of questions:

> Why is the book called *Charlie Anderson*?—A
> Who is that cat in the yard?—A
> Why was the door open just a crack?
> Do cats really like French fries?
> Where does the cat go every morning?—A
> Are these girls twins?
> Does Sarah get jealous that he likes Elizabeth's bed best?
> Why did he get fatter and fatter every day?—A
> Did they miss Charlie when they went to their dad's on the weekends?
> Do they like their dad's house better?
> Why didn't Charlie come home one night?—A
> Is he going to be all right?—A
> How come Anderson looks just like Charlie?—A
> Which family does Charlie like better?

As Mary read through the questions, she asked the kids to come up and put an A for answered next to the questions that were explicitly answered in the text. After reviewing and coding the questions, the class discussed them. In most cases, the unanswered questions were the more intriguing ones, the questions that dug toward deeper themes and bigger ideas. The question about where the girls preferred to live sparked a lively conversation. We have discovered that unanswered questions often stimulate the most stirring discussions.

Categorizing Questions

We can start helping kids categorize questions in primary grades. As we move up through grade levels, we can add different categories of questions. Some question categories and corresponding codes include

◆ Questions that are answered in the text—A
◆ Questions that are answered from someone's background knowledge—BK
◆ Questions whose answers can be inferred from the text—I
◆ Questions that can be answered by further discussion—D
◆ Questions that require further research to be answered—RS
◆ Questions that signal confusion—Huh? or C

The endearing question about whether cats eat French fries would likely require further research, although someone may have the background knowledge to provide an answer. As we look at the questions, we can work together as a class to code them. Since we adhere to the gradual release of responsibility approach to instruction, we are likely to introduce these question categories slowly and deliberately, adding new ones as kids develop facility with them.

Knowing When You Know and Knowing When You Don't Know

Purpose: Monitoring comprehension to clarify confusion or answer questions about the text

Resources: Any number of picture books and magazines or a piece of self-selected text the student is currently reading

Responses: Sticky notes coded Huh? for confused or with a lightbulb for the reader's illumination after being confused

One of our favorite techniques for monitoring comprehension involves the code Huh? We have noticed that when kids become confused by their reading or when they have a question, they are likely to stop, scrunch up their noses, and say Huh? as Steph did when reading *The God of Small Things* (see the strategy lesson on pages 82–83).

We can't stress how important it is for teachers to realize when kids are confused and to help them do something about it. We encourage kids to code a sticky note Huh? and place it at the point of confusion in the text. We model this ourselves, and we write Huh? on the top half of the sticky note, leaving the bottom half blank.

As kids continue reading or rereading to clarify meaning or answer a question, they often clear up their confusion or find the answer in the text. At this point, we encourage them to move their original sticky note to the place where their confusion is clarified or their question is answered. There, hot on the heels of Huh?, we encourage them to sketch a lightbulb on the bottom half of the sticky note. Most of our students are so excited to have resolved the difficulty that they happily take time to draw a lightbulb to mark their point of success. This coding technique supports their effort to monitor their own comprehension as they move toward independence.

Gaining Information Through Questioning

Purpose: Writing in Wonder Books (nonfiction notebooks that support inquiry) to explore thinking and wondering

Resources: Wonder Books and assorted nonfiction trade books

Responses: Written question lists; two-column note form headed Questions/Facts

Eleanor Wright begins the year in her fifth-grade classroom at Ellis Elementary in Arlington, Texas, by sharing her own questions, those things she wonders about and longs to explore further. Kids are encouraged to share their questions in notebooks reserved for wonder and exploration. Eleanor asks her students to choose at least three things they wonder about. Cassie is nothing if not curious! Eleanor asks Cassie's permission to make an overhead transparency of her question list to share with the class (see Figure 7.2). Eleanor understands that questions are contagious and that kids who are struggling to come up with a question may just catch the wonder bug from Cassie. In classrooms that value wonder, kids come up with terrific questions.

In Mary Urtz's fourth-grade classroom, questions abound. Kids refer to their nonfiction notebooks as Wonder Books, and they explore questions on topics of interest, questions from their reading, and questions for research. Most begin by simply listing a wide range of topics they wonder about, as Jonathan did when he wrote the following in his Wonder Book:

Anacondas. How can an anaconda squeeze so tight when it looks all fat and lazy and isn't all bulked up like Arnold Schwarzenegger?

Hurricanes. How do they form? What season? Where?

Spinal cord. How can breaking your spinal cord paralyze or kill you?

Allergic reactions. How can a bee sting kill a person? How can nuts make you all puffed up? How come hair and fur make you sneeze a lot?

Monkeys and gibbons. How do they have such good balance? How can they stand on a branch that is so thin or swing on branches with speed and not hit another branch or fall off?

Matt's curiosity grew as he investigated space. In a letter he wrote to Mary Urtz, he burst with questions (see Figure 7.1). When Mary talked to Matt, she found that his questions were especially useful to help him narrow the broad topic of space. We have found that the easiest way to guide students to focus research topics and pare them down is through their questions.

As kids read books on a specific topic, they acquire information and record new questions in their Wonder Books. Some code their questions on sticky notes. Some simply list their questions in their Wonder Books. Others record them in a variety of two- and three-column note forms (see Part III, Appendix F). Mary teaches the class to use a two-column form headed

Figure 7.2 Cassie's List of Questions

Questions/Facts. Amanda chose it to record questions and facts as she did research on Queen Elizabeth II (see Figure 7.3). Others chose listing, webbing, or mapping to record questions and new information. Matthew recorded his questions and left room to answer them as he read (see Figure 7.4).

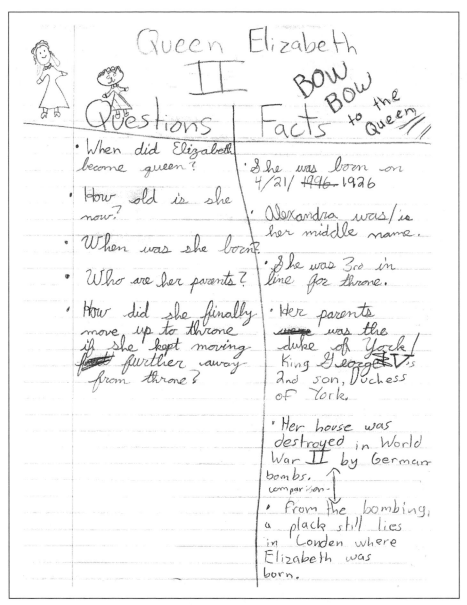

Figure 7.3 Amanda's Questions and Answers in Two-Column Format

In sum, Eleanor and Mary expose their students to a variety of possibilities for asking questions, organizing thinking, and responding in writing. In addition, the kids come through with a wide range of original ideas and forms for sharing their own questions. Mary and Eleanor frequently ask the kids' permission to make transparencies of these organizational forms to

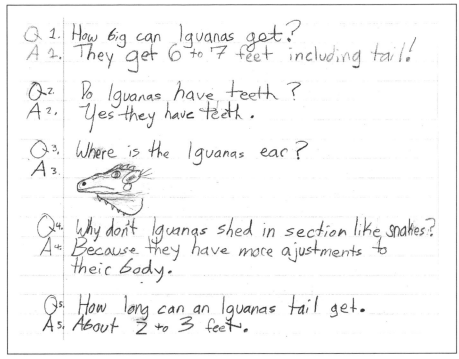

Q 1. How big can Iguanas get?
A 1. They get 6 to 7 feet including tail!

Q 2. Do Iguanas have teeth?
A 2. Yes they have teeth.

Q 3. Where is the Iguanas ear?
A 3.

Q 4. Why don't Iguanas shed in section like snakes?
A 4. Because they have more ajustments to theic body.

Q 5. How long can an Iguanas tail get.
A 5. About 2 to 3 feet.

Figure 7.4 Matthew's Questions and Answers

share on the overhead projector. These teachers know that twelve-year-olds often learn best from each other, so they invite kids up to teach other class members how to use these forms.

Thick and Thin Questions

Purpose: Differentiating between large global questions and smaller clarification questions in a content area

Resources: Science textbook, nonfiction trade books

Responses: Thick questions on the front of 3 x 3″ sticky notes, thin questions on the front of sticky flags; attempted answers on the reverse sides of the sticky notes and flags

Horace Mann Middle School teacher Margaret Bobb uses many different types of texts to teach seventh-grade physical science: newspaper and magazine articles, trade books, and yes, the dreaded science textbook. She knows that textbooks don't usually go deep enough to give kids the background they need to understand important science topics, so she surrounds her kids with science print of every type. But she also knows that her students will be steeped in textbooks for at least five more years, and she would be doing them a disservice if she ignored teaching them how to read these bastions of American secondary education.

A technique she uses that helps her students sift large global questions from smaller clarification questions is the thick and thin question approach. Thick questions in Margaret's class are those that address large, universal concepts and often begin with Why? How come? I wonder? Or they address large content areas, such as What is photosynthesis? The answers to these questions are often long and involved, and require further discussion and research.

Thin questions are those primarily asked to clarify confusion, understand words, or access objective content. Questions that can be answered with a number or with a simple yes or no fit into this category. How many moons does Neptune have? is an example of a thin question. The answers are typically shorter than those for thick questions.

Kids in Margaret's classroom code for thick and thin questions in trade books as well as in textbooks. As they read, they code for thick and thin questions with different-sized sticky notes. For thick questions, they use the larger 3 x 3" sticky notes, mark them with the word Thick, and write the question on the front. For thin questions, they use the skinny, sticky flags with room only for small questions. In both cases, Margaret encourages her students to take a stab at the answer on the back of the sticky note. They may have no ideas about the answer, which is fine. But if they do, they can attempt an explanation on the reverse side of the sticky note.

Margaret has noticed that the visual marker of 3 x 3" sticky notes for thick questions and small sticky flags for thin questions has an immediate impact and helps students categorize questions more quickly than before. In the content areas particularly, these question categories, which separate broad concepts from smaller issues of clarification, seem to guide students down the path to further insight.

Questioning That Leads to Inferential Thinking

Purpose: Making meaning through asking questions
Resource: Langston Hughes's poem "Dreams"
Response: Chart of poem with questions written on it

Poetry, with its images and metaphors, provides students with ample opportunities to exercise their powers of interpretation. When planning a lesson on questioning with poetry, Anne chose Langston Hughes's poem "Dreams" because it is one of her favorites. She wondered if it might prove a little too abstract for third graders. But if she'd learned anything in her years of teaching, it was to never underestimate the kids' potential.

Hughes's poem uses the metaphors of "a broken-winged bird" and "a barren field" to describe what life would be like without hope. His first line,

"Hold fast to dreams," could be interpreted as an admonishment to remain hopeful in the face of obstacles. Anne knew more about Langston Hughes's difficult life than these third graders, and she wondered if their lack of background knowledge would hinder their understanding.

Anne copied the poem on a large chart and placed it on an easel set up in front of the kids. When the students started thinking out loud about the poem, they used the questioning strategy to help them better understand it. They had experience with questioning, and the poem evoked many questions.

Unlike most lessons in this book, this particular lesson was launched without modeling the comprehension strategy itself. What Anne did model was her own struggle to understand the poem. She read the poem and told the kids that she had some ideas about the poem but wasn't entirely sure of the meaning. Sharing her own doubts about the meaning of the poem opened up the opportunity for the kids to risk sharing their own interpretations and inferences. Their questions were quite sophisticated and attempted to unlock the poem's meaning. Anne wrote their questions on the chart next to the place in the poem where they asked them or at the end of the text for less specific questions.

> What does "Hold fast to dreams" mean?
> Could "Life is a broken-winged bird" mean that life is sad and miserable?
> When dreams go, do you die?
> The poet seems to want to hold on to his dreams. Is he hopeful or sad?
> Is this about a dream, like a sleeping dream?
> What's a barren field?
> Why is nothing growing?
> Could the author or poet be thinking of dying?
> Did his wish come true?
> Was this a broken dream of the author?
> Did he have a hope that didn't come true?
> When did he write this?
> Does he mean that if we don't have dreams, we don't have hope?

The children's questions ranged from the literal What's a barren field? to thoughtful inferences about the poet's feelings, such as Was this a broken dream of the author? Rather than stopping to answer each question as it was asked, Anne and the students continued reading the poem, returning later to look again at the questions. The questions served as prompts to the interpretation of the poem and inferences about its meaning. Students didn't always agree. Some argued over whether the poem's message was ultimately hopeful or discouraging. Two students offered to find out more about Langston Hughes in the hope that learning something about his life would help them resolve this difference of opinion. In this lesson, the kids asked more questions than they answered, and they learned that there are no absolute answers when interpreting poetry. But in the end their questions took them deeper into the poem and inspired a thoughtful conversation.

Although the lesson ended without a comfortable sense of closure, the students now viewed questions in a new way. Questions didn't always have to be answered. Questions prompted their inferences and guided their interpretations. Questions opened their minds.

Using Question Webs to Expand Thinking

Purpose: Organizing content knowledge to answer a specific question

Resources: Civil War picture books and young adult magazines (see Part III, Appendix B, for Civil War text set and Appendix D for magazines)

Response: Question web

We are always searching for different ways to help students make meaning through questioning. It is not easy for children to pick out essential questions from a long list of unrelated questions. One way we have found to highlight the most essential questions is to construct a question web. Similar in form to other semantic webs, a question web differs in that it has a question at its center. The lines that emanate from the center are used to add information that relates in some way to the question, with the ultimate goal of building an answer from all of the various bits of information. Kids can use question webs individually to answer specific questions when reading. Or, additionally, question webs have proven useful for small groups studying a content area.

As kids study a specific content area, small research teams can explore a common question of their choice and construct meaning through a question web. One such informational study group was doing research on the Civil War. After reading a wide variety of picture books and young adult magazines on the Civil War, one member raised the question Why was it called the Underground Railroad? No one was completely sure. From that point on, members of the research team read to answer that question and added pertinent information to the question web as they came upon it in their reading. They drew their web on a large piece of butcher paper and added new web lines when they found new information. By the end of the inquiry, they had amassed enough information to answer the question (see Figure 7.5).

Sincere Questions vs. Assessment Questions

When we were in school, the teachers asked the questions, and we supplied the answers, or tried to anyway, whether we knew them or not. The teachers knew the answers to the long litany of questions they asked or the questions we faced at the end of the story in our reading textbooks. And they asked these questions to check on us, to see whether we had done the homework,

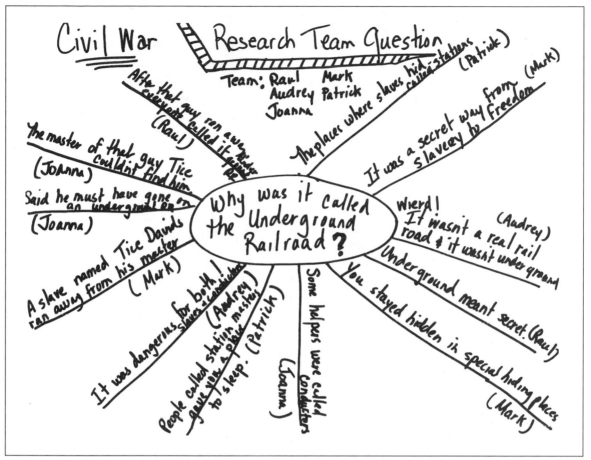

Figure 7.5 Question Web About the Civil War

read the chapter, or memorized our facts. Those were the only questions we remember in school. Our own important questions were reserved for recess, walking home after school, or the dinner table that night. School was not to be mucked up with a lot of tangential kid questions.

Fortunately, in the classrooms portrayed in this book, authentic student questions are encouraged and valued. We call these "sincere questions." Many schools, however, still focus primarily on what we have come to call "assessment questions."

Assessment questions are

◆ Questions we know the answers to
◆ Questions we ask in order to check or monitor our students

Sincere questions are

- ◆ Questions we don't know the answers to
- ◆ Questions we ponder and wonder about
- ◆ Questions that require further research by both teacher and student

Now, before launching a full frontal attack on assessment questions, we recognize that we are teachers and that we have both the right and the responsibility to ask assessment questions to monitor our kids' progress. Asking assessment questions represents one way to measure academic growth and follow kids' progress. But do we need to ask so many? Right now, most of the questions asked in schools fall into the assessment category. Sincere questions are still rare in classrooms. We need to balance this by allowing more time for kids and teachers to ask and explore sincere questions.

We are explicit about these two question categories to the kids. Why fake it? When we ask assessment questions, we might tell our students, "This is an assessment question. I know the answer. Here comes the question." With younger primary kids, we might call these "checking questions." "I know the answer to this question. I'm asking it to check and see if you do." When we encounter sincere questions, our response is something like, "I don't know the answer, but let's see if we can find out."

When we ask sincere questions, our "puzzle drive" kicks in. We make connections to what we already know. We generate ideas. We ask more questions. And we visualize and infer to make sense and to find answers.

When all is said and done, the sincere questions kids have are more likely to enhance understanding and construct meaning than the assessment questions we have. In his enthusiastic response to his teacher Eleanor Wright, fifth grader Brandon reminds us how questioning helps him in both reading and life (see Figure 7.6). We think that's terrific!

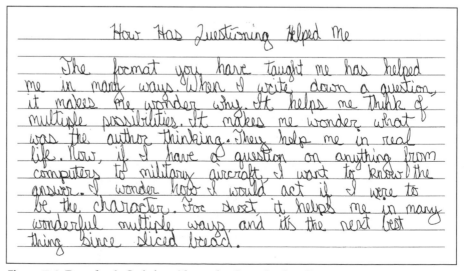

Figure 7.6 Brandon's Opinion About the Questioning Strategy

Chapter

8 Visualizing and Inferring
Strategies That Enhance Understanding

One day Steph walked into a staff developers' meeting and mentioned that she was in search of a fresh, new picture book to teach visualizing. Our colleague and friend Chryse Hutchins suggested Estelle Condra's *See the Ocean*, a beautiful book filled with stunning water color illustrations, striking poetic words, and a moving narrative.

It is the tale of a little girl who travels to a beach house with her parents and her brothers each summer. As we read through the story, we soon notice that something is different about Nellie. She never begs to sit near the window in the car, she describes the ocean as an old white-bearded man, and she asks her parents endless questions. Near the end, we discover that she is blind. As Steph read through it, she, too, had endless questions.

"I wonder why Chryse recommended this for visualizing?" she asked Anne the next day. "I think it's perfect for questioning." Anne read it and commented that she thought it was just what she was looking for to teach inferring. When we talked with Chryse later, she said that from her perspective the poetic language, metaphoric writing, and stunning imagery best lent itself to teaching visualizing.

Different readers rely on different strategies to help them gain better understanding. We mention this because well-crafted picture books can be used to teach and practice just about any strategy. To gain the best understanding of *See the Ocean*, readers are likely to activate several strategies, including visualizing, questioning, and inferring.

Many teachers we know introduce this book after their students have spent considerable time practicing different strategies. They encourage their kids to think about which strategies they are using to make sense of *See the Ocean* and to mark sticky notes with whatever strategy seems to help them gain meaning. Eighth grader Veronica's sticky notes show how she activates all three of these strategies and more as she reads and thinks through *See the*

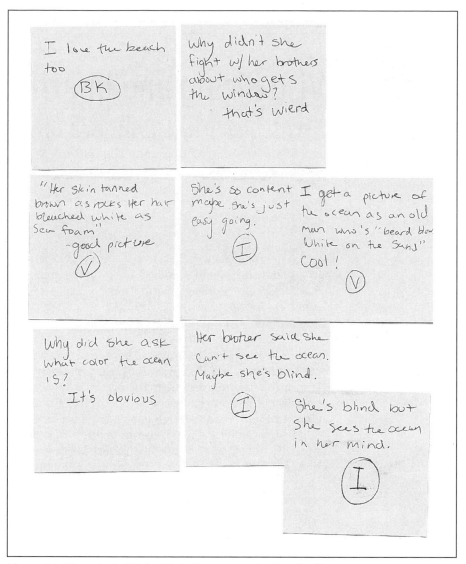

Figure 8.1 Veronica's Sticky Note Responses for *See the Ocean*

Ocean (see Figure 8.1). These sticky notes provide strong evidence of her flexibility with strategy use. She activates multiple strategies to comprehend.

Visualizing and inferring don't occur in isolation. Strategies interweave. Inferring occurs at the intersection of questioning, connecting, and print. Visualizing strengthens our inferential thinking. When we visualize, we are in fact inferring, but with mental images rather than words and thoughts. Visualizing and inferring are first cousins, the offspring of connecting and questioning. Hand in hand, they enhance understanding.

Visualizing: Movies in the Mind

Visualizing brings joy to reading. When we visualize, we create pictures in our minds that belong to us and no one else. As more and more books are routinely churned into movies, we are not surprised that most people prefer the book over the movie, kids included. One problem inherent in transforming text to film is that Hollywood routinely takes a four-hundred-and-fifty-page novel and converts it into a one-hundred-page script. Not surprisingly, depth and texture suffer. Another common complaint relates to the characters. Steph could never sit back and enjoy the film *Seven Years in Tibet* (Harrer 1997), one of her favorite books, because Brad Pitt, no matter how cute he was, did not jibe with her image of Heinrich Harrer, the book's protagonist.

Several years ago, a short-lived program about Beverly Cleary's beloved character, Ramona, hit TV. Kids were outraged. Each had clear, yet very different, pictures of Ramona in mind. Not one we spoke to could relate to the televised image of Ramona. When we visualize, we create our own movies in our minds. We become attached to the characters we visualize. Visualizing personalizes reading, keeps us engaged, and often prevents us from abandoning a book prematurely. When we introduce visualizing, we are likely to facilitate a conversation about books and movie adaptations in an attempt to make the strategy concrete. Kids relate and quickly weigh in with their own opinions.

STRATEGY
LESSONS

Visualizing

Visualizing with Wordless Picture Books

Purpose:	Visualizing to fill in missing information
Resource:	*Good Dog Carl,* by Alexandra Day
Response:	Drawing what you visualize

We teach visualizing in many different ways, but one surprising way is through wordless picture books. One might think that when a book has only pictures with no written text, visualizing is rendered unnecessary. Not so. We take the clues revealed in the illustrations and combine them with the missing pictures we create in our minds to make meaning.

Alexandra Day's picture books about Carl, the baby-sitting rottweiler, are wonderful examples of wordless books that kids love and that we can use for the purpose of teaching visualizing. *Good Dog Carl* tells the story of a household adventure in which Carl leads the baby on a romp through the house while the mother is out shopping.

Midway through the book, we find a picture of the baby sitting in front of a laundry chute with Carl standing right behind her. The very next page (picture) shows Carl dashing down the stairs. The kids' expressions are priceless. Many erupt with laughter. We ask them what they visualize between the two pictures and then have them draw, write, or talk about their response. Angie Carey's first-grade class visualized an array of scenarios, including the baby falling down the laundry chute, the baby sliding down on purpose, and Carl pushing the baby down.

Cristina and Max had different mental pictures, but both had the baby headed down the chute, which is exactly what happened one way or another. Cristina visualized an elaborate floor plan of the house in relation to the laundry chute (see Figure 8.2). Max created a less complicated image

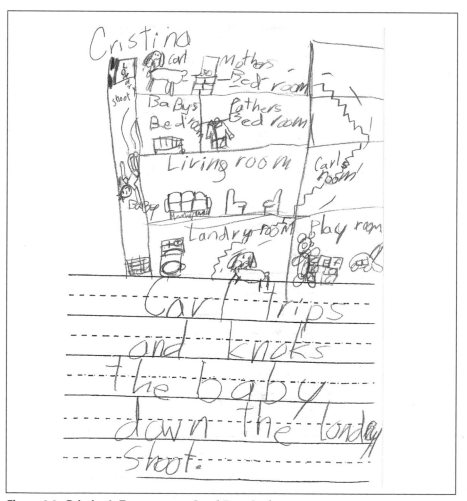

Figure 8.2 Cristina's Response to *Good Dog Carl*

Figure 8.3 Max's Response to *Good Dog Carl*

but used the phrase "shot down the shoot" to convey how the baby got down (see Figure 8.3). As with all comprehension strategies, we bring our schema to our mental images to make sense of things. Both Cristina's and Max's images make perfect sense.

We can alert ourselves to misconceptions by looking at student work. For instance, if a drawing had the baby sprouting wings and flying into the clouds, we would talk to the child about whether that was reasonable given the context of the story. We don't want kids to go too far afield because the purpose of visualizing is to help them better understand the actual text. One student in Angie's class drew a picture of Carl carrying the baby down the stairs. While this was closer to reality than a baby sprouting wings, it was still a misconception. The first picture clearly showed the baby at the edge of the laundry chute followed by the next picture of Carl running down the stairs, no baby on his back. In either case, we would confer with the child to help clear up any misconceptions.

Visualizing with wordless books helps readers build meaning as they go. Visualizing with text does the same thing. This lesson might become an anchor to help kids remember how visualizing helps them better comprehend. Although the examples here are from first graders, we have used wordless picture books for teaching visualizing with older kids as well, to give them a concrete sense of the strategy and how it works. They are frequently amazed at how their notion of visualizing is clarified when we show them wordless picture books.

Visualizing from a Vivid Piece of Text

Purpose: Merging prior experience and the text to create visual images
Resource: The lead to Chapter 3, "Escape," in *Charlotte's Web,* by E. B. White
Response: Drawing visual images with small groups

We work on and practice strategies with small groups as well as with large groups and individuals. A group of six fourth graders had chosen to read E. B. White's *Charlotte's Web* in their book club. Steph saw this as a great opportunity to talk to them about visualizing because E. B. White writes in such a strikingly visual way.

Chapter 3, "Escape," begins with a vivid, detailed description of the barn where Charlotte, the magical spider, lives with all of the other animals in the story. The passage describing the barn is about a page and half long and is filled with specific nouns and compelling descriptions:

The barn was very large. It was very old. It smelled of hay…. It smelled of the perspiration of tired horses and the wonderful sweet breath of patient cows…. It smelled of grain and of harness dressing and of axle grease and of rubber boots and of new rope…. It was full of all sorts of things that you find in barns: ladders, grindstones, pitch forks, monkey wrenches, scythes, lawn mowers, snow shovels, ax handles, milk pails, water buckets, empty grain sacks, and rusty rat traps. It was the kind of barn that swallows like to build their nests in. It was the kind of barn that children like to play in.

Steph read the passage out loud to the group and asked them to close their eyes and visualize the scene. When she finished, she asked them simply, "Tell me about your barn." Jon said that the barn was rickety and old and in need of a coat of paint. Jessica said she visualized a red barn with white trim. Jason mentioned beautiful green pastures with cows and horses grazing peacefully. Others mentioned farmers pitching hay and kids jumping from the hayloft. E. B. White had not explicitly written these details. The kids' comments reflected the movies running through their minds.

After about ten minutes of discussing their images of the barn, Steph asked them to sketch their barn. Each drawing was unique. The drawings included kids swinging on tire swings, riding the horses, and driving tractors. Some of the barn roofs were rounded; one was pointed with a rooster weathervane on top. Some pictures had farmers working and birds flying in and out of a small opening on top. Others had no people or animals. Some included wheat and corn fields. One was a detailed drawing of the interior of the barn loaded with mousetraps, milk pails, and water troughs. In some cases, none of the items drawn were mentioned in the text. As the kids shared, it became clear that many of their pictures came from their own prior knowledge of barns combined with the words of E. B. White.

This is what visualizing is all about—taking the words of the text and mixing them with the reader's preconceived ideas to create pictures in the mind. Good writers like E. B. White act like old-time movie projectionists who crank up the projector with their vivid words and then sit back as the reel runs unfettered for the viewer. The movie becomes the reader's own. In this case, if we were raised on a farm, we have the most detailed movie of all. If we lived around farms or have seen pictures of farms, we pick up on those. Combining the author's words with our background knowledge allows us to create mental images that enhance our understanding of the text and bring life to reading.

Visualizing in Nonfiction Text: Making Comparisons

Purpose: Visualizing to better understand the dimensions of size, space, and time
Resources: Nonfiction trade books that use illustrations to make comparisons
Response: Drawing a comparison between one object and another

Teachers frequently tell us that they have a good handle on how to teach and use visualizing in narrative text but that they are less confident about how the strategy helps kids better understand expository text. Nonfiction text often features illustrated comparisons to help readers better understand the concepts of size and distance. Slavens Elementary first-grade teacher Michelle Meyer shows her students examples of comparisons in nonfiction text. When Michelle read that a *Tyrannosaurus* tooth was the size of a banana, Sean could visualize it more accurately than if he had read that a *Tyrannosaurus* tooth is six and a half inches long; a banana's size made more sense to Sean than the more abstract inches or feet. Michelle encourages artistic responses in her classroom, and Sean drew the image Michelle described, which further shows his understanding of the concept (see Figure 8.4).

Much nonfiction expository text relies on the concepts of size, weight, length, distance, and time to explain important information. Illustrations, graphs, charts, time lines, and diagrams provide visual support to students as they try to understand and acquire information from nonfiction text. Search for examples of nonfiction comparisons, both written and drawn. They flourish in nonfiction trade books, and they provide needed support to help readers grasp difficult concepts of time and space.

Figure 8.4 Sean's Drawing of a Comparison in Nonfiction Text

Visualizing in Reading, Showing Not Telling in Writing

Purpose: Creating images with compelling nonfiction

Resources: Baseball, the American Epic series, including *Shadow Ball: The History of the Negro Leagues* (Ward, Burns, and O'Connor 1994), *25 Great Moments* (Ward, Burns, and Kramer 1994), and *Who Invented the Game?* (Ward, Burns, and Walker 1994)

Responses: Class discussion; charting of responses

Several years ago, hoards of American baseball fans switched their channels from ESPN for several nights and glued themselves to their local public broadcasting system affiliate to watch documentary film maker Ken Burns's series entitled *Baseball, the American Epic.* Later, much to our delight, Knopf published a series of three nonfiction trade books based on the compelling documentary programs.

The print series includes *Shadow Ball, 25 Great Moments,* and *Who Invented the Game?* and comprises one of the most comprehensive young adult trade book accounts of baseball history. We love the entire series, but *Shadow Ball: The History of the Negro Leagues* stands out as one of the finest pieces of narrative nonfiction that we have ever encountered. It is striking not only for its content but also for the quality of the writing.

This book is multifaceted. We have used it to build background knowledge about the black experience in America, to develop a greater sense of the American civil rights movement, and to teach questioning and inferring. But above all, we found it to be a terrific model for writing. *Shadow Ball* is written in such a vivid and compelling way that readers can't help but create stirring visual images in their minds when reading it. It begins this way:

> The crowd stirs with anticipation as the Indianapolis Clowns, an all-black team, take the field for their warm-ups. The second baseman's glove snaps back when he snags a quick peg from first. He hurls the ball to the third baseman, whose diving catch brings the fans to their feet. Then a batter steps to the plate. The pitcher sets, gets his signal, winds up, and throws. The batter swings. He hits it! The shortstop leaps to his right and makes a tremendous backhand stab. He jumps up, whirls, and throws to first just ahead of the sprinting runner. The low throw kicks dirt up by the first baseman's outstretched glove. The runner is out! The crowd roars.
>
> But wait! There's no ball in the first baseman's glove. The batter didn't really hit it. The Clowns were warming up in pantomime—hurling an imaginary ball so fast, making plays so convincingly, that fans could not believe it wasn't real.
>
> They called it shadow ball—and it came to stand not only for the way the black teams warmed up, but the way they were forced to play in the shadows of the all-white majors. Many black ballplayers were as good—if not better—than the big leaguers. All that kept them out was the color of their skin.

After overcoming our surprise at the pantomime warm-up and the rich shadow ball metaphor, we can't get over the compelling writing. This is a terrific piece to point out how active, visual verbs and specific nouns enhance writing quality and paint pictures in our minds. After discussing the content, we reread it and ask the kids to close their eyes, visualize the scene, and then comment on what makes this scene come alive for them. We write their comments on a large chart:

The running
The sliding
The kicked-up dirt
The outstretched glove
The tremendous back-hand stab
Snagging a quick peg from first
Hurling the ball

In this excerpt from *Shadow Ball* all of these images and more combine to create a realistic movie in the mind. Nouns and verbs give writing its life. We label the nouns and verbs, and ask kids to think about how these parts of speech bring such striking visual imagery to the piece. Before we finish, we encourage them to think about this vivid piece the next time they try to recount a true event in writing.

Creating Mental Images That Go Beyond Visualizing

Purpose: Using all the senses to comprehend text

Resource: A *National Geographic* article (Rudloe and Rudloe 1994),"Sea Turtles in a Race for Survival"

Responses: I see…, I hear…, I can feel…, I smell…, I can taste…

The term *visualizing* implies seeing pictures. Proficient readers create images from all of their senses when they read. We have all read an article about a pie baking in the oven or a steak crackling on the grill. Suddenly, our mouths water and hunger overcomes us. We can practically taste the meal.

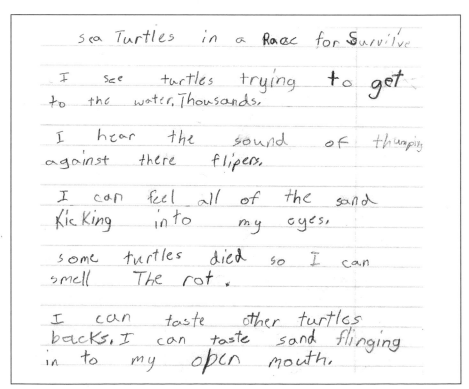

Figure 8.5 Robert's Response to "Sea Turtles in a Race for Survival"

Well-written text allows us to taste, touch, hear, and smell images as well as see them when we read.

After his teacher read aloud an article in *National Geographic* called "Sea Turtles in a Race for Survival," Robert, a fifth grader, envisioned himself as one of the turtles in the piece. Over thirty thousand endangered sea turtles had come from miles around to mate on the sands of a Costa Rican beach. The article vividly describes this extraordinary scene. His teacher gave Robert the magazine and asked him to look again at the words and write what he heard, smelled, tasted, and felt as well as saw. Robert brought all of his senses to bear in his response, which clearly deepens his understanding of the text and shows his level of interaction with it (see Figure 8.5).

Inferential Thinking: Reading Between the Lines

Inferring is the bedrock of comprehension, not only in reading. We infer in many realms. Our life clicks along more smoothly if we can read the world as well as text. If our boss looks grumpy in the morning, it might not be the best day to ask for a raise. If a kid's lips are quivering, it might be a sign to give him a hug. To help students understand the nature of inferential thinking, we might feign a terrified look and ask them what they can infer from our facial expression. If they mention scared or frightened, they've made an accurate inference. Inferring is about reading faces, reading body language, reading expressions, and reading tone as well as reading text.

STRATEGY LESSONS

Inferring

Inferring Feelings with Kindergartners

Purpose:	Helping kids to better understand their own and others' feelings; introducing inferential thinking
Resources:	A feelings chart and a card with the word *sad* written on it. The card is pinned on the back of one student who doesn't know what it says.
Response:	Child with card on back goes to the middle of the circle, and kids give him clues as to how they feel when they are sad to help him guess the feeling word on the card.

Slavens Elementary kindergarten teacher Sue Kempton organizes a game with a twofold purpose. She wants her students to have an opportunity to explore feelings, and she hopes to help them get a beginning handle on the notion of inferential thinking. Every few days, Sue introduces a new emotion and writes it on a card. At this point, the kids have *mad, sad, happy, disappointed,* and *frustrated* in their repertoire of cards. Sue reviews the nature of these feelings and then chooses one of the cards. She pins it on the back of a class volunteer; on this day Andrew wears the card. Andrew stands in the middle of the circle and turns around several times slowly so that everyone has an opportunity to see his card. Andrew doesn't know which card he wears on his back.

"Who has a clue for Andrew?" Sue begins. Kids raise their hands and give clues that might help Andrew figure out what word he is wearing on his back. Each student begins with "I felt that way when…" and completes the clue:

> …my sister hit me with a golf club
> …my dog died
> …my mom said we couldn't go to the Children's Museum
> …my dad didn't let me go to the movies
> …my grandpa Nick died

After five or six kids have shared their clues, Sue asks, "Okay, Andrew, can you infer what the feeling is?"

"Sad," Andrew answers triumphantly.

"Good thinking, Andrew. How did you know?" Sue asks.

"Because people get sad when animals and grandparents die," Andrew answers.

And he was right, of course. The kids love this game. As they play more often, they clarify their feelings and predict which situations might lead to one feeling or another.

Inferring from the Cover and Illustrations as Well as the Text

Purpose: Using all aspects of a book to infer meaning

Resource: *Tight Times,* by Barbara Shook Hazen

Response: Two-column note form headed Quote or Picture from Text/Inference

One of our favorite picture books for teaching inferring is Barbara Shook Hazen's *Tight Times.* It tells the story of a boy, about four years old, who desperately wants a dog for a pet. Tension pervades the household as his dad loses his job and the family struggles to make ends meet and stay intact. With picture books, readers can use the illustrations as well as the text to help them infer. Emergent readers frequently use picture clues to gain meaning, particularly when they come to a word they don't know. Older students can use pictures to enhance meaning, too.

Trina Schart Hyman's black-and-white illustrations convey moods that run the gamut from despair to hope. There's dad with his downturned mouth, furrowed brow, and head in hands at the dining room table and mom too busy to look up at her son as she sews a button on her blouse in the mad morning rush. These pictures say it all.

Steph joined with fifth-grade teacher Jennifer Jones at Denver's Pioneer Charter School to work on inferential thinking. Jennifer's students had begun learning about inferring earlier that week when they attempted to infer the nature of some unusual kitchen utensils (see Chapter 3). On this day, Steph read *Tight Times* while the kids crowded around on the floor with clipboards and pencils at the ready. She held up the cover of the book, which shows a boy with a plate of lima beans, his fork two inches from his mouth holding one lonely lima which he refuses to even look at. Knowing that covers and titles are a good place to start with inferring, Steph asked what they could infer from the cover.

"He doesn't like those beans," Curtis answered.

"How do you know?" Steph asked.

"Look at his face and how he won't put the fork in his mouth," Curtis said.

"Yeah, and his plate is still full of beans," D. J. added as the others nodded.

"What does *Tight Times* mean?" Les asked.

This proved tougher. No one seemed to have adequate background knowledge for this term. Steph hung up a large piece of chart paper and divided it into two columns, one headed Quote or Picture from Text and the other headed Inference. "Let's read the story and find out," she suggested. "We'll record the information here as we find it." After hearing several pages, Audra burst out, "I got it! 'Tight times' is when you don't have enough money to do the stuff you want to do."

"Good thinking, Audra. Did the author tell you that?" Steph asked.

"No, not exactly."

"So, how did you know?" Steph asked.

"I sort of guessed it when his dad said they didn't get roast beef anymore and his mom went back to work because of tight times," Audra answered.

"She inferred it," Curtis said.

"That she did, Curtis. Let's record it on the chart," Steph suggested.

Audra came up and wrote her response on the chart.

When Curtis came upon a picture near the end of the story of the dad reading the want ads, he headed up to the chart and wrote that the dad was going to get a new job.

Quote or Picture from Text	Inference
Tight Times are why we don't have beef on Sunday.	They are short on money.
Picture—The dad is reading the want ads.	He's going to get a new job.

When Jennifer asked Curtis how he knew that, he answered, "Because he's got a smile on his face in that picture and he's a hardworking guy. I'm predicting it."

"Right on, Curtis," Jennifer told him. At that point, she and Steph released the kids to work in pairs as the teachers moved about the room, eavesdropped, and chatted with individuals who were working their way through the text and responding on an identical form on their clipboards. The kids relied on both pictures and text to predict outcomes, infer ideas, and construct meaning in the story.

Prediction or Inference?

When Curtis stated that he was making a prediction, it gave Jennifer and Steph an opportunity to discuss the relationship between prediction and inference. Predicting is related to inferring, of course, but we predict outcomes, events, or actions that are confirmed or contradicted by the end of the story. Inferences are often more open-ended and may remain unresolved when the story draws to a close.

To help our students understand the difference, we encourage them to consider the outcome of an event or action each time they make a prediction

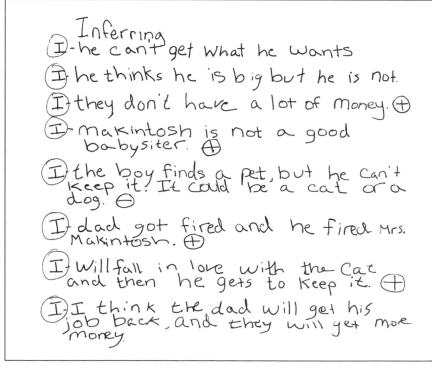

Figure 8.6 Curtis's Inferences in Response to *Tight Times*

and notice whether there has been a resolution. Curtis continued reading and found that the book ends before resolving whether the father finds a new job. But the story ends hopefully, and Curtis wasn't wrong to infer that the dad would find employment. He had good reason to believe it. Curtis made a list of inferences in his notebook as he read *Tight Times*. When he finished reading, he went back and marked those that were confirmed (+) and those that were contradicted (–). He left those that were unresolved coded with only I for inference (see Figure 8.6).

When readers look carefully at the illustrations in picture books and combine them with words from the text, they are helped to make insightful inferences to better comprehend the narrative. ·

Recognizing Plot and Inferring Themes

Purpose: Differentiating between plot and theme, and inferring the big ideas or themes

Resource: *Teammates,* by Peter Golenbock

Responses: Class discussion; chart of themes; theme boards

Literature, both fiction and nonfiction, is rife with themes. Books and articles rarely promote just one main idea but rather several themes for readers to ponder and infer. When we talk to students about themes, we help them discern the difference between theme and plot. We explain that the plot is simply what happens in the narrative. The themes represent the bigger ideas of the story. The plot carries those ideas along. To demonstrate plot, we choose a simple narrative that everyone is likely to be familiar with. We might recount the plot of *Goldilocks and the Three Bears* by summarizing the events of the story as follows. A girl named Goldilocks was wandering through the forest and entered an unfamiliar, empty house. She tasted porridge that didn't belong to her, broke a chair, and slept in a bed that wasn't hers. She was caught when the bears returned, and she ran out of the house scared to death.

We explain to our students that themes are the underlying ideas, morals, and lessons that give the story its texture, depth, and meaning. The themes are rarely written out in the story. We infer themes. Themes often make us feel angry, sad, guilty, joyful, frightened. We tell kids that we are likely to feel themes in our gut. To help students more clearly understand the difference, we might ask, "What are the bigger ideas in *Goldilocks and the Three Bears*?" Kids tend to identify taking things that don't belong to you, selfishness, thoughtlessness, and so on. They have experienced these notions and they understand them.

Inferring Themes in *Teammates*

A nonfiction picture book we have used to demonstrate inferring themes is Peter Golenbock's *Teammates*. It is the moving story of Jackie Robinson's courageous breakthrough into the all-white major leagues. It goes beyond the history and describes the personal relationship between Jackie and his white teammate Pee Wee Reese. Pee Wee was the only player on the Brooklyn Dodgers team that supported Jackie's quest.

To continue their study of inferring, Steph demonstrated a think-aloud with *Teammates* to the fifth graders in Jennifer Jones's class the day after taking them through the Goldilocks exercise. After describing the hard, segregated life of players in the Negro leagues, Golenbock writes that life was much better for players in the major leagues. They were paid well, and many were famous all over the world. Steph coded her sticky note I for inference while noting that this kind of racial inequality might breed anger. She suggested that both racial inequality and anger might be themes in the story even though the writer hadn't written those very words. On a large piece of chart paper she wrote the words *racial inequality* and *anger* under the heading Themes.

When Curtis heard that Branch Rickey, the manager of the Brooklyn Dodgers, was looking for a man who "would have to possess the self-control not to fight back when opposing players tried to intimidate or hurt him," he suggested that self-control might be a theme. Steph concurred and added it to the chart. When Steph finished reading the story, she facilitated a discussion about the bigger ideas in the narrative.

"Jackie was really brave," Chantal said.

"How?" Steph nudged as she wrote *bravery* on the theme chart.

"He was all alone without a single friend until Pee Wee, and he never gave up no matter how badly they treated him," Chantal answered.

"So, would loneliness be a theme?" Steph asked.

"Yeah. I know how he felt. When I moved here I didn't have one single friend," Rogers said, as Steph added *loneliness* to the theme chart.

"But Pee Wee was his friend," Jaquon added.

"So, is friendship a theme?" Steph asked.

"Sort of, but most of the team would not be his friend because he was black," Jaquon continued.

"That's racist," Curtis added.

"It sure is racist, Curtis. Are racism and friendship both themes in *Teammates*?" Steph asked.

The kids nodded and added both of those themes to the chart. And so the discussion went for nearly forty-five minutes, culminating in the following theme list:

Themes

racial inequality	segregation
anger	heart
self-control	self-determination
bravery/courage	teamwork/working together
loneliness	sadness

racism	taking a stand
friendship	living up to the best of your ability
fairness/unfairness	violence
internal pain	self-respect

Steph reiterated that all of these themes represented the bigger ideas in the story and that most of them evoked strong feelings. We have noticed that kids are more likely to remember important themes when they derive the ideas themselves and feel them deeply. It is our role to help draw students out through engaging discussions about the bigger ideas in the story. Often, the kids used their prior knowledge to infer themes and better understand the narrative, as Rogers did when he mentioned being the new kid on the block. As students talk about the bigger ideas, it is our responsibility to help them label the ideas and articulate the themes. For instance, they may understand the concept of self-determination, but they may not know the word for it. As teacher facilitators, we can help them put language to their thoughts and feelings.

Theme Boards: Hey, What's the Big Idea?

Jennifer continued to work on surfacing themes throughout the year. She reported that her students became quite adept at inferring themes as well as labeling them. They even began to notice when certain themes appeared over and over. To reinforce theme identification and the connections between themes in one text and those in another, Jennifer established a theme board headed Hey, What's the Big Idea? Each time the class read a book, they developed a theme list and added the list to the theme board. Themes identified from Sherry Garland's *The Lotus Seed* included

keeping traditions alive	cooperation
sharing traditions	sadness
courage	loneliness
internal pain	

It didn't take kids long to notice the overlapping themes in certain books, such as *Teammates* and *The Lotus Seed.* This was a great literary lesson. Experienced readers know that the same themes are likely to appear over and over in literature. Why not begin to teach this in elementary school?

Visualizing and Inferring to Understand Textbooks

Purpose: Using reading comprehension strategies to better understand content area textbooks

Resource: *Merrill Earth Science* (1993), seventh-grade textbook

Responses: Two-column note form headed Facts/Inferences; ongoing discussion about how comprehension strategies help readers understand textbooks

Throughout this book we have talked about using authentic literature and trade nonfiction to teach content. Still, many classrooms across the United States rely primarily on textbooks to teach content in subjects such as science and social studies. Textbooks have their advantages but also their limitations. The advantages derive primarily from the organization of the material. Each chapter usually has a number of sections, which are organized around headings and subheadings. The text provides factual information in the paragraphs that follow, sometimes information that is difficult to find elsewhere. The writing is predictable; most paragraphs begin with an introductory sentence followed by several supporting sentences and a conclusion. Textbooks are chock full of framed text, boldface print, underlined concepts, diagrams, and definitions, which scaffold the reader's understanding.

The disadvantages of using only textbooks to teach are many. First and foremost, kids get bored. The problem with textbooks isn't getting information out of them; the problem is staying awake while reading them! Because few books outside of school are written in the same style as a textbook, reading textbooks doesn't prepare kids for much of the authentic nonfiction reading they will do in their lifetimes. Textbooks cram too much information into one book. And even though many are six hundred pages long, it would take thousands of pages to do justice to the whole of, say, European history, and therefore textbooks go for breadth rather than depth.

Although authentic trade nonfiction—newspapers, books, videos, and magazines—is the mainstay in science teacher Margaret Bobb's classroom, she also uses a science textbook, *Merrill Earth Science,* to supplement instruction. The textbook frequently offers the information Margaret needs to share with her students. But she recognizes that all is for naught if her students can't understand what they read.

Although Margaret is a specialist in earth science, she knows that she must be a literacy teacher first. She must explicitly teach students how to read content area textbooks to gain information, rather than just telling them to read the fossil chapter and answer the questions. The unfamiliar terms and concepts in textbooks combined with the dry writing sometimes sink students. As Margaret studied strategic reading comprehension, she quickly realized how useful these strategies could be in helping her students better understand their textbooks as well as trade nonfiction.

Margaret teaches her seventh graders several comprehension strategies to help them understand textbook writing. She explains that when we read, we have to be able to tell the difference between facts and opinions. "In science, we observe facts," she explains. "Your opinion is your own idea, but in science we call it a hypothesis. This is really an interpretation or inference about something." Margaret labeled a two-column overhead transparency Facts (Something We Can See and Observe)/Inferences (Interpretation).

Juan read out loud from the textbook: "The dense forest thunders as the *Tyrannosaurus rex* charges forward in pursuit of her evening meal. On the other side of the swamp, a herd of apatosaurs moves slowly and cautiously onward. The adults surround the young to protect them from predators. Soon night will fall on this prehistoric day, 70 million years ago" (*Merrill Earth Science* 1993). Margaret asked the class what they visualized and if they could infer anything from the text. Jana visualized a group of slow dinosaurs, peacefully hanging around, while the *Tyrannosaurus* raced toward them undetected in the woods. Raul commented that he thought the *rex* would get these plant eaters. Margaret commented that he was making two inferences—first, that the *rex* would eat them, and second, that the apatosaurs were plant eaters. Both were strong possibilities.

As they read on, they came to the following passage: "Usually the remains of dead plants and animals are quickly destroyed. Scavengers eat the dead organisms or bacteria cause them to decay. If you've ever left a banana on the shelf too long you've seen this process begin. Compounds in the banana cause it to become soft and moist, and bacteria move in and cause it to quickly decay." Margaret asked what the writers were doing here. "Making you visualize again," Luz called out.

"You bet they are," Margaret said. "You can just picture that black, shriveled, smelly banana. It reminds me of how the fridge smells when food is rotting in there. I can use my background knowledge to get a better picture." In reading just several paragraphs, Margaret and her students had explicitly activated background knowledge, visualized, and inferred to better understand the textbook. These strategies brought the science textbook to life. The students filled in the following chart as they read:

Facts (Something We Can See and Observe)	Inferences (Interpretation)
Apatosaurs are slow.	The *T-rex* will catch them.
Adults protect young.	The apatosaurs are plant eaters.
Took place 70 million years ago.	
Bacteria decay the banana.	Bananas get rotten when you leave them out too long.

As Margaret shows us, these comprehension strategies can improve textbook reading. By stopping and activating the strategies, her seventh graders increased their store of knowledge and stayed alert rather than sinking into boredom.

It should be noted that Margaret looks very closely at the writing in textbooks when it is time to choose a new textbook or adopt a new series. Although content and organization are important, writing style and presentation are important, too, so that kids will stay alert, monitor their comprehension, learn, and retain information. Margaret is not seduced merely by a new copyright date. She compares the older textbook to the newer one to determine if the new one is truly better or simply newer. She looks for organizational features such as framed text and appealing photographs that scaffold the reader's understanding. For her earth science course, she chooses the best written and best organized textbook she can find and then teaches her students the comprehension strategies that will enhance their understanding.

Inferring and Questioning to Understand Historical Concepts

Purpose: Inferring and questioning go hand in hand to build understanding
Resource: *Encounter,* by Jane Yolen
Responses: Discussion; two-column note form headed Questions/Inferences

In Paula Windham's fourth-grade class, the students speak many languages in addition to English, including Spanish, Japanese, Arabic, and Vietnamese. When studying explorers in social studies, Paula and Anne selected Jane Yolen's *Encounter* to read aloud because it provided a fictionalized account of Columbus's meeting with the Taino people. Written from the perspective of a Taino child, *Encounter* is a difficult picture book requiring readers to infer what is going on in the story. The young Taino boy, unlike any of his elders, is suspicious of Columbus and his men. He is unable to convince his people of the potential danger until, of course, it is too late. The young boy's questions and fears about the strange ships and men who "hid their bodies in colors, like parrots" prompt many questions. At first, Paula and Anne wondered if it would be a wise choice given the eight children in the class for whom English was a second language.

The more they studied *Encounter* themselves, however, the more convinced they became that it could be a powerful way to introduce the children to ideas and issues about the "discovery" of the Americas. Rather than starting out by reading about a succession of explorers, they thought the children would more easily understand the issues surrounding exploration by reading historical fiction. Most important, Anne and Paula wanted students to move beyond traditional ideas about exploration to an awareness of the perspectives of indigenous people.

Paula was curious to see how her fourth graders, who had been introduced to inferring and questioning with realistic fiction, would transfer these reading comprehension strategies to social studies content. To provide a scaffold for the ESL students, they began reading the book as a whole class. Anne and Paula modeled their own questions first and jotted these down on an overhead transparency under a column headed Questions. When the children began to make inferences, Anne added a second column headed Inferences and recorded the children's thinking.

After she had recorded children's questions and inferences for several pages, the children continued to read the text and note questions and inferences with a partner. In some cases, more fluent readers worked with their ESL classmates. Kathy's copy of the text included her questions about the illustrations and text under the heading Questions. Under a separate heading for Inferences she kept a running commentary explaining her interpretations of story events.

Questions	Inferences
First picture: What is the name of the ship?	The boy daydreamed and saw a bird.
Is it a dream or a daydream?	The little boy is telling the story.
Are they Columbus's boats?	They think the white men are weird and come from the sky.
Do Native Americans think the boats are giant birds or spirits?	The white men turned giving into trading.
Is this a biography of Columbus?	The white men want gold.

With *Encounter,* questioning and inferring worked in tandem to enhance the children's understanding of the story. As they read, students asked questions to clarify their uncertainty and made inferences about the Taino boy's thoughts and actions. The students' language provides a clue to their thinking. When a student says, "Well, maybe it means..." we are quick to label his thinking as inferring. Or, when a student says, "I wonder...," she is posing a question. With questions like those Kathy and the other children asked, an inference was rarely far behind. Inferring and questioning are next of kin. In *Encounter* they go hand in hand.

Paula and Anne had originally planned to focus on the questioning strategy because they thought the book lent itself to that. Changing the modeling and guided practice portion of the lesson to include inferring illustrates how important it is to observe children's responses and adapt our teaching to their thinking. Children certainly asked lots of questions, but inferring was essential to figure out the story's puzzling events as well. Students' interpretations continued all the way to the story's ambiguous ending. Reading through the text in a deliberate manner ensured that all of Paula's students, especially the ESL students, gained a clearer understanding of the story.

Rereading to Clear up Misconceptions

When we come across information that surprises us, such as Nellie's blindness in *See the Ocean* or the phantom baseball game in *Shadow Ball,* we can't help but flip back through the pages and search for the clues we missed that might have led us to draw a more accurate inference earlier in our reading. Readers need to stay on their toes to make meaning, checking for misconceptions as they go. And teachers need to look closely at student work and listen intently to student comments to nip misconceptions in the bud.

As a little girl, whenever Steph heard the Christmas carol "Silent Night," an image of a large, round Friar Tuck sort of character appeared in her mind. It wasn't until later that she realized that this misconception had originated in her confusion about the words of the song. Where it actually said "round yon Virgin," Steph had always heard it as "round John...." She visualized a fat, jolly monk. This misconception disrupted meaning and kept her from fully understanding the carol.

Encourage your kids to go back through the text to check their mind pictures and inferences, and remind them to check their thinking with someone else if it doesn't seem to make sense. A good reality check can go a long way toward keeping Friar Tucks at bay. Visualizing and inferring are strategies that enhance understanding, but if ill conceived, they can just as easily hinder understanding. Rereading is one of the best ways to check for meaning. It all makes so much sense the second time through.

Chapter 9

Determining Importance in Text
The Nonfiction Connection

A dozen or so years ago, a large footlocker arrived at Steph's door. Her parents, their kids grown, had sold the house where she had grown up and moved to another. In the move, they boxed all of her remaining possessions and sent them out to Steph in Denver. As the padlock clicked free, the top of the trunk burst open and childhood treasures of every imaginable size and shape poured out. Stuffed animals, glossy black-and-white photographs of Hollywood movie stars, her collection of Nancy Drew books, a well-loved Raggedy Andy doll, a 1954 edition of Dr. Seuss's *If I Ran the Zoo*, and even her kindergarten report card cascaded over the sides.

As Steph peeled away the layers of her life, she came upon several hulking college textbooks lining the bottom of the trunk. When she opened a tome titled *Modern European History*, a blast of yellow blinded her. Page after page of white space and black print had been shaded neon yellow, the result of Steph's bout with mad highlighting disease!

Throughout her education, teachers had instructed Steph to highlight the important parts. But no one had shown her how. She assumed that if the writers of these massive textbooks had written it down, it must be important. So she highlighted just about every letter of print. Highlighting is easy; determining what to highlight is the challenge.

For years in schools, students everywhere have been asked to pick out the most important information when they read, to highlight essential ideas, to isolate supporting details, and to read for specific information. This is easier said than done. The strategy lessons in this chapter are designed to help readers sift and sort information, and make decisions about what information they need to remember and what information they can disregard.

The Link Between the Strategy of Determining Importance and the Genre of Nonfiction

Determining important ideas and information in text is central to making sense of reading and moving toward insight. Much of this chapter shows how teachers support readers in their efforts to sift and sort essential information. When we teach the strategy of determining importance, we often introduce it in nonfiction. They go together. Nonfiction reading is reading to learn. Simply put, readers of nonfiction have to decide and remember what is important in the texts they read if they are going to learn anything from them.

When readers determine importance in fiction and other narrative genre, they often infer the bigger ideas and themes in the story, as the kids in Jennifer Jones's fifth grade did when they read *Teammates* (see Chapter 8). Getting at what's important in nonfiction text is more about gaining information and acquiring knowledge than discerning themes. Nonfiction is full of features, text cues, and structures that signal importance and scaffold understanding for readers. These features, specific to nonfiction, provide explicit cues to help readers sift essential information from less important details when they read expository text. We explicitly teach readers how to use these cues to extract salient information. But first we need to ensure that they have a wide range of nonfiction at their disposal.

Beverly Kobrin, author of *The Kobrin Letter,* a quarterly publication that reviews nonfiction trade literature, tells us that "life is nonfiction." We agree. We are completely captivated by the realm of nonfiction. For us, the real world is rich, fascinating, and compelling. Young kids know this, which is why furry caterpillars, sparkling rocks, and medieval knights sweep them away. Kids can't resist the real world. We encourage them to explore a topic of interest, ask questions about it, and read for information to add to their store of knowledge.

Steph and Anne both have wonderful memories of having been read aloud to in school. We can still hear the words of *Black Beauty* (Sewell 1941) and *The Secret Garden* (Burnett 1938) as our teachers lured us in from recess for read-aloud time. But neither of us can ever recall having had a piece of nonfiction read aloud to us or even seeing it in school. It was as if the genre didn't exist—outside of textbooks, that is.

A number of years ago, we joined a group of fourth- and fifth-grade teachers in a classroom book audit to determine whether their classroom book collections included a wide variety of genres. To our surprise, we found very little trade nonfiction among the novels and textbooks. Over 80 percent of the classroom books fell into the fiction category. Considering that about 80 percent of the reading we do outside of school is nonfiction, it wasn't hard to recognize a disconnect. More nonfiction needed to be shared, explored, and taught in these classrooms and in classrooms everywhere.

Classroom book audits are invaluable tools to ensure that classrooms balance their collections with respect to genres as well as other categories.

Nonfiction picture books and young adult magazines and newspapers fire kids up, especially if text quality matches the compelling photographs, charts, and illustrations. There's nothing like a photograph of the jaws of a great white shark clamping down on the front end of a surfboard to spark kids' interest in ocean life. Interesting authentic nonfiction fuels kids' curiosity, enticing them to read more, dig deeper, and search for answers to compelling questions. When kids read and understand nonfiction, they build background for the topic and acquire new knowledge. The ability to identify essential ideas and salient information is a prerequisite to developing insight.

Distilling the Essence of Nonfiction Text

In *Nonfiction Matters* (Harvey 1998), Steph wrote about overviewing and highlighting the text to help students determine important ideas and information while reading.

Overviewing

When students read nonfiction, they can be taught overviewing, a form of skimming and scanning the text before reading. Reading comprehension researcher Jan Dole suggests focus lessons on the following to help students overview the text:

◆ Activating prior knowledge
◆ Noting characteristics of text length and structure
◆ Noting important headings and subheadings
◆ Determining what to read and in what order
◆ Determining what to pay careful attention to
◆ Determining what to ignore
◆ Deciding to quit because the text contains no relevant information
◆ Deciding if the text is worth careful reading or just skimming

A careful overview saves precious time for students when reading difficult nonfiction text. The ability to overview eliminates the need for kids to read everything when searching for specific information. Overviewing represents an early entry in the effort to determine importance. Teachers can model these components of overviewing in their own reading and research process.

Highlighting

To effectively highlight text, readers need to read the text, think about it, and make conscious decisions about what they need to remember and learn. They can't possibly remember everything. They need to sort important information from less important details. They need to pick out the main ideas and notice supporting details, and they need to let go of ancillary information. We encourage students to consider the following guidelines when they highlight, and we provide explicit instruction in each of these points:

◆ Look carefully at the first and last line of each paragraph. Important information is often contained there.
◆ Highlight only necessary words and phrases, not entire sentences.
◆ Don't get thrown off by interesting details. Although they are fascinating, they often obscure important information.
◆ Make notes in the margin to emphasize a pertinent highlighted word or phrase.
◆ Note cue words (see Part III, Appendix F). They are almost always followed by important information.
◆ Pay attention to the vast array of nonfiction features that signal importance.
◆ Pay attention to surprising information. It might mean you are learning something new.
◆ When finished, check to see that no more than half the paragraph is highlighted. As readers become more adept, one-third of the paragraph is a good measure for highlighting.

Nonfiction Features That Signal Importance

When a word is italicized, a paragraph begins with a boldface heading, or the text says "Most important,…" readers need to stop and take notice. This may sound obvious, but it's not. No one ever taught us to pay attention to these nonfiction conventions. Steph was so textbound as a young reader that to this day she still skips over the title to get to the text. This is a shame. Titles, headings, framed text, and captions help focus readers as they sort important information from less important details. Nonfiction is one of the most accessible genres for reluctant and less experienced readers because the features scaffold the reader's understanding. A photograph and a caption sometimes synthesizes the most important information on the page, rendering a complete reading of the text unnecessary. Nonfiction features are user-friendly. Some that we teach follow.

Fonts and effects Teachers can note examples of different fonts and effects, such as titles, headings, boldface print, color print, italics, bullets, captions, and labels, which signal importance in text. We can remind kids that font and effect differences should be viewed as red flags that wave "This is important. Read carefully."

Cue words and phrases Nonfiction writing often includes text cues that signal importance. Signal words, like stop signs, warn readers to halt and pay attention. Proficient adult readers automatically attend to these text cues. Less experienced readers don't. We need to remember to point these signal words out to readers. Writers choose phrases such as *for example, for instance, in fact, in conclusion, most important, but, therefore, on the other hand,* and *such as* so that readers will take note. As students come across signal words, they can add them to a classroom chart of text cues to guide readers through difficult expository text (see Part III, Appendix F). Standardized tests as well are full of cue words, and familiarity with these signals may boost scores.

Illustrations and photographs Illustrations play a prominent role in nonfiction to enhance reading comprehension. Nonfiction trade books and magazines brim with colorful photographs that capture young readers and carry them deeper into meaning.

Graphics Diagrams, cut-aways, cross-sections, overlays, distribution maps, word bubbles, tables, graphs, and charts graphically inform nonfiction readers of important information.

Text organizers Teachers cannot assume that kids know concepts such as index, preface, table of contents, glossary, and appendix. When kids are surveying different texts for information, knowledge of these text organizers is crucial for further research.

Text structures Expository text is framed around several structures that crop up in both trade and textbook publications and standardized test forms. Understanding different expository text structures gives readers a better shot at determining important information. These structures include cause and effect, problem and solution, question and answer, comparison and contrast, and description and sequence. If students know what to look for in terms of text structure, meaning comes more easily. Grappling with nonfiction text structure and coming to understand it helps readers determine essential ideas.

STRATEGY
LESSONS

Determining Importance

In the classrooms portrayed here, teachers at various grade levels surround their students with nonfiction trade books and other materials to help them build background knowledge of the genre—how certain features signal importance; and to model interesting as well as accurate writing. The first three lessons that follow illustrate these goals.

Nonfiction writing does not have to be boring. All we have to do is pick up a newspaper, look through a *National Geographic,* or read a nonfiction best-seller to see that nonfiction writing can be rich in voice. Sometimes, indeed, it is so compelling that sifting important information from the overall text can be challenging. Readers are likely to become so engrossed in authentic trade nonfiction that they may get carried away by the rich details and miss the essence of the text. But the first purpose of real-world nonfiction is to convey factual information, important ideas, and key concepts. The remaining strategy lessons in this chapter show how teachers help students read to extract important information and essential ideas from nonfiction text.

Building Background Knowledge of Nonfiction Conventions

Purpose: Building background knowledge of nonfiction conventions by creating books that illustrate these conventions

Resources: *Hungry, Hungry Sharks,* by Joanna Cole, photographs from home or school, 8 x 11" booklets containing six blank pages folded in half and stapled

Responses: A different nonfiction convention on each page; a two-column class chart headed Convention/Purpose, which serves as a record for all of the kids

To help her first graders become aware of the features of nonfiction, Michelle Meyer had them create nonfiction convention books. These little booklets were made up of six sheets of 8 x 11" paper folded over and stapled together with a construction paper cover. The kids wrote the title "Nonfiction Conventions" on their books and decorated them (see Figure 9.1). To help build their background knowledge for nonfiction features, Michelle filled her room to capacity with nonfiction books and read them aloud each day, pointing out various nonfiction conventions as they came up.

The first feature Michelle presented for these nonfiction convention books was captions. She pasted a photograph of her and her cat, Madison, on the first page, and wrote the following caption under the picture: "Here I am with Madison wearing her princess look as she drapes herself over the pillow while lounging on my bed." Then Michelle labeled the page "Caption." Later, the kids brought in a photograph, pasted it on the first page, wrote a caption under the picture, and labeled the page "Caption." (Michelle had a Polaroid camera for those kids who were unable to come up with a photograph from home.) The photograph and the caption made for a very appealing page to begin the nonfiction convention books.

Each day as she read a nonfiction book out loud, Michelle added a new feature to her own book. The kids joined in the search, and when they came across an unfamiliar nonfiction feature, they shared it with the class and added it to their booklets as well as to a large two-column class chart headed Convention/Purpose. Along with Michelle, the kids recorded the new nonfic-

Figure 9.1 Cover of a Nonfiction Convention Book

tion conventions in the first column and indicated their purposes in the second column.

One day, while flipping through Joanna Cole's *Hungry, Hungry Sharks*, Catie found an illustration of a whale shark stretched across the roof of a bus, a visual marker of its great size. Michelle suggested that Catie teach the other kids about this new feature, called a comparison. Catie drew the whale shark on top of a school bus and labeled her new page with the heading "Comparisons" (see Figure 9.2). The next day she taught the class about

Figure 9.2 Catie's Illustration of a Comparison in Nonfiction Text

the notion of comparisons by sharing her illustration. Michelle reinforced this by reading a written example of a size comparison between a *Tyrannosaurus* tooth and a banana. Sean's drawing (see Figure 8.4) illustrates his rendition of those words.

Michelle pointed out to the class that Catie and Sean used different words to compare these items. Catie wrote "a little bit bigger than" and Sean wrote "as big as." The class discussed the difference in these phrases and their meanings because Michelle wanted them to begin to notice the language of comparison. Just telling kids about the special features and language of nonfiction is not enough. But having them search for their own examples and talk about nonfiction characteristics scaffolds their nonfiction reading and enhances their understanding of the genre.

Becoming Familiar with the Characteristics of Nonfiction Trade Books

Purpose: Acquiring information about an interesting topic, asking some questions, and designing pages based on authentic pages in nonfiction trade books

Resources: Nonfiction trade books, students' own nonfiction convention books, paper, and markers

Responses: Prior knowledge form; question form; 11 x 17" paper for page design

Slavens Elementary teacher Barb Smith led her second graders through a nonfiction study. After surrounding them with nonfiction material, teaching them about nonfiction features, encouraging them to choose a topic for exploration, having them read for information and write down what she called WOW facts (striking information that makes one say Wow!), Barb helped her students design nonfiction pages that looked very much like the pages we find in nonfiction trade books.

Barb thought about having her students write nonfiction picture books, but wisely decided to have them create single pages instead as a first effort. These pages included both factual content about a chosen topic and the nonfiction features that kids had noticed in trade books. These topics ran the gamut from Sherman tanks to the life of Elvis Presley.

Barb asked her students to begin their research by recording what they already knew about their topic on a Prior Knowledge form. Turner listed five things he already knew:

Research Topic: Elvis Presley
Prior Knowledge: Write down facts that you already know about your topic

1. Elvis was the king of Rock and Roll.
2. He was very famous.
3. He sang many great songs.
4. He was very tall.
5. He died of drugs.

Next, Barb asked her students to record their questions on a Questions form. After thinking through what he already knew about his topic, Turner made a list of questions:

Research Topic: Elvis Presley
Questions I have before I begin my research are...

1. Did Elvis have any other jobs?
2. Did he have children?
3. Did he have brothers and sisters?
4. What were his parents' names?
5. What instruments did he play?

Figure 9.3 Turner's Nonfiction Page

An additional sheet asked the kids to list five new facts they learned as they conducted their research. In their final form, these nonfiction pages included interesting factual information, answered questions, resembled published nonfiction, and were visually striking (see, for example, Figure 9.3).

This was a terrific project that helped build background knowledge about the genre of nonfiction as well as demanding that kids sift through interesting information and choose what they deemed most important to include on their page. This would serve as an important step in creating nonfiction picture books at a later date.

Determining What's Important When Writing Information

Purpose: Becoming a specialist on a favorite topic, choosing what is important to include in a piece of writing, and writing informational teaching books.

Resources: Nonfiction trade books, magazines, and former students' work; 8 x 11″ construction paper booklets containing about twelve pages folded and stapled

Responses: Teaching books that replicate authentic nonfiction trade books, features and all. The writers write about their specialties, something they know about, care about, and would like to teach someone.

On a visit to Jacqueline Heibert's third grade classroom at Crofton House School in Vancouver, British Columbia, Steph worked with the students on writing important information about a topic of choice in the form of a "teaching book." Jacqueline had surrounded her third graders with nonfiction trade books, and they were becoming increasingly knowledgeable about the characteristics of the genre. When Steph arrived, she encouraged them to flip through nonfiction books, magazines, and examples of former students' teaching books and note the features and the writing. After they perused the resources for twenty minutes or so, Steph talked to the kids about writing books whose purpose is to teach something. "Everyone is a specialist in something," she told them as she wrote the following on a large chart:

A specialist is someone who
◆ Cares a lot about a topic, is passionate about it
◆ Knows a lot about the topic
◆ Wants to teach someone about the topic

She then made a list of several topics she knew and loved. Her list of specialties included

◆ Teaching and learning
◆ Reading and writing
◆ Her family
◆ Snorkeling
◆ Snow skiing
◆ The country of Tibet
◆ Hiking in the Colorado mountains

After sharing the topics she specialized in and choosing snorkeling for further exploration, she asked the kids to think of at least three specialties of their own. She asked for at least three in the belief that one will almost always emerge, even from more reticent kids, and that three or more would be a welcome bonus. The kids jotted down their specialties and shared them in pairs.

Next, Steph modeled writing her own teaching book. She wrote different information on each page of a construction paper booklet containing about twelve pages of paper, lined on the bottom half and unlined on the top for illustrations. She explained that since the purpose of nonfiction writing is to teach something, writers need to choose the most important information to include in the writing. To do this, writers ask themselves, "What information will best help my reader understand the topic?"

Steph began with snorkeling equipment on the first page, wrote about getting into the water on the next page, and followed with safety, coral, fish, and hazards on subsequent pages. Writing these parts on a page served as a preamble to later paragraphing. Steph explained that she chose these particular components of snorkeling because she felt they represented the most important information she could teach on the topic. She illustrated each page and included some nonfiction features, such as labeling her illustrations and marking each page with a heading.

The kids leaped at the chance to share their considerable information in the teaching book format. They filled their teaching books with interesting content as well as an array of nonfiction features, including illustrations. Creating these nonfiction books gave kids opportunities to draw as well as write. Hillary C. used labeling to enhance her informational book about skiing (see Figure 9.4), and Hilary W. headed each section in her manatee book with a pertinent question, which she answered on the page (see Figure 9.5).

Figure 9.4 Hillary C.'s Teaching Book Page on Skiing

Figure 9.5 Hilary W.'s Teaching Book Page on Manatees

Making these teaching books provided a terrific follow-up to the earlier nonfiction convention books and page designs.

Later that week, after they had completed the teaching books, Jacqueline gave the kids plenty of time to share their information with each other. Sharing their specialties built community. The kids came to see each other as specialists in a particular area. Some specialties were expected. Some were a complete surprise. Everyone learned new information on fresh topics as well as building background for nonfiction features. Because the kids included information they deemed important, their classmates learned essential content. When kids do the teaching, their peers take note.

A thought occurs to us here. To model outcomes, share student work as well as trade publications. One of the most effective ways to give our students an idea of what a project looks like in the end is to share completed examples of other students' work. Copy and save kids' work. Ask their permission to share it with future students. Flattery will get you everywhere! Student work is more authentic and powerful than any model we can think of. Kids love to read the work of other students, and they learn from it, too.

Coding Important Information on Unfamiliar as Well as Familiar Topics

Purpose: Noticing and selecting new information on familiar and unfamiliar topics

Resource: The picture book *The Unhuggables,* published by the National Wildlife Federation

Responses: Sticky notes coded L for learned something new about a familiar topic, or ∗ for important information about an unfamiliar topic

Our background knowledge plays a major role when we read informational text. As an avid lover of the country of Tibet and a passionate reader about the plight of Tibetans, Steph has extensive background knowledge for the topic. Each time she picks up an article about Tibet, she focuses on new information to add to her store of knowledge and develop further insight into this wonderful country. Much of what she reads about Tibet she knows already. On the other hand, if she were to pick up an article about Colorado water conservation, she would likely be overwhelmed with a mass of new, unfamiliar information, since she knows so little about the topic to begin with.

Kids are no different. Every teacher has met a kid who knows practically everything there is to know about dinosaurs, black holes, or the Civil War. The amount of background knowledge we have on a topic has a lot to do with what we deem important about it. If we already know the information, we are less likely to consider it important when we read it again.

When kids are reading about topics they know a great deal about, we encourage them to notice when they've learned something new and code the text L for learned. That new information means a lot to students with considerable background knowledge about a topic. When kids read about a little-known topic, however, coding the text L for learned is useless because the text would likely disappear under a sea of Ls. We encourage these readers, instead, to code parts they deem important with ∗, a kind of a universal code for importance. We suggest that they use the same criterion for coding with ∗ as they use to highlight important text.

Nick, a sixth-grade spider specialist, was reading *The Unhuggables,* a collection of short text pieces about animals you wouldn't want to cuddle up to. The compelling content, the rich writing style, and the engaging short text combine to make *The Unhuggables* one of our favorite books. In the section on spiders, he coded the text and wrote the following comments:

L Tarantulas protect jewelry stores at night. Burglars are scared just by
   the look of them.

L Spiders are a sign of good luck in some countries.

L Of 30,000 spiders, only a dozen are dangerous.

Nick was delighted to have this additional information. No topic intrigued
him more than these eight-legged creatures. For someone who knew little
about spiders, the ratio of poisonous to harmless might not be so important,
but for Nick this was essential new information to add to his arachnid arsenal.

After reading about spiders, he turned to the section titled "Octopus," a
sea creature he knew next to nothing about. His teacher encouraged him to
read the text and code information he thought was important with ∗. She
suggested that information that surprised him might be important. The
response on several of his sticky notes included surprising information:

∗ Octopuses are the one of the shyest sea creatures.

∗ Octopuses do not grab swimmers and suck them in with their arms.

∗ Most of their bodies are the size of a grown man's fist and none are
   bigger than a football.

Nick's reading exploded octopus myths right and left. He knew so little
about them that this new information was very important to him. In *The
Unhuggables*, Nick experienced reading both as a spider specialist and as an
octopus novice. These were two different experiences, and determining
what was important in the text was related primarily to his background
knowledge and interest in the topic.

Finding Important Information Rather Than Just One Main Idea

Purpose: Understanding that there are often several important ideas in a piece of text rather than a single main idea

Resource: A piece of like kind text for each student

Responses: Three sticky notes, each one coded ∗ to mark three important ideas in the text

When we are trying to wean kids from the one and only main idea mental-
ity, we give them three sticky notes and ask them to draw a big asterisk on
each one. Sound a little hokey? We thought so, too, until we saw how well it
worked, particularly when students are reading the same text.

Our point is to show students that there is more than one important idea
in anything they read. So we ask them to place the sticky notes at three different points in the text that they deem important. We model this, too, and
when we come back together to discuss the reading, each child and the
teacher shares what he or she has determined to be important in the text.
Naturally, we aren't all in agreement, and that is the point. We ask kids to

defend their stance and explain the thinking behind their decision. This contributes to our students' capacity to speak out about what they think, and it reminds them that text includes many important concepts and issues, not just a single main idea.

Reading for Answers to Specific Questions

Purpose: Reading to find specific information

Resource: *Exploring the Titanic,* by Robert Ballard

Responses: Class discussion, circling key words, underlining and writing in the margins on a page of text

Long before the blockbuster movie, people were transfixed by the sinking of the *Titanic*. The question that continues to plague all of us is how this could have happened. Why did the *Titanic* sink? One of the primary purposes for reading nonfiction is to answer specific questions. Robert Ballard's *Exploring the Titanic* gives one of the most in-depth and engaging accounts of the ship's fateful voyage of any book we know. It's a great book for reading aloud, full of suspense and interesting details that build knowledge about the plight of this great vessel.

As Steph read the book to a class of seventh graders, they couldn't stop asking why it sank. They learned in the first two chapters that the ship was sturdily built and that the captain had thirty-eight years of experience at sea. So they were even more perplexed about the ship's demise than before.

These seventh graders set out to read Chapter 3, "That Fateful Night," with the specific intent of discovering information that might lead them to understand what went wrong. They each had a copy of the text attached to their clipboards. "As we read, let's think about whether there are any clues as to why this happened. We will underline those places in the text that give us important information about our question. We can circle key words that help us understand and write our thinking in the margins," Steph suggested.

"Who wants to read?" Steph asked. Jennifer came forward. "As Jennifer reads the first few paragraphs, listen for some possible clues to answer our question and then share any information that might help us answer it." William spoke up as soon as Jennifer read the sentence, "It's another iceberg warning."

"How many warnings did they have?" William asked. "How many did they need? Why didn't they pay attention?" We coded the text and recorded William's questions.

"I circled *wearily*," Jill added. "It sounds as if these guys were tired and I underlined where it said that they had been working for hours sending personal messages."

"*Wearily* is a key word for you, Jill. It made you think about how tired they were, one more possible piece in the puzzle," Steph commented. And so the conversation went, with kids discussing the clues and Steph under-lining phrases, circling key words, and coding the margins with their responses (see Figure 9.6). When they reached the end of the page, the kids continued reading in pairs, searching for specific clues that addressed their basic question and underlining and circling important points in the text.

By the time these kids finished the chapter, they had a pretty good idea as to why the *Titanic* sank. They determined that exhaustion and a general

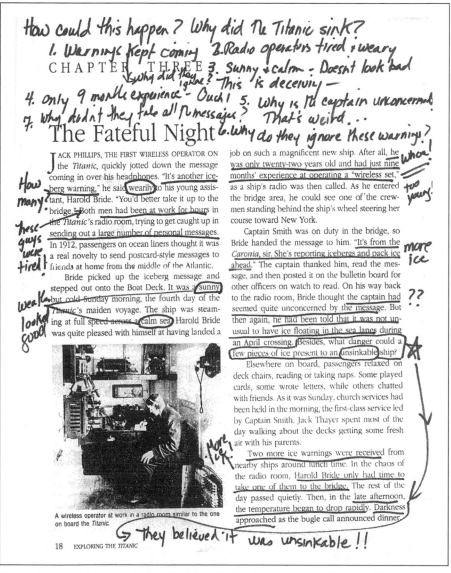

Figure 9.6 Text from *Exploring the Titanic,* Marked for Questions and Information

lack of concern about serious issues led to this grave tragedy. This nonchalance seemed to stem from the belief of everyone involved that this ship was unsinkable. These students identified important signals in the text. When they finished reading, they were no longer completely in the dark about why this had happened. Their close reading of the text enhanced their understanding and led to new insight.

Sifting the Topic from the Details

Purpose: Discriminating between key topics and supporting details

Resource: "Howling Again," an article from *Wild Outdoor World*

Responses: Two-column note form headed Topic/Details; three-column note form headed Topic/Details/Response

Mary Urtz generally uses a young adult magazine to introduce two-column note-taking to her fourth-grade class. We have found the Topic/Details note form to be particularly effective at helping students organize their thinking as they read for information. The most difficult part of this form is figuring out the primary topics. Mary introduces this two-column note-taking with nonfiction text that is structured around sections with separate headings. She explains that the headings represent the topics and that the text is full of details that give information about the topic. Much nonfiction text is structured this way.

To introduce two-column note-taking, Mary found an article in *Wild Outdoor World*, "Howling Again." This article was structured around a series of six headings followed by two or three paragraphs of details under each heading. The headings were

> Fifi, Is That You?
> They Run in Packs
> They Have Babysitters
> They Howl to Communicate
> They Use Body Language
> They Stay Out All Winter

Mary began by reading the first section. "Fifi, Is That You?" didn't provide much in the way of clues for a topic. The first few sentences read, "Wolves belong to the canine family. All dogs are descended from wolves. That means that your pet poodle, basset hound, retriever, or mutt developed from wolves." The section went on to discuss canine behavior and some basic wolf information. Mary mentioned that when you can't infer the topic from the heading, you should take a look at the first sentence or two to help ascertain what the section is primarily about. She decided that her first topic could be "Dog Family." As she wrote that on an overhead transparency, kids wrote it in their Wonder Books on a page headed Topic/Details.

The next topic she explored was "Packs," taken directly from the second heading. As kids read through the paragraphs that followed, they included details supporting the topic. After reasoning through the first few sections, the kids continued on their own with a partner, using each section heading as a topic on their Topic/Details form (see Figure 9.7).

These headings support students as they practice two-column note-taking. Not every nonfiction article is written in this user-friendly way, although many are. When introducing a new concept or strategy, we choose the most accessible material so that grasping the concept will be relatively easy.

As Mary continued teaching two-column note-taking, she sought out articles in which it was harder to sort the topics from the details because, for instance, the text was not broken up into sections by headings. We move to

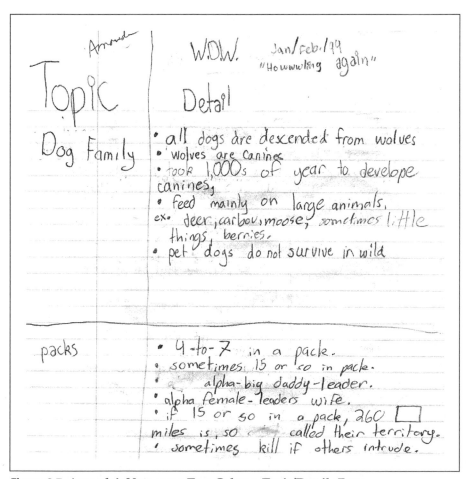

Figure 9.7 Amanda's Notes on a Two-Column Topic/Details Form

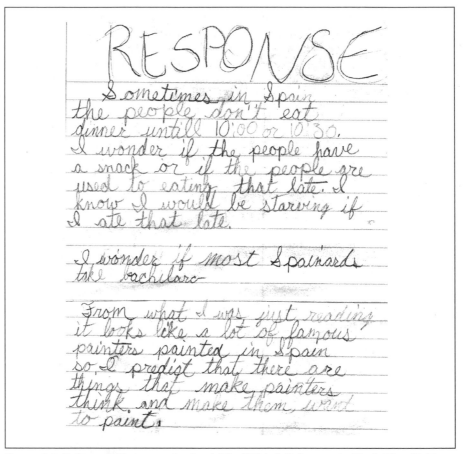

Figure 9.8 Rebecca's Response in the Added Third Column of a Topic/Details Form

more challenging material after students have had practice with more accessible material. This reflects our ongoing commitment to the gradual release of responsibility approach to instruction. Eventually, students use the two-column Topic/Details note form independently.

Adding a Third Column for Personal Response

As her students gain facility with two-column note-taking, Mary introduces a third column for personal response. Her kids let her know that the Topic/Details form was effective for listing essential information but lacked a place for their responses. A third column for response allows kids to interact with text personally and ensures that they have a place to record their thoughts, feelings, and questions. Since it is impractical to place three columns on one page of notebook paper, Mary's students divide one page of their Wonder Books into two-columns headed Topic and Details, and use the entire opposite page as a third column for **Response**. We have found that the more space we allow for responding in writing, the longer and more in-depth the responses are likely to be. Rebecca listed the following topics and details for her research on Spain on the first page:

Topic	Details
Employment	Work hours—9 A.M.–1 P.M. and 3 P.M.–6 P.M.
	Go home for lunch
	Spanish sometimes eat dinner at 10:30 P.M.
Education	In 1900, sixty out of one hundred people could not read.
	1987—Only 3% could not read.
	1st—Pre-Primary
	2nd—Primary
	3rd—Secondary
	4th—Bachillerato (optional)
Art	Great tradition in art, architecture, and music

Clearly, Rebecca was much impressed by the late dining hour favored by Spaniards because she started her third-column response on this theme (see Figure 9.8).

Reading Opposing Perspectives to Form an Opinion

Purpose: Reading persuasive material carefully to make an informed judgment

Resource: "Should Cities Sue Gunmakers?," an article from *Junior Scholastic*

Responses: Group discussion; a three-column note form headed Evidence For/Evidence Against/Personal Opinion

Junior Scholastic magazine includes a regular feature called "News Debate," which presents an issue in the news and gives two opposing perspectives (see, for example, Figure 9.9). *Junior Scholastic* is one of our favorite magazines. We remember it fondly from when it floated around our own junior high classrooms, and it has only improved with age. It covers a spectrum of issues and does not steer clear of controversy.

Helen Wickham, an eighth-grade teacher in Atlanta, explained to her social studies class that essays and editorials are written to promote a certain perspective and persuade the reader of that view: "It is the job of readers to read carefully and weigh the evidence to make a thoughtful decision regarding their own opinion." She provided her students with a three-column note form headed Evidence For/Evidence Against/Personal Opinion. She passed out the magazine to each class member and asked the kids to read the piece silently and record their thinking about the issue. Helen read along with the students silently and completed the task, also.

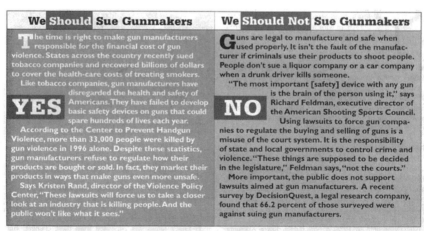

Should Cities Sue Gunmakers?

New Orleans is suing gun manufacturers. Mayor Marc Morial wants them to pay for police and health-care costs resulting from gun violence. The city's lawsuit claims that gunmakers manufacture "unreasonably dangerous" guns that lack effective safety devices.

Although gun sales are banned in Chicago, gun violence remains a big problem. The city has filed a $433 million lawsuit accusing the gun industry of "negligent marketing." The lawsuit argues that gunmakers deliberately flood nearby suburbs with more guns than law-abiding citizens can buy. The guns end up in the hands of Chicago's criminals.

A similar lawsuit, known as the "Hamilton Case," has been filed in Brooklyn, New York. The suit claims that gun manufacturers "negligently market" too many guns to states that have weak gun-control laws. Gun traffickers then sell the guns in states that have strong gun-control laws, such as New York and Massachusetts.

Other cities planning to sue the gun industry are closely watching the Hamilton Case. They hope the threat of expensive lawsuits will force the gun industry to better regulate itself.

What do you think? Should gun manufacturers be held legally and financially responsible for gun violence in cities? Read both arguments below, then decide.

We Should Sue Gunmakers

YES

The time is right to make gun manufacturers responsible for the financial cost of gun violence. States across the country recently sued tobacco companies and recovered billions of dollars to cover the health-care costs of treating smokers. Like tobacco companies, gun manufacturers have disregarded the health and safety of Americans. They have failed to develop basic safety devices on guns that could spare hundreds of lives each year.

According to the Center to Prevent Handgun Violence, more than 33,000 people were killed by gun violence in 1996 alone. Despite these statistics, gun manufacturers refuse to regulate how their products are bought or sold. In fact, they market their products in ways that make guns even more unsafe.

Says Kristen Rand, director of the Violence Policy Center, "These lawsuits will force us to take a closer look at an industry that is killing people. And the public won't like what it sees."

We Should Not Sue Gunmakers

NO

Guns are legal to manufacture and safe when used properly. It isn't the fault of the manufacturer if criminals use their products to shoot people. People don't sue a liquor company or a car company when a drunk driver kills someone.

"The most important [safety] device with any gun is the brain of the person using it," says Richard Feldman, executive director of the American Shooting Sports Council.

Using lawsuits to force gun companies to regulate the buying and selling of guns is a misuse of the court system. It is the responsibility of state and local governments to control crime and violence. "These things are supposed to be decided in the legislature," Feldman says, "not the courts."

More important, the public does not support lawsuits aimed at gun manufacturers. A recent survey by DecisionQuest, a legal research company, found that 66.2 percent of those surveyed were against suing gun manufacturers.

Figure 9.9 "News Debate" Article from *Junior Scholastic*

When they had finished reading, the students had a lively discussion, which bordered on a raucous debate. Callie's form shows the factual information she acquired as well as her personal opinion:

Evidence For	**Evidence Against**	**Personal Opinion**
Tobacco companies can be sued. No safety devices on guns. 33,000 people dead in a year.	Liquor companies can't. The best safety device is the person using the gun. The public doesn't agree with suing gun manufacturers; 66.2% against.	Guns kill way too many people. Guns should have safety locks and checks, but I'm not sure we should sue the gun companies. There are too many lawsuits already. Hot coffee and all that stuff. But if suing would make a difference in people dying, maybe we should do it.

This form and the ensuing discussion helped kids sort out their thinking and informed their opinions. Some wrote more in the Personal Opinion column after participating in the discussion. Much of the short text adults encounter is written with a slant. Readers must be trained to recognize persuasive writing and exercise judgment as they read it. Elementary school is not too soon to start.

Reasoning Through a Piece of Historical Fiction to Determine the Essence

Purpose: Using questioning and inferring to determine the essence of the text

Resource: *Bull Run*, by Paul Fleischman

Response: Conversation between five members of a book club reading this book to learn more about the Civil War

As a history major in college, Anne had to learn how to read historical sources and documents. This was a big switch from high school, when history appeared only in a textbook. Now Anne realizes the importance of teaching younger students to learn to read history in many different genres, for instance, historical fiction. Unlike fiction about topics close to students' own lives, historical fiction creates a clear context for different times, places, and people. Historian Linda Levstik (1993) argues there is no better way to learn about other times and places than through carefully researched, well-written historical fiction. She suggests that portraying human experiences from the past in realistic, engaging narratives enables students to understand perspectives and ideas that would be difficult if they were first encountered in summary form in a history textbook.

When students read historical fiction, they gain practice reading like historians, constructing interpretations based on the words and ideas in the text. More challenging historical fiction requires students to proceed slowly and carefully, taking time to reason through new ideas and information.

In one seventh-grade class, students were studying the Civil War by reading Paul Fleischman's *Bull Run* in small groups. Questioning and inferring were the strategies of choice for determining the important ideas and issues in the text. Anne designed several lessons to provide students with practice in thinking through the text together. In this way, they built their collective knowledge about the time period. Through conversation and sorting and sifting the details, they came to an understanding of the important ideas in the text.

Bull Run, a fictionalized account of the first battle of the Civil War, introduces students to ordinary people, all of whom have a clear connection to this moment in history. The vignettes explore how war profoundly affects these individuals. Fleischman's characters include a doctor, a woman slave who has gone to war with her Confederate officer master, and a twelve-year-old Southern boy "desperate to kill a Yankee."

Each character tells his or her story through a first-person narrative that draws students to ask questions, such as Who was this person? How was he or she connected to this battle and this war? What was he or she doing, thinking, and feeling about it all? Figuring out each person's perspective and connection to the battle encouraged several levels of questioning and thoughtful discussion. This excerpt from a discussion captures how students pieced together the story of Carlotta King, a young slave who was forced to journey to Virginia with her Confederate soldier master. Carlotta's words are represented in italics.

Anne: Right now, let's read Carlotta King's first-person narrative. Think about who she was, where she was, what was happening to her and why. Let's read the first few sentences and jot down any questions we have. It's not really clear what's happening to her, so we have to draw inferences from her words.

I come up from Mississippi with the master. He was a lieutenant or some such thing. I heard him bragging to another man that he had five thousand acres and loads of slaves, which was a bare-headed lie. And that his slaves would sooner die than run off and leave him, which was a bigger lie yet. Lots of the soldiers brought their slaves with 'em. We washed and cooked and mended same as back home. Except we weren't back home.

Carla: What?! Why did the officers bring their slaves to war with them?
Lynda: She said they cooked and did the laundry just like on the plantation, but it doesn't sound like she liked her master.
John: So she was in the North now, or close to the North? So they were at Bull Run or not yet?
Anne: Remember, Bull Run was a stream in northern Virginia, where the Union and Confederate troops first met on the battlefield.

The Union men weren't more than a few hills away. I'd look at them hills. They did call to me powerful. I was a young woman and fast as a fox. I knew I'd surely never get another chance and made up my mind and picked the night I'd go. My heart beat hard all that day. I didn't tell nobody.

Mike: It sounds like she's going to try to escape.

Anne: Which words made you think that?

Mike: She said, "Them hills, they did call to me powerful" and she also said she could run fast with the words, "I was a young woman and fast as a fox."

Amber: Won't that be dangerous if there's fighting? Won't somebody notice her?

Lynda: But she says it's her only chance.

Then at supper another slave told how those that crossed over were handed back to their owners by the Yankees! My bowl slipped right out of my hands. I thought the Yankees had come to save us.

Anne: What does it mean… "those that crossed over were handed back to their owners by the Yankees"?

John: So they return slaves who escape. Couldn't she have used the Underground Railroad and gotten away?

Carla: I bet not every Yankee did that; maybe some of them helped the slaves.

Mike: Remember in the Aunt Harriet book [Ringgold 1992] there were those people—the bounty hunters—who would try to spy on runaway slaves and catch them and return them?

Lynda: And at the end it said something about a law which made people in the north do that.

Anne: Do you mean the Fugitive Slave Act?

John: Well, maybe that's why they have to return the slaves that escape, maybe that's why northerners couldn't just help them escape.

Carla: Or that's why they have to go all the way to Canada to be free.

Amber: So why didn't they just hide until the battle was over?

Mike: I wonder if she'll try to escape at all, she might have just given up.

Anne: So what do you think happened to her? What do you think she decided to do?

Lynda: I think she might have escaped, at least for a while, but I wonder if she ever made it to freedom.

As it turns out, Carlotta did try to escape during the heat of the Battle of Bull Run, but Fleischman left us hanging with Carlotta's last words: "If Union soldiers sent slaves back, I'd just have to keep clear of 'em. When I came to Bull Run, I just waded across and kept movin' North."

In order to understand the dilemma Carlotta faced at Bull Run, the students needed background knowledge about many aspects of the Civil War, such as the Fugitive Slave Act and the Underground Railroad. Reasoning through the text meant that students built a clear understanding of historical issues and events as seen through the eyes of one person.

Reading for Details

Throughout this chapter we emphasize reading to answer questions and reading for important information. We tend to downplay reading for details, perhaps because we spent so much time doing it in school ourselves. But authentic reading experiences remind us that there are many reasons to read, often for the big ideas and sometimes for the details. Just recently, Steph read in the *New York Times* that more and more bright young people were choosing teaching as a career. Well aware of a predicted future teacher shortage, she was thrilled to see an increase in education majors at colleges across the country. When she mentioned this to her husband, his immediate question was, "How much of an increase?" She couldn't remember. She had skimmed the statistic and ignored it.

"It would be nice to know," he commented. "To determine how significant it really is."

And he was right, of course. Once again, we see the value in all kinds of reading. Reading is about purpose, and there is a time and place for every type of reading, reading for details as well as reading for the big picture. And often it's the details that we piece together to arrive at the bigger picture.

The next chapter focuses on that most complex of strategies, synthesizing information. When readers synthesize, they read for the gist of a piece and apply a variety of strategies that nudge their thinking. They notice how the details fit together to form a whole. Choosing important information and sifting essential ideas from text moves readers further down the path to insight. Synthesizing is the final step in this evolution of thought.

Chapter

10

Synthesizing Information
The Evolution of Thought

Among Steph's fondest childhood memories are the summer afternoons spent in the great room of her grandparents' log house on a lake in northern Wisconsin. The musty smell of worn Oriental carpets, the shiny pretzel log walls, the Scott Joplin tunes on the player piano, and the continuous whir of the ceiling fan filled her senses as she whiled away those lazy days, in tandem with her grandmother, working jigsaw puzzles of every size and shape. A cardtable in the far corner of the room housed all the action. One week a Bavarian castle, the next a nineteenth-century painting of the Grand Canyon. As the years went by, a portrait of Captain Hook, a can of Coca-Cola, and a pepperoni pizza materialized on that cardtable. A battalion of two, grandmother and granddaughter attacked the puzzles together and were delighted as entire pictures slowly emerged from the hundreds of scattered cardboard pieces.

Isn't that what synthesizing is all about? When we synthesize information, we take individual pieces of information and combine them with our prior knowledge. We begin to see a pattern emerge, and we form a new picture or idea from the pieces of information. Our thinking evolves as we add information from the text. Each bit of information we encounter adds a piece to the construction of meaning. In the same way that a jigsaw puzzle moves toward completion piece by piece, our thoughts become more complete as we add more information. At its best, synthesizing involves merging new information with existing knowledge to create an original idea, see a new perspective, or form a new line of thinking to achieve insight.

How Thinking Evolves

Synthesizing is the most complex of comprehension strategies. To be honest, as staff developers engaged in strategy instruction, we often failed to get to synthesizing before the end of the year, and not because of time constraints. Rather, when we faced the strategy head on, we were not completely sure of how to tackle it. So we have broken synthesizing down. A true synthesis is an Aha! of sorts. We have these lightbulb occurrences when we read, but they don't come around every day. And they only happen if we are taking stock of meaning throughout our reading. As we take in information, we enhance our understanding. Our thinking is likely to evolve slowly over time, as Steph's jigsaw puzzles did.

Synthesizing lies on a continuum of evolving thinking. Synthesizing runs the gamut from taking stock of meaning while reading to achieving new insight. Introducing the strategy of synthesizing in reading, then, primarily involves teaching the reader to stop every so often and think about what she has read. Each piece of additional information enhances the reader's understanding and allows her to better construct meaning.

The agreement between Steph and Alverro, the incredulous giraffe reader, meant that Alverro would view the end of each page as a red light to stop and think about what he had read and digest the parts to construct meaning before powering on through the text. This is synthesizing at its most rudimentary. There may not be an original thought in it, but stopping and thinking about meaning as one goes helps readers stay on track with the text and allows their thinking to evolve.

Synthesizing at the highest level goes beyond merely taking stock of meaning as one reads. A true synthesis is achieved when a new perspective or thought is born out of the reading. In *Nonfiction Matters* (Harvey 1998), Steph included an excerpt (Brantley 1996) from a review of Savion Glover's Broadway musical *Bring in da Noise, Bring in da Funk*. It describes a high level of synthesis revealed through Glover's new style of dance: "Almost all the numbers trace an arc from tentativeness to full-blown assured performances. This is most evident in Glover's splendid second-act solo in which he demonstrates the techniques of legendary tap artists of the past, and then *synthesizes* them into an exultant style of his own."

Through his inventive dance form, Savion Glover put his personal stamp on the art of tap dancing. When thinking evolves to this point, students personalize the outcome by integrating their thinking with new information to achieve a new perspective. This is the insight we have spoken about throughout this book.

So how does this type of insight come about in reading? Nonfiction text, for example, often conveys information that helps the reader form a particular viewpoint. A reader's thinking changes as he ingests new information gleaned from the text. An article on rain forest deforestation might point a finger at governmental forestry policies. A synthesis could involve forming an opinion about the shortsightedness of the government in question. This constitutes an evolution of thought; the new information combined with the reader's thinking leads to new insight.

The following strategy lessons support an evolving notion of synthesizing. We explicitly teach our students to take stock of meaning while they read and use it to help their thinking evolve, perhaps leading to new insight, perhaps not, but enhancing understanding in the process.

To nudge readers toward synthesis, we encourage them to interact personally with the text. Personal response gives readers an opportunity to explore their evolving thinking. Synthesizing information integrates the words and ideas in the text with the reader's personal thoughts and questions and gives the reader the best shot at achieving new insight.

Synthesizing Information

Making Synthesizing Concrete

Purpose:	Using baking to help students make the abstract synthesizing strategy more concrete
Resources:	Ingredients for making a cake
Response:	A discussion about how synthesizing in reading is similar to baking

Kindergarten teacher David Harris thinks carefully about how to make abstract comprehension strategies concrete for kids. Aware that synthesizing requires combining a number of parts to form a new whole, David uses baking to demonstrate synthesizing for little kids. He tells his young scholars that reading is about taking in a lot of different facts, thinking about them, and learning something new.

David decided to use baking a cake to demonstrate the notion of synthesizing. Together with the kids, he measured out the different ingredients and set them on a table in front of the class. The kids counted seven ingredients in all. David left what remained of the packages of flour, sugar, and other ingredients on the table. Together, they poured each ingredient into the bowl and blended it with a spatula. When they finished mixing the batter, David pointed out that those seven separate ingredients were now blended into one thick, gloppy mixture ready for the oven. They slid it in, waited an hour, and out popped a golden cake.

"What do we have here?" David asked them.

"A cake," they answered in unison, their eyes wide.

"That's right," David told them as he pointed to the remnants of the ingredients. "All of these different parts mixed together became a whole new thing, that delicious cake you baked. When you read and listen to stories, there are a lot of different parts and characters, but in the end all of those parts come together to make up the whole story, just like this cake."

David didn't expect kindergartners to talk about "synthesizing," but he would remind them to think about the ingredients and the cake baking when he next read out loud to them. He hoped this would help them think about the different parts of the story and how they fit together to make the whole story. Kids love to bake. This rather offbeat way of making synthesizing concrete fired them up about the strategy and scaffolded their understanding of the nature of story.

Some other activities for making synthesizing concrete include making orange juice, doing jigsaw puzzles, and building with Legos. All are activities that involve putting together assorted parts to make a new whole, which is what synthesizing is all about.

Retelling to Synthesize Information

Purpose: Providing a basic framework to help students begin to synthesize information through a brief retelling of a story

Resources: Assorted picture books, including *For Every Child a Better World*, by L. Gikow

Responses: Recording brief syntheses on sticky notes or charts, or through discussion; one-word lists of a synthesis

When first-grade teacher Debbie Miller introduces synthesizing to her students, she provides them with a basic framework for thinking and talking about synthesizing. She tells her students that when readers synthesize, they

◆ Remember to tell what is important
◆ Tell it in a way that makes sense
◆ Try not to tell too much

Over the next few weeks, Debbie models this with a variety of well-loved picture books. After she finishes reading a story, she shows her students how she synthesizes the story by following the above guidelines. Sometimes she records her synthesis on a chart, sometimes on a sticky note. At other times she merely talks about her synthesis. But she always keeps it brief, salient, and to the point.

Young kids in particular have trouble with brevity when they attempt synthesizing. We've all heard a retelling of *Star Wars* that lasted longer than the movie itself. But as Debbie models extensively, kids begin to get the hang of it.

Several weeks into the teaching of this strategy, Kent shared his synthesis of the book *For Every Child a Better World*. During sharing time, he took out a piece of paper and began to read his synthesis: "Every child needs food, but sometimes there isn't any. Every child needs clean water, but sometimes they can't find it. Every child needs a home, but some don't have one." When he finished reading, Debbie commented on his good thinking and asked him about his writing. Kent explained that after he read, he thought about what was important and how it would make sense and then he made some notes to help him remember. His notes, translated from his temporary spelling, follow:

food
clean water
home
clean air
medicine
school

Kent went on to explain that when he finished reading, he went back through the book and thought about the most important information and then wrote only a word to help him remember. "Then when you tell some-body, you can just look at your paper and put in all the rest of the words that are in your head." Kent's note-taking to aid synthesis helped all of the kids in the class who tried it the next day. This early attempt at synthesizing shows how Debbie's students began to learn how to pick out what is impor-tant when they read and keep notes short enough to help them remember the information at a later time, a valuable skill as they move on through school and life (Harvey et al. 1996).

Synthesizing While Reading Expository Text

Purpose: Making margin notes in your own words to synthesize sections of the text

Resource: "In Sickness and in Health," an article in *Kids Discover Magazine*

Responses: Brackets in the margins for synthesizing information; sticky notes coded S for synthesize; two-column note form headed What's Interesting/What's Important

One of our absolute favorite magazines for kids, *Kids Discover,* addresses a specific science or social studies topic each month. We couldn't keep the April 1999 issue, titled *Blood,* out of kids' hands. Along with articles on how to make fake blood and on blood typing was a longer article, "In Sickness and in Health," which discussed the importance of blood in the battle to stay healthy. Horace Mann sixth-grade teacher Gloria Mundel lifted a section of that article to practice the synthesizing strategy with her class.

Gloria explained that she would read a paragraph or two and then write about the essence of the text *in her own words.* Gloria knew that if kids could use their own words to describe what they read and the words made sense, then the kids understood the text. She said that to synthesize what she was reading, she would try to write the *most important* information and keep it *brief.*

She also told her students that there was no need to write full sentences, as long as what they wrote made sense. As she read out loud, Gloria explained the concept of bracketing to the kids. On an overhead trans-parency, she bracketed off a section of the article and then wrote in her own words what that section meant (see Figure 10.1).

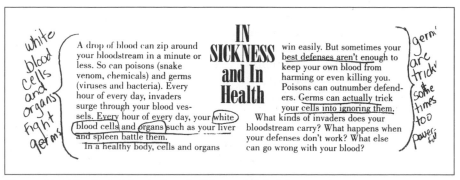

Figure 10.1 Bracketed Part of an Article, and Brief Summaries

After Gloria showed her students her thinking, she encouraged them to do the same on the following page of the article. The kids attached sticky notes to synthesize the sections. They coded the sticky notes S for synthesize and then wrote down the gist of the passage in their own words.

Ashley's notes hit the nail on the head (see Figure 10.2). Ryan, on the other hand, coded the same text with two sticky notes, one that said, "People eat blood sausage" and another that said, "It's also called blood pudding." Ryan had picked out the *most interesting* rather than the *most important* information on the page. The trouble was that this response captured rich details rather than key ideas. To accurately synthesize when reading, readers need to get at the essence of the text. When readers respond in their own words, teachers can quickly tell if they are getting the key ideas.

A two-column form that helps kids focus on the difference between what's important (the essence) and what's interesting (the rich details) is headed What's Interesting/What's Important (Harvey 1998). Sometimes they are one and the same, sometimes not. Gloria shared this response form with Ryan so that he would have a place to record the compelling details while also recording the important information and synthesizing for the essence as he read.

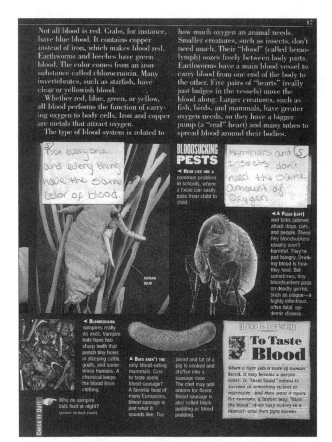

Figure 10.2 Ashley's Synthesis on Sticky Notes

Making Comparisons in Science and Synthesizing the Similarities

Purpose: Comparing and contrasting properties to better understand their essence

Resources: Science trade books or science textbooks on marine biology

Response: Three-column note form headed Compare and Contrast

Seventh-grade science teacher Margaret Bobb has developed an interesting form that supports synthesizing in the content areas. She uses a three-column Compare and Contrast note form. The first and third columns are headed with the content to be compared, in this case Kelp in the first column and Coral in the third column as Margaret explores marine biology with her students. The middle column is headed Alike. As Margaret and her students read, they record the properties of kelp in the first column and the properties of coral in the third. When they encounter similarities between the two, they record that information in the middle column. The middle column is a synthesis of the similarities between coral and kelp. Margaret explains to the kids that this three-column form is similar to a Venn diagram, since they both report similarities in the middle.

Teachers have used this form with social studies as well. For example, in a Revolutionary War study, the first column could be labeled The British and the third column could be headed The Colonists. The middle column would once again be reserved for the similarities between the two. Middle school content area teachers have found this form to be invaluable when trying to help their students make sense of two different properties or concepts.

Showing Evolving Thinking by Summarizing the Content and Adding Personal Response

Purpose: Summarizing the content of a piece of text and responding personally

Resources: Young adult magazines, including *Kids Discover, Wild Outdoor World,* and *Time for Kids*

Response: A page of notebook paper divided horizontally with the top half marked Summary and the bottom half marked Response

Fourth-grade teacher Mary Urtz models summarizing and responding in her own Wonder Book. First, she divides a notebook page in half horizontally and labels the top half Summary and the bottom half Response. She summarizes a piece of text in the summary portion and then gives her personal response below. When she demonstrates summarizing, she tries to pick out the most important ideas in the text and keep the writing to a minimum. Brevity is a virtue when summarizing, and Mary wants her fourth graders to learn this. She explains to them, however, that synthesizing is about more than summarizing. It's also about integrating thinking with the content and getting the reader's personal take on a piece of text. In the response portion, she mentions her use of comprehension strategies and the process by which she constructs meaning along with her personal reflections on the text itself.

Jonathan picked up on this in the most delightful way. He describes the content of an article on muskies in his summary and then explains how he visulizes with a "picture in your mind" in the response portion (see Figure 10.3). Jonathan's response shows how he summarizes the content, responds

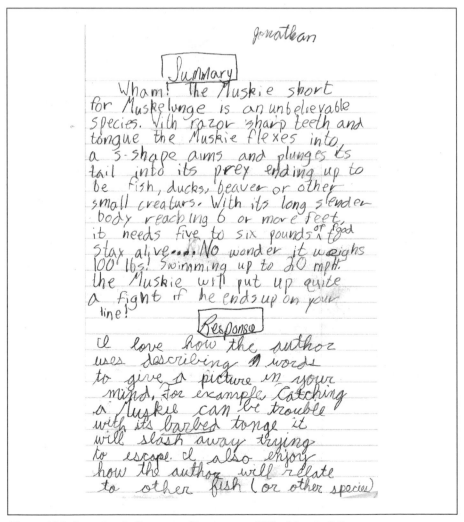

Figure 10.3 Jonathan's Summary/Response of Muskies Article

personally to reading, and reflects on his process as a reader. The kids in Mary's room use this form to acquire content as well as to respond to their own reading process.

Reading for the Gist

Purpose: Taking notes and using a variety of strategies to synthesize

Resource: The picture book *An Angel for Solomon Singer,* by Cynthia Rylant

Responses: Lists of notes and strategies; one-page written responses

Near the end of a two-year loop through fourth and fifth grade, the kids in Glenda Clearwater's class had become increasingly adept at reading strategically, having practiced strategies over the course of two years. They understood that reading was about constructing meaning, and they read for that purpose. Glenda knew that writing while reading can show the reader's evolution of thought. Although her students had been coding the text and writing in margins while they read independently, they hadn't done much note-taking while she read. This was more of a challenge.

Glenda decided to up the ante and have them take notes as she read. She chose to read them Cynthia Rylant's picture book *An Angel for Solomon Singer,* the story of a sad, lonely old man who lives in a New York boarding house and laments his station in life. Things change when he wanders into a twenty-four-hour café and sees a friendly waiter with a smiling face.

Glenda began by having her students list the comprehension strategies they'd studied, and reiterated that these strategies could help them make sense of the text. She asked them to write down their thinking as well as story events as they took notes. She believed that notes of their questions, predictions, important ideas, and visual images would be of more use to them than mere content notes as they tried to synthesize the material. She knew that this book was difficult to understand and required questioning, visualizing, and inferential thinking to gain meaning.

As Glenda read *Solomon Singer* out loud, she stopped and took notes in her own journal periodically and then shared her writing with the kids. Some of the students wrote practically nonstop throughout the read-aloud. Others needed a few moments to collect their thoughts and record their thinking. So Glenda paused intermittently to allow them to jot down some notes and complete their thoughts. When they finished, their notes revealed that they had visualized, asked questions, made connections, inferred, and synthesized while Glenda read.

Jessica's notes, which follow here, include examples of her flexible use of multiple strategies, a requirement when readers synthesize:

He doesn't like where he lives.
I think all of his wishes will come true.
His life isn't that great.
The café has made him happy.
He is poor.
I think the waiter is an angel.
He is lonely/I've been lonely before.
He wants to go back home.
He likes to dream.
He really likes to go to the Westway Café.
He's starting to like New York better now.
The Westway Café brightened up his life and made him feel like New
    York was his home.
Why is he in New York City if he loves Indiana so much?
How come he is so poor?

When Jessica wrote that she thought the waiter was an angel, she was inferring. When she mentioned that she'd been lonely before, she was making a connection. When she commented that the Westway Café made New York feel like home, she was synthesizing.

Claire drew a barn on her notes, which showed she was visualizing. She labeled the barn, and wrote notes, predictions, and questions (see Figure 10.4).

When Glenda's students finished their note-taking, they wrote responses in their response journals based on their notes, their memories of the story, and their thinking. These notes and responses show how thinking evolves as kids read. As they derive more information from the text, they begin to synthesize it into the bigger picture. Claire's response follows:

> I think Mr. Singer has a horrible place to live. He hates everything in New York until he wanders into the Westway Café, "where dreams come true." This is a wonderful book about feelings, dreams, and angels. When our teacher was reading, it made me visualize. I had a picture of a perfect home for Solomon, in Illinois where I used to live. It had a balcony, bouncy grass, everlasting fields of corn and wheat. At night, he could lie down and stare at the stars in the sky. He would have three cats, two dogs, five fish, ten hamsters, etc. They would be free to run all over and Mr. Singer wouldn't be lonely. The sun would shine all day long. But New York isn't that bad, now that he found the Westway Café, especially when the angel watches over him.

In her response, Claire shows how she activates multiple strategies to understand the story. Ultimately, she reads for the gist of the story, how the Westway Café changes Solomon Singer's life. When readers synthesize, they get the gist.

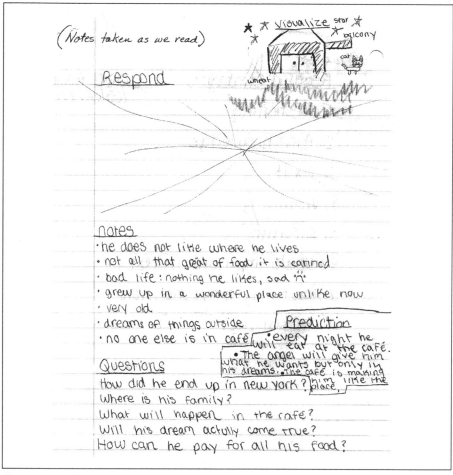

Figure 10.4 Claire's Response to *An Angel for Solomon Singer*

Writing as Synthesis: Personalities from the Past

Purpose: Writing from a first-person perspective to better understand the contributions of historical figures

Resources: Picture book biographies

Responses: Two-column note form; note-taking

When we're studying famous people, we try to gain insight into their lives. It makes sense to ask, What's important to remember about them? What lessons can we learn from their lives? Columbine Elementary third-grade teacher Barbara Munizza wanted to take a thoughtful approach to the study of biography, so she asked her students to read and think about famous people who had made a difference in the world or who had overcome adversity or obstacles in their lives.

Barbara's goal was for each child to read about and research a person of their own choosing, using their responses and notes to eventually write a thoughtful "first-person" sketch. Knowing that she would need to support her students as they explored a new genre, took notes, and developed their written pieces, Barbara planned out a series of lessons. These included modeling thoughtful responses to reading, taking notes on important ideas rather than trivial details, and organizing notes to support writing. Making sure that children's voices weren't lost in the midst of all this information was important, and a tall order for these third graders.

Barbara chose Joseph Bruchac's *A Boy Called Slow,* the story of Sitting Bull's transition from childhood to adulthood. As she modeled her own reading, thinking, and responding with the book, it dawned on her that she was teaching her students about synthesis. As the class read Sitting Bull's story of learning to be brave, Barbara pointed out that thinking can change during reading. After completing their own responses, the children discussed how their thinking about the "boy called Slow" had changed over the course of the story. Dylan's response illustrates that although he originally was incredulous that Slow had the courage to scare his tribe's enemies away, by the end of the story he realized that Slow deserved his new name. He states, "I can't believe that Slow scared the Crow warriors away. I think Slow was very brave. If I were there, I would give him a big reward and I would give him a new name."

When the children began to read their biographies independently, they responded to important events and details, often with honesty, amazement, or outrage. Kevin's response to David Adler's *A Picture Book of Anne Frank* noted his personal reactions to important events in Anne Frank's life. He recorded them on the following two-column form:

Facts from the Text	Response
Six million Jews were murdered.	I wish there were no Nazis because it's not fair that others couldn't have food and homes.
They were cold and suffering.	I wonder how it felt to hide and to be tortured by the Nazis.
Margot died.	I felt bad for them when she died because I wouldn't like to be killed or get sick and die.
Anne hid for more than two years.	I can't believe that she hid for more than two years because some of them got caught right away.
Anne died.	I wouldn't want to be Anne Frank because she died in a death camp and hid for most of her life.

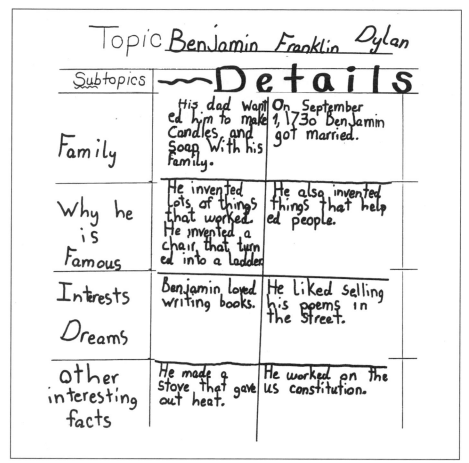

Figure 10.5 Dylan's Notes on Benjamin Franklin

Dylan's note-taking sheet on Ben Franklin illustrates the next step in this process. The Details form (see Figure 10.5) illustrates how the children sorted their notes, ensuring that categories such as "Why He Is Famous" and "Interests and Dreams" are covered.

Donald Graves has said that "writing is the ultimate act of synthesis." Dylan collected a lot of fascinating information that captured his imagination, including the surprising fact that Ben Franklin liked to sell his poems in the street. His genuine interest in and engagement with Ben Franklin, as well as his thoughtful and clearly organized notes, helped him internalize the information over time. This excerpt from Dylan's "first-person" biography illustrates how Dylan synthesized interesting details about Ben Franklin's life, making it possible for him to write convincingly from Ben's point of view:

In the 1700s your father could pick what you learned in school and what your job was. When I was little, my dad told me to be a preacher. Later, he told me that they are poor. At school I learned to write well, but I failed arithmetic. Two years later, my dad told me you will work for me and your family making soap and candles. It was hard smelly work, but I did it for two years. Then one day I said, "I want to go to sea." But my father said "No, your brother drowned at sea. You will stay in Boston!"

When I was seventeen, I decided to run away. I ran away to Philadelphia, Pennsylvania. There I worked for a printer. Then I started my own print shop. Later I owned a newspaper and a store. I was a busy man. But I wanted to do more, so I started a library and a fire department. I did experiments and wrote about science and I sold my poems in the streets. Later, I invented a chair that turned into a ladder and a stove that gave heat away. I called it the Franklin stove. Everyone wanted one! Then I wrote a book about farming and weather and holidays. For twenty-five years, each year I would write a new one.

Moving from Short Text to Chapter Books

Purpose: Using comprehension strategies to read and synthesize longer chapter books

Resource: *The Devil's Arithmetic,* by Jane Yolen

Responses: Beyond-the-Line Question form; Beyond-the-Line Answer form; two-column form with page number and strategy in the first column and a one-paragraph synthesis in the second column

Tiffany Boyd and Joe Kolodziej's fourth and fifth graders at Mapleton Elementary in Boulder are seasoned book group participants. The students begin the year reading and discussing realistic fiction and thinking about connections between the text and their own lives. Tiffany and Joe typically introduce a comprehension strategy using short text and then guide children to transfer the strategy to chapter books as part of small book group discussions. It's important that children use comprehension strategies in longer, more difficult text, but we've learned the hard way that it's more effective to have them practice in short text first. Otherwise they may just get lost in a big, fat book.

Over the course of the year, Tiffany and Joe had the students practice questioning, inferring, and determining importance with a variety of short stories, gradually moving into longer novels. By the end of the year, the students were using and recording responses that included all of these comprehension strategies in their literature journals. At this point, Tiffany and Joe felt that the students were ready to attempt the most sophisticated and challenging strategy of all: synthesizing.

One way to approach teaching synthesizing is to ask students to record how their thinking evolves over time. Introducing the students to the idea of synthesizing made sense with book clubs, so that students could discuss their changing ideas and insights with their peers. Using thoughtful historical novels about World War II, Tiffany modeled her own response to the beginning of Jane Yolen's *The Devil's Arithmetic,* in which a young girl at a Passover Seder finds herself transported back in time to a concentration camp. Tiffany didn't merely talk through the lesson on synthesis, she also provided her students with her written definition and an example of how she combined several different comprehension strategies to make sense of the beginning of the book. The following excerpt from Tiffany's notebook explained synthesis and showed the kids how she expanded upon her understanding of familiar strategies, including questioning and determining importance, to synthesize the story.

Synthesis: The combining of separate ideas into a new whole.

Writing a synthesis should help to fix the meaning of what you read into your mind. You are weaving together what you read and your own ideas into new complete thoughts.

Use any or all of the comprehension strategies we have learned this year. Write down each one in the right-hand column and write the page number down in the left. Use the information to write a synthesis when you finish.

Use T-S, T-T, and or T-W for the connection strategy, Q for questioning or wondering, I for inferring, Imp for determining importance, Char for looking at character. My example follows.

Page	Strategy
3	Q What is the meaning behind the Passover Seder?
4	T-W When Hannah says her mother's lectures are so annoying, it reminds me of how discouraged kids can get with what adults want them to do.
4	Imp "It's about remembering." I think that is going to be the lesson that Hannah learns in this book.
5	Char Hannah is the type of person who needs to experience things in order for them to be meaningful.

Synthesis

I am going to learn a lot about Jewish traditions from this book. I know a little bit about Passover and Seders, but I'm sure I will learn a lot more. Hannah's attitude reminds me of some kids that I know. She seems irritated that adults are telling her what is important and what she needs to remember about the Holocaust, which she did not even experience. It is hard for many of us to connect to things in history that we did not experience. That's why I love historical fiction; it weaves interesting events from history into a story with characters we can relate to.

Claire's response included a summary of the characters, setting, and plot as well as her beyond-the-line question (see Figure 10.6). Throughout

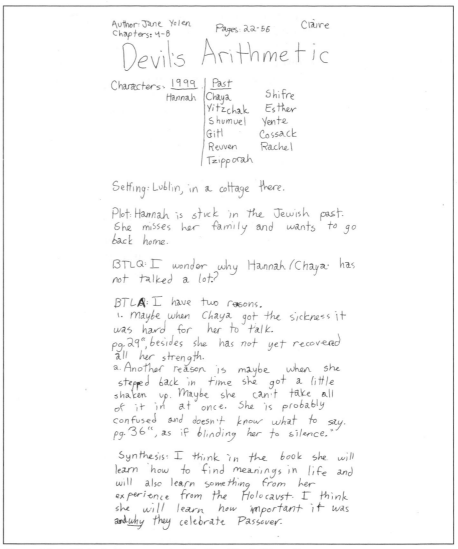

Figure 10.6 Claire's Response to *The Devil's Arithmetic*

the year, Tiffany and Joe had modeled what they call beyond-the-line questions (BTLQ), questions that move students beyond a literal interpretation of the text. Claire asked the BTLQ I wonder why Hannah/Chaya has not talked a lot? Citing evidence from the text, Claire poses two possible answers to her question, which she labels her beyond-the-line answer (BTLA). She infers that Chaya became sick or that she was shaken up from stepping back in time. In her synthesis, Claire uses what she has read to anticipate the lessons the story will teach Chaya, such as how experiencing the Holocaust will help her "find meaning in life."

A week later, when Claire is further along in her reading, we see evidence of her evolving thinking. Her response includes two questions: I wonder what it would be like to be in a concentration camp? and Why couldn't you wear your own clothes in the showers? Claire predicted what she thought was going to happen at the end of the book. She wrote in her notebook, "I think Hannah is going to go home, and at the end, one person in her family, such as her aunt, is going to have some resemblance to a person in the past."

Her final synthesis of the story, written in her notebook, follows:

This book has surprised me. I thought I would learn more about Passover, but I really learned more about the concentration camps. Here's an example. I didn't know you couldn't wear your own clothes and all the good clothes and stuff went to the Germans. I think I would be scared to take all my clothes off and dive into a garbage dump. I think when I read next time I will learn about both, Passover and the concentration camps. If Hannah ever comes back to real life, I think one person in her family will resemble a person in the concentration camp.

Her evolving thinking in her journal illuminates how a combination of comprehension strategies allowed her to synthesize the information and achieve new insight. Looking back over the year, Tiffany and Joe believed that their extensive modeling of short text to teach comprehension made a significant difference in their students' understanding of longer chapter books later on.

Synthesizing to Access Content

Purpose: Noticing the thinking we do to access content and acquire knowledge

Resource: "Moonstruck Scientists Count 63 and Rising" (Boyd 1999), an article in the *Denver Post*

Responses: Two-column note form headed Content/Process; class discussion

Content area reading demands that readers pick up factual information as they read. One of the things we hope for our students is that the reading strategies described in this book will help in their quest for information. As we mentioned in Chapter 2, we want our students to become aware of their thinking process as well so that they can call up a strategy to access content, particularly in difficult, more challenging text.

In Kim Worsham's fifth grade at Ford Elementary in suburban Atlanta, Steph and Kim decided to test a form they thought might help students articulate their thinking as they read for information. The form was simple enough—two columns, with the first column headed Content (Facts) and the second column headed Process (Thinking). They added the terms *facts* and *thinking* in parenthesis to provide more explicit language.

Knowing that this might not be the mini-lesson to end all others, from the kids' perspective at least, Steph chose the most compelling piece of expository text she could find. A rule of thumb we have tried to adhere to for many years is that the more boring the task, the more compelling the text must be. So Steph was delighted when she happened upon the article "Moonstruck Scientists Count 63 and Rising" (Boyd 1999), the majority of which is reprinted here from the *Denver Post:*

Here's a trivia question sure to stump your friends: How many moons are there in our solar system?

It's a rare person who knows the answer—63 moons and climbing.

Just last year, two more satellites were discovered circling counter-clockwise around Uranus, the seventh planet from the sun.

"It's almost inconceivable there aren't more moons out there," said Brett Gladman, an astronomer at Cornell University in Ithaca, NY, who detected the new Uranian moons in October 1997. "Almost every time there is an advance in detector efficiency, we find more satellites."

The search for new moons—as well as planets, comets, asteroids, rocks, and dust littering the starry skies—is part of humankind's age-old quest to understand the universe we live in. By studying them, scientists have learned much about how the solar system, including our own Earth, formed and what its fate may be.

Moons Everywhere
Besides, as poets, lovers, and mystics know, moons are cool.

Earth and Pluto, the ninth planet, are the only members of our sun's family to have just one moon each. Mercury and Venus have none. But Mars has two, Jupiter 16, Saturn 18, Uranus 17, and Neptune eight.

Even a little asteroid, Ida, floating between Mars and Jupiter, has its own pet moonlet, named Dactyl, only 1 mile wide.

The giant planets—Jupiter, Saturn, and Neptune—have so many moons that they resemble miniature solar systems. Astronomers have assigned them romantic names culled from Greek mythology and the plays of Shakespeare: Atlas, Pandora, Ophelia, Ariel, Juliet, and the like.

This burgeoning horde of satellites indicates that moons may be common around other planets in the universe, offering more potential habitats for life.

The moons in our solar system come in a rich variety of sizes, temperatures, atmospheres, and behaviors.

Mighty Jupiter boasts the biggest and the smallest satellites detected so far. Little Leda is only 6 miles across, while Ganymede, 3,266 miles in diameter, is half again as big as Earth's moon, which measures 2,155 miles. Saturn's Titan, 3,193 miles wide, is the next biggest. Ganymede and Titan are actually bigger than two planets, Mercury and Pluto....

Unlike our own dead moon, some satellites lead active lives.

Io, a moon of Jupiter, is so volcanic that it "glows in the dark," said Paul Geissler, an astronomer at the University of Arizona in Tucson. A NASA photo caught one volcano in mid-eruption, shooting a plume of hot gas hundreds of miles into space.

"Io glows green, blue, and red," said Geissler. "It looks like a Christmas tree, colorful and mysterious."

Moons also perform useful tasks, such as helping to preserve the shiny rings, composed of small rocks, dust, or ice, that surround some planets. A ring around Uranus is shepherded by two moons, one on either side. Four of Jupiter's moons cling to the edge of that planet's faint rings. Saturn's gorgeous rings also may have shepherded moons, but they have not been detected yet.

Our own moon probably deflected a number of asteroids that might have smashed into Earth, causing enormous damage. The huge craters on the moon bear witness to its service as a shield for our planet.

As Steph lifted the text for overhead display, the kids followed along with the Content/Process form on their clipboards. They began by reviewing some of the thinking readers do when they read. The class had spent time on several strategies, including questioning, connecting, and inferring. This form required readers to keep track of their evolving thinking. Commenting on their process of synthesizing information by noting information on the content side of the form and noticing what they did to access that information on the process side of the form.

When Steph read the title of the article, James immediately asked, "What does moonstruck mean?" Steph recorded his question in the Process column, coding it Q for question, and then tossed it out to the crowd. The kids looked puzzled. Steph asked them to stop and turn to another student and try to construct meaning together. After a few moments, Ryan and Jessica raised their hands and said, "Maybe it's scientists who like moons a lot." Steph acknowledged their good thinking, coded their inference I, and wrote it down on the transparency in the Process column as the kids recorded it on their forms. She read the first paragraph and paused after, "It's a rare person who knows the answer—63 moons and climbing."

She asked if anyone noticed any factual information here. "There are sixty-three moons in our solar system," Julie called out. Astonishing information, to say the least. Steph quickly showed her amazement. She wanted to fire the kids up about the content so that they would stay engaged in the task. She wrote the information down on the Content column as the kids followed her lead. Soon the form looked as follows:

Content (Facts)	Process (Thinking)
There are 63 moons and more to come.	What does moonstruck mean? (Q)
	Maybe it's scientists who like moons. (I)
	Wow! 63 Moons! No kidding!

Uranus is seventh from the sun.

Why didn't they know if they launched those satellites? (Q)
Maybe when they say satellites, they mean moons. (I)
A moon could be a natural satellite. (I)
What is detector efficiency? (Q)

As we reasoned through the text, the kids' conversation helped them build answers to questions, clear up misconceptions, and immerse themselves in the content. Misconceptions arose, such as confusion surrounding the term *satellite*. The kids' background knowledge for that term had more to do with telecommunications. Most had no idea that the term could be

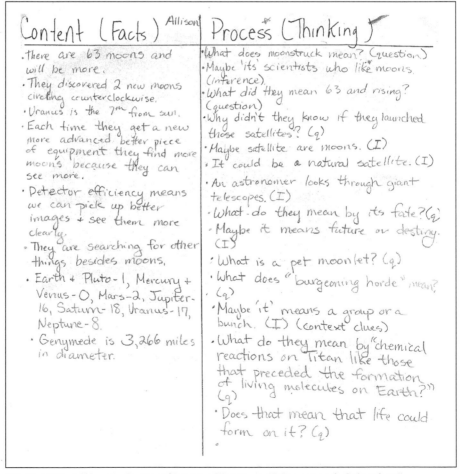

Figure 10.7 Allison's Content/Process Notes on "Moonstruck Scientists"

used interchangeably with the word *moon*. They talked it through and came to understand. Not surprisingly, the notion of detector efficiency was difficult, but as they thought it through, they made sense of it from the context. After about twenty minutes of discussion, Steph and Kim released the kids to work in groups of two or three around the room. The kids loved working through this article. It completely captivated them.

Allison's form is typical of many of the responses (see Figure 10.7). Reading and understanding requires a great deal of ongoing thinking. This form gave us a window into that evolution of thought.

Reading Like a Writer

Purpose:	Noticing the craft of a piece as well as the content and the reading process
Resources:	"Moonstruck Scientists Count 63 and Rising"(Boyd 1999) and "Rhino Dehorned by Rangers"(Edlin 1992), articles in the *Denver Post*
Response:	Three-column note form headed Content/Process/Craft (CPC)

When Steph returned from Atlanta, she talked to fourth-grade teacher Mary Urtz about the Content/Process form and about the "Moonstruck" article. Mary wanted to try it as soon as she heard about it. As Mary read the lead at the overhead, Ryan blurted out, "The writer just hooks you when he says 'Here's a trivia question sure to stump your friends. How many moons in our solar system?' What a great way to start the article!" The kids nodded in agreement as Mary commented that Ryan was "reading like a writer," noticing the words and the structure of the language in the piece as well as the content. Mary proceeded to model the Content/Process form, but as the kids continued to comment on the writing quality, Mary wondered how she and Steph might improve upon the two-column form. The first two columns were concerned solely with reading. Upon reflection, Steph and Mary decided that maybe they needed a third column that would allow responses to the writing style as well.

The next day Mary presented a new form, the first two columns as before but with a third column headed Craft (Writing). She explained that kids could comment on the writing quality in this third column. She modeled it first, noting her observations about the writing as well as about content and process. They thought through several paragraphs together and then Mary released them in pairs to practice. Mary and Steph were astounded by their attention to the third column. The kids were immediately drawn to the engaging writing style, and they commented on it at length, as Kaitlin's three-column CPC form shows (see Figure 10.8).

Mary continued to let kids practice with this form. The CPC form required them to read as writers. Later, as they read a *Denver Post* article independently about the devastating problem of rhino poaching in Zimbabwe (Edlin 1992), their comments in the Craft column included the following:

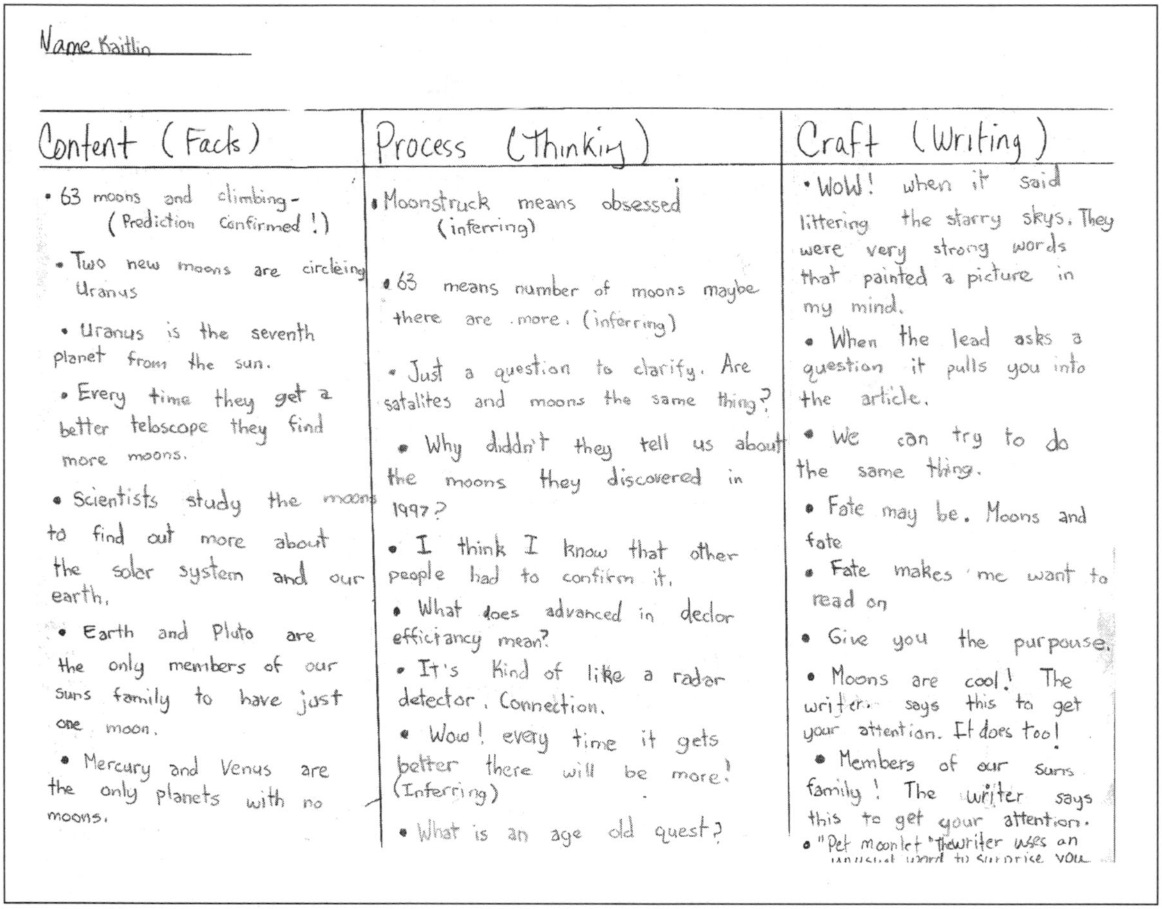

Name Kaitlin

Content (Facts)	Process (Thinking)	Craft (Writing)
• 63 moons and climbing - (Prediction confirmed!)	• Moonstruck means obsessed (inferring)	• Wow! when it said littering the starry skys. They were very strong words that painted a picture in my mind.
• Two new moons are circleing Uranus	• 63 means number of moons maybe there are more. (inferring)	• When the lead asks a question it pulls you into the article.
• Uranus is the seventh planet from the sun.	• Just a question to clarify. Are satalites and moons the same thing?	• We can try to do the same thing.
• Every time they get a better teloscope they find more moons.	• Why diddn't they tell us about the moons they discovered in 1997?	• Fate may be. Moons and fate
• Scientists study the moons to find out more about the solar system and our earth.	• I think I know that other people had to confirm it.	• Fate makes me want to read on
• Earth and Pluto are the only members of our suns family to have just one moon.	• What does advanced in declor efficiancy mean? • It's kind of like a radar detector. Connection.	• Give you the purpouse. • Moons are cool! The writer says this to get your attention. It does too!
• Mercury and Venus are the only planets with no moons.	• Wow! every time it gets better there will be more! (Inferring) • What is an age old quest?	• Members of our suns family! The writer says this to get your attention. • "Pet moonlet" the writer uses an unusual word to surprise you

Figure 10.8 Kaitlin's Content/Process/Craft Notes on "Moonstruck Scientists"

I like how the writer used the word *slaughtered* instead of *killed;* it's stronger.

The beginning paragraph pulls you in when it says "In a desperate attempt to save the rhino."

I like how he put the numbers of all the rhinos in the world and then used the word *dwindling* instead of something boring.

The author jumps right into what is happening.

It is creative when the writer says "under cover of darkness."

The words really grab you, like *dugout canoe* instead of just plain *canoe.*

Mary's kids read and wrote every day and studied writing, which is why they noticed the writer's words. They were writers themselves. This form gave them an opportunity to reflect on the writing, which could only help them as they continued with their own nonfiction writing. In subsequent work with this form, we have found that most kids need extensive practice with the two-column Content/Process form before exploring a third column for Craft. But after practicing the Content/Process form with three or four articles, we launch and begin to explore the Craft column, or the kids lead us there, as Ryan did.

The three-column CPC form is the ultimate synthesizing response form. The three columns cover the major bases. If readers can record factual content, explain their thinking process while reading, and reflect on writing, they are well on their way to becoming truly literate thinkers.

Trying to Understand: Seeking Answers to Questions That Have None

Purpose:	Synthesizing information by attempting to answer difficult questions
Resource:	*The Triumphant Spirit: Portraits and Stories of Holocaust Survivors, Their Messages of Hope and Compassion,* by Nick Del Calzo
Responses:	Sticky notes with questions

The genre of narrative nonfiction personalizes the human experience for readers in ways other genres simply can't. Personal tales of triumph and tragedy become indelibly etched in our brains when we read it. Sometimes these experiences are horrific and unthinkable. The Holocaust, above all else, reflects the worst, most grotesque aspects of human nature. Teachers understandably shy away from topics that are almost beyond comprehension. We feel ill-equipped to deal with such horrendous information, and we are at a loss to explain reasons for this behavior when children ask how such a thing could happen. Anne and Steph believe, however, that children deserve to know about what has really happened in the past. Furthermore, there are clear connections between historical events such as the Holocaust and situations of intolerance and genocide in many parts of the world today. In some ways, not to deal with these tragic events is to prevent children from learning about the strength of the human spirit and the triumph of survival.

Seventh-grade teacher Carla Mosher understands that it is easier not to think about unthinkable acts. And she knows that if we don't think about them, we will forget them. Carla wants her students to leave her class with an understanding of, and a personal commitment to, the warning "Never Again." To do this, she and her students build background knowledge about these times by reading a wide range of literature, including novels, picture books, poetry, editorials, essays, and feature articles. Their inquiry culminates with each student entering a local writing contest named in honor of Anne Frank. Carla's commitment to the vow of "Never Again," along with a message of compassion and hope, is central to their exploration.

Carla subscribes to the *Denver Post*'s Newspaper in Education Multicultural Program. As a subscriber, she receives occasional special student supplements published by the Post. One such supplement included multiple copies of a student edition of *The Triumphant Spirit: Portraits and Stories of Holocaust Survivors, Their Messages of Hope and Compassion*. Available locally to teacher subscribers free of charge, it is an excerpt from a book by the same name written by Nick Del Calzo, which can be purchased at your local bookstore. The *Denver Post* excerpt includes fourteen inspirational portraits of Holocaust survivors. To preserve this treasure, Carla cut up each copy and laminated every page. In that way, there were more than enough to go around.

Carla asked her students to think about the title as they read these portraits. She recognized that the text would be shocking and disturbing, and she wanted her students to keep the notion of the triumphant spirit of survival in mind. She gave them sticky notes and encouraged them to record their thinking as they read, reminding them to use the strategies they had practiced to help comprehend text.

Carla was not surprised that most of her students were recording questions as they read. Marcus was reading the story of Harry Glazer, who at age 22 arrived at Auschwitz from his native Romania. His tragic story tells the horrors of becoming separated from his family and never seeing them again, of being forced to drag dead bodies to mass graves at Auschwitz and Bergen-Belsen, and of triumphant survival and eventual liberation by the British in 1945. A photograph taken by the British liberators accompanies the written portrait and shows Mr. Glaser holding a newspaper photograph of mass graves and dead bodies.

When Carla stopped to confer with Marcus, his sticky notes were jammed with written questions, beginning with What is in that photograph he's holding? As Carla began to help him look at the horrifying photo and work through it with him, he told her that he had thought those might have been bodies, but he couldn't believe it. Each sticky note he wrote began with "I wonder" and included his own reaction (see Figure 10.9). Most of what he read was inconceivable to him. Carla realized that his questions were so prolific because he was trying desperately to make sense of this tragedy. He just couldn't comprehend it. These questions seemed to have no answers.

As the students shared their disbeliefs, most were overwhelmed with questions. It soon became clear to Carla that the discussion spawned by these questions helped the class construct meaning. Their questions led them to synthesize their thoughts and feelings. These questions nudged their thinking and gave them insight into personal feelings that they had not explored before. The more the students shared their questions and talked about these portraits, the more they knew about the Holocaust, and the more they came to realize that some things can't be explained and some questions can never be answered.

What they did come to understand, however, was the spirit of triumph that tied these survivors to one another and the sense of hope and compassion that is still with them today. Their stories live on. They bravely speak

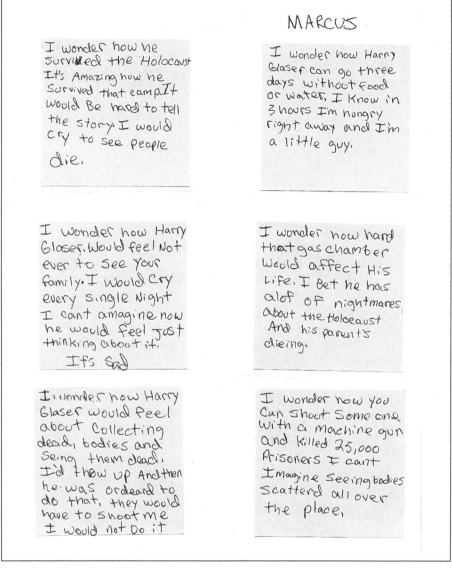

Figure 10.9 Marcus's Questions About *The Triumphant Spirit*

out about the unspeakable horror they endured to ensure that people will not forget. Carla's students read the survivors' personal stories, and remember never to forget. This was their synthesis.

Chapter

11 Strategy Instruction in Context
Three Classroom Portraits

I t's 3:30 P.M. and the classroom is quiet for the first time all day. Books and papers are piled on the rug, chairs are scattered, topless markers dry out on the desk tops. Drawings and children's notes about the sun hang from the chalkboard tray. The first graders are gone, but Kelly Daggett and Anne sit down to rehash the day's lesson—launching a study of space by observing and asking questions about the sun.

"The kids did a great job asking questions, and they know a lot already," Kelly points out. "But the space books are too hard for them to read. And the one I started reading today talked about nuclear fusion and hydrogen atoms. So how do we find information that will make sense to them?"

"Maybe we have to paraphrase the information in the books so they'll understand it," Anne suggests. "We can't read every book to them, but look at what they learned from just that little bit of information and those few pictures you shared today. And maybe there's a way to take their questions, which are really good, and help them find answers."

"So, where do we go next?" Kelly wondered.

Teachers ask this question countless times each day. Indeed, Steph and Anne spend much of their time as staff developers sitting down with teachers and planning what's next. There's no easy answer. What's next depends on the kids, the topic, and the teacher's goals for instruction. And we can't forget about things like keeping kids interested and engaged, or making sure we design instruction that meets the needs of each student. Planning is everything, but we don't always know just where we're going.

This chapter tackles the question What's next? in the context of three different classrooms. Each classroom portrait reveals how teachers think about instruction and teach comprehension strategies. Each portrait describes how teachers, using the gradual release of responsibility approach, design and implement instruction over time. The format for each classroom portrait begins with teacher modeling, moves on to guided practice, and culminates with students applying strategies independently.

In the first portrait, Kelly Daggett's first graders study space, building background knowledge by asking questions and visualizing as they prepare to research the planets. The second portrait finds a librarian, Nell Box, and two teachers, Dave Shinkle and Susan Prentiss, using picture books to teach reading comprehension strategies to help their fifth graders better understand issues surrounding the Civil War. In the third portrait, a small group of seventh graders works with Anne on making connections around immigration themes and issues. Each portrait illustrates how teachers create and reflect upon their instruction, supporting their students as they move toward independence. Although these portraits show three different grade levels, with a little creative thinking the instruction, strategies, and resources can be adapted for use in grades K–8.

CLASSROOM
PORTRAIT

Investigating Space

Grade 1

Strategies: Questioning and visualizing to build background knowledge

Duration: Four weeks

Responses: Constructing class charts with questions; writing and drawing webs to organize thinking; artistic, written, and dramatic responses through posters, short reports, and other projects

Resources: Picture books about space
Do Stars Have Points?, by Melvin Berger and Gilda Berger
Dogs in Space, by Nancy Coffelt
My Picture Book of the Planets, by Nancy Krulik
Postcards from Pluto, by Loreen Leedy
Saturn, by Seymour Simon
The Sun, by Seymour Simon

"You're doing research on space? With first graders?" a fellow teacher asked Kelly Daggett in the lounge at lunchtime. Undaunted, Kelly knew her first graders were ready to learn about, among other things, newly discovered moons, red giant stars, and the asteroid belt. Kelly understood that before kids can ask thoughtful, informed questions, they need to have enough information to ground those questions in reality. Aware that many young students have misconceptions about this conceptually challenging topic, Kelly made sure the space study was developmentally appropriate for her students.

She launched the study by suggesting students observe the one heavenly body she thought children might take for granted—the sun. After a trip outside with clipboards to take notes, Kelly asked the children to share what they had noticed about the sun and the sky. They shared not only their observations but their questions:

What We Observed About the Sun	Questions
The sun could make you blind if you stared at it.	Why is it so bright? (Verita)
	What is the sun made of?
The sun could burn your skin.	Is it made of fire? (Sean)
The sun makes you squint.	Why is it so hot? (Natasha)
It feels hot.	How hot is the sun? (Diego)
I saw two birds and one airplane.	Why is it yellow? (Destiny)
The sun could cause fire.	Why is the sun a star? (Sean)
It makes shadows.	What would happen if there were no sun? (Phillip)

To support these young researchers, Kelly planned a lesson on how to use picture books to begin to find the answers to these questions.

Modeling

"Sometimes," Kelly began, "learning a lot of new information makes us think of lots of questions. That's what researchers do best—ask questions. When scientists noticed those new moons around Jupiter, they wondered what the moons were made of, or why no one had noticed them before. The more we know about something, the more questions we have." Pointing to the chart of observations and questions about the sun, she continued, "I was amazed at your observations and your questions. I think we should do some reading so we can answer our questions. Let's start with Sean's question, What is the sun made of? I'll read a few pages from this book [*The Sun*, by Seymour Simon]. Listen for information that might answer this question and raise your hand when you hear some information we should remember."

Kelly read the text, paraphrasing slightly: "The sun's photosphere is a sea of boiling gases. The sun's light and heat come from fires and explosions deep within it. But the sun doesn't burn like a fire on Earth. It is more like a continuous explosion, and it will continue for another 5 billion years."

Worried that this explanation of nuclear fusion would be beyond the kids, Kelly tentatively asked, "So, what did we learn about what the sun is made of?"

Natasha's hand shot up. "It's made of hot gases and lots of explosions; no wonder it looks like fire in the sky."

"But it says that it's not like the fire we have on Earth. So, what is it again?" Sean wondered.

"Hot, hot, really hot gases that keep exploding," ventured Phillip.

As the children responded to the question, Kelly jotted down their answers next to Sean's question. Next, she called on Phillip, who had a puzzled look on his face. "I'm still wondering about that question—What would happen if there were no sun? said Phillip. "My mom said we couldn't live without the sun."

A small group gathered to investigate this question, and Kelly helped the group read the last page of *The Sun:* "The sun is all important to life on Earth. Our weather and climate depend upon the sun. Green plants need sunlight to grow. Animals eat plants for food, and we need plants and animals to live....Without the sun there would be no heat, no light, no clouds, no rain—no living thing on earth."

Combining their background knowledge with the information from the book, the children constructed the following responses:

What Would Happen If There Were No Sun?

We wouldn't need sunglasses.
Elephants would die first because they don't have fur.
Polar bears maybe could live a little longer.
We would have to wear lots of clothes to keep warm.
You wouldn't know if it was day or night.
We would be cold. We would be hungry.
The whole world would be ice.
It would be really dark and cold.
The stars wouldn't shine.
No animals would live long. No plants, either.
All living things would die.

Kelly was surprised at these six-year-olds' elaborate answers. Although the answers might not all be exactly right, and the kids might not have grasped the idea of nuclear fusion, they were able to integrate their own knowledge with the information she had read to them and construct thoughtful, reasonable responses. They were ready for research.

Guided Practice with Questioning

Kelly continued working with small interest-driven groups to guide the children's questions and information seeking. She knew that small-group instruction would allow her to be more responsive to the needs of these beginning readers. And students had definite interests they wanted to explore. When Sara brought in a book from home about Saturn (*Saturn*, by Seymour Simon), Kelly read the book to a small group of interested children who loved the ringed planet. The text was difficult for the children to understand, and Kelly noticed that the children's questions were focused primarily on the pictures. Kelly jotted their questions down, anticipating that the children would want to answer them.

Why are there those rings around it?
What are they made of?
What are those little dots around the planet?
Could those be moons?
Why does Saturn have one side dark and one side sunny?
Why are the rocks falling down?

Why do some planets have rings and others don't?
What color is Saturn really?
Why are there planets?

Some questions were easily answered, such as Why does Saturn have one dark side and one light side? Other questions, such as Why are there planets? involved complicated explanations. Kelly and the children found information about one question on Saturn's rings, What are the rings made of? but had trouble answering the question Why are there those rings? After reading to answer their questions, Kelly helped the children put what they had learned into words, writing their thoughts on a large chart:

> The rings are made of ice and rock and dirt. They are very thin—the book says astronomers can see distant stars through them. We were surprised to learn that Saturn has moons, too. We wondered why the picture doesn't have the moons showing. Are they inside the rings?

Fortunately, it didn't bother the children that they couldn't come up with definite answers to all of their questions. Rather than wanting simply to find answers, Kelly realized, the children asked questions as a way of expressing their curiosity and excitement about learning. Questions, for most of these six-year-olds, were an entrée into a fascinating topic, not formal queries requiring absolute answers.

Guided Practice with Visualizing

After the students had asked and answered questions in small groups, Kelly knew it was time to help them record some of the many facts they encountered each day as she read aloud to them. Straightforward note-taking, she anticipated, would be problematic for these beginning readers and writers, so Kelly took a different approach to recording information. Sketching an outline of a planet web on chart paper and labeling it "Mars," she decided to ask the children to record what they were learning by drawing.

As Kelly read aloud Loreen Leedy's *Postcards from Pluto,* she asked the children to think carefully about the information in the book. "Listen for facts you think are really important. See if you can make a picture in your mind of what Mars looks like. Stop me by raising your hand when we come to a fact that you think is important enough to write down or draw on our web," she directed. Upon hearing information they wanted to add to the web, children came up to the chart to write or draw their contribution.

Moving Toward Independence

Excited by the idea of drawing and writing what they knew, Kaitlin and three other children created a poem about Jupiter. They already knew quite a bit about Jupiter, and their drawing included the features they thought important—its red spot, swirling clouds, even the thin rings of ice and dust that circle it (see Figure 11.1).

Figure 11.1 Children's Poem About Jupiter

As children clamored to draw and write about their favorite planet, Kelly knew that some groups needed more information. She talked with them about what researchers do when they need more information. To support further efforts at research the kids brainstormed questions that were important to answer about a planet:

Research Questions

What color? (describe your planet)
What size is it? (big or small?)

Is it hot or cold?
Does it have rings?
Why are they round?
How far is it from the sun?
Why do they float?
What is it made out of? (rocks, gases, what else?)

As the children added more information to their planet webs, some asked if they could create a poster and model of their planet. David got the idea to write a weather report from outer space. McKenna decided to write a newspaper published on Venus. Several children wanted to write a play about their planet. Having anticipated that most kids would write a report with an illustration, Kelly was amazed at the wide range of ideas for projects.

Application

A week or so later, Eric and Destiny put the finishing touches on their poster of blue-green Neptune, surrounded by glittering stars and a distant asteroid belt made out of pipe cleaners. They wrote:

> Neptune is almost too far for us to see. It is 320 degrees below zero, so Eric and Destiny have decided not to visit. It is just too cold. Its gravity is almost the same as Earth's.

Kaitlin and Linda wrote a report on Jupiter to accompany their beach-ball size model of the planet:

> Jupiter has 16 moons. It is the biggest planet of all. Jupiter is made of gases, and clouds swirl all over it. The red spot you can see is a big, big storm. It has stripes, which we put on it. It is far, far, far away from the sun.

On the final day of the space study, the children presented their projects to their parents and classmates. The following script for the play *A Trip to Pluto*, written by Jacob and Ashton, describes their journey:

Ashton: 5...4...3...2...1...0—BLAST OFF FOR PLUTO! Gosh, this is bumpy. Are we going through the asteroid belt?

Jacob: No, we are not there yet. I see Mars. There is a huge volcano. And I see a giant dust storm. It is about to blow our rocket ship away! AAAaaa!

Ashton: Yes, let's get out of here. I'm getting scared.

Jacob: Watch out—here comes an asteroid!

Ashton: We are almost to Pluto. Look, there is Uranus and Neptune.

Jacob: Oh, there is Pluto. Let's get the space ship ready to land.

Ashton: OK, Jacob. Get in the space shuttle. Be careful. I will see you when you get back. (*Ashton puts on her Pluto costume.*)

Jacob (*jumping to land on Pluto*): Whoa! Pluto is small.

Ashton: Yes, I am the smallest planet in our solar system.

Jacob: Pluto is icy cold.

Ashton: Yes, I am cold because I am so far away from the sun that I do not get any heat.

Jacob: Is there another planet out there?

Ashton: Yes, I think so. I call it Planet X!

The play continued until Ashton and Jacob climbed back into their space ship and blasted back to Earth. Songs, more plays, and the weather report from space followed. As Kelly reflected on the space investigation, she was amazed that the children had been able to absorb and remember so much sophisticated information. And they were only in first grade! Asking and answering their own questions about the planets spurred them on.

These projects were conceived solely by the kids because their teacher let them know the sky was the limit when it came to creating a final product. As their engagement soared, they thought of one idea after another. Kelly was there to support them all the way: to help them find a book, share information, procure materials, and organize their thinking. Projects of this scope are a lot of work, but the students' expectations were high because their teacher believed they could do it, and they had learned so much about space. The weeks spent building the kids' background knowledge paid off, freeing them to dream up a variety of ways to share their knowledge.

CLASSROOM

PORTRAIT
Understanding Historical Issues Surrounding the Civil War

Grade 5

Strategies: Asking questions and determining important ideas

Duration: Two weeks

Responses: Three-column note form headed Facts/Questions/Response (FQR)

Resources: Picture books relating to the Civil War
Aunt Harriet and the Underground Railroad in the Sky, by Faith Ringgold
Follow the Drinking Gourd, by Jeanette Winter
Nettie's Trip South, by Ann Turner
Now Let Me Fly, by Dolores Johnson
Sweet Clara and the Freedom Quilt, by Deborah Hopkinson

Louisville Elementary fifth-grade teachers Susan Prentiss and Dave Shinkle were ready to try something new as they planned their yearly Civil War study with the school librarian, Nell Box. They were concerned that students spent so much time learning about the facts and details of this period that they seldom had time to focus on history as the experiences and narratives of individual people. Although the social studies textbook and other materials provided the students with interesting information, Susan, Dave, and Nell wondered if reading historical fiction picture books might present issues, dilemmas, and perspectives missing from the sources the students typically read. Understanding the stories of people living long ago, they hoped, would bring historical facts from this time period to life.

Planning Instruction with Civil War Picture Books

Guided by Nell's expertise in linking literature with the curriculum, the trio met one day to plan lessons using historical fiction picture books sophisticated enough to challenge fifth graders. Nell suggested they launch the study with Faith Ringgold's *Aunt Harriet and the Underground Railroad in the Sky*, a complicated narrative of two modern-day kids who find themselves on a journey on the Underground Railroad with Harriet Tubman. The book was full of interesting information about slavery, and Nell anticipated its puzzling narrative would hold the children's attention and prompt lots of questions.

Paging through Dolores Johnson's *Now Let Me Fly*, Dave pointed out that this was the only book in their collection that began in Africa, recounting how some Africans captured their fellow villagers, taking them to the coast to be put on slave ships sailing west. Dave knew this book would make gripping reading and broaden students' perspectives on slavery. Susan recommended Ann Turner's *Nettie's Trip South*, having read this picture book to students in prior years. She remembered how the deceptively simple text jolted students with the story of a northern girl, Nettie, traveling in the South, who came upon a slave auction and was outraged by it.

Nell, Susan, and Dave were confident that these and other picture books would provoke their students to think about historical issues and ideas. If their students were to really grapple with these issues, however, they would have to do more than simply read through the books. The teachers knew that these fifth graders, who had already been introduced to several reading comprehension strategies, would think more carefully about the information they encountered in the books if asked to record significant facts and ideas. A two-columns note form headed Facts/Questions would elicit important information and provide opportunities for questions. A third column, labeled Response, was added to encourage the students to think about their reactions, opinions, and feelings about the books.

Nell and each teacher planned to first model their thinking for the students with *Aunt Harriet and the Underground Railroad in the Sky*, writing down information, questions, and responses on a large chart headed Facts/Questions/Response (FQR). After the teachers modeled reading the picture book out loud and showed students their own thinking by jotting down facts, questions, and responses, students would do the same in their book groups. Over the next ten days, groups of six to eight students would read and respond to several picture books, eventually rotating through all the books. Dave, Nell, and Susan initially planned to guide the book group discussions and gradually release the groups to ask questions and determine important ideas on their own.

Modeling

To launch the study, Nell and Susan began reading *Aunt Harriet* aloud. After reading a few pages, they modeled the kind of thinking they expected from the students, discussing what they had just read and jotting down important facts and questions on a large chart. As Susan continued reading, the students chimed in with their own facts and questions. Nell recorded their comments for all to see, and each student wrote down facts and questions on his or her own three-column FQR form. Once students understood how to gather facts, ask questions, and respond with their own opinions, they finished reading *Aunt Harriet* in pairs and continued to fill out the three-column FQR forms on their own. At the end of the session, students were eager to share their own personal responses based on facts they gathered and the questions they asked. They added some of their thoughts to the following chart.

Title: *Aunt Harriet and the Underground Railroad in the Sky*
Author: Faith Ringgold

Facts	Questions	Response
Harriet Tubman escaped and started the Underground Railroad.	How did she escape?	I would be afraid of getting caught.
Black people were taken as slaves from Africa.		I think slaves' spirits died on those ships.
More slaves died on those ships than reached the shore.		If they made it alive, they had probably given up hope.
Slaves weren't allowed to learn to read.	Why were they stopped from learning?	Reading was a power that white owners did not want slaves to have.
People would jump brooms to get married.	What is "jumping the broom?" Why couldn't they go to a church?	
The Underground Railroad was a way for slaves to get to the free land.	Were they dreaming in this story?	

Nicole and her partner's three-column FQR form illustrates their in-depth reading of the text (see Figure 11.2).

Guided Practice

The next day, eight children crowded around a table, sharing multiple copies of Ann Turner's *Nettie's Trip South*. After deciding they would read the book out loud together, Nell watched as her group of students zipped through the pages, seldom stopping to record facts or questions. To slow them down, Nell suggested that they stop after each page or so to discuss their ideas and note information and questions. As a result, they thought more carefully about their reading. This sample of one student's Facts/Questions/Response form illustrates how students focused on the important ideas in each book and shared their opinions.

Title: *Nettie's Trip South*
Author: Ann Turner

Facts	Questions	Response
Slaves weren't allowed to learn. I can't believe the Constitution could say that slaves were 3/5 of a person.* (*How could I check this?)	Who is Addie? Who is writing the letter? Why were slaves considered to be only 3/5 of a person? Were the husband and wife split apart?	I think Nettie is writing to her friend Addie. She didn't expect to see what she saw. It makes me angry that slaves were sold away from families who were in tears because they were split apart and sold. You can tell Nettie had a mind of her own.

Some of the students were able to connect information learned during a study of the Constitution to the information they encountered in the picture books. Joanne said, "I thought the Constitution was written to protect people. Didn't the Bill of Rights give people rights like freedom of religion and freedom of speech?" Her background information, accurate to a point, did not include the knowledge that the states compromised and counted slaves, for the purposes of congressional representation, as "3/5 of a person." Like Nettie, Joanne was outraged at the slave auction and subsequently investigated why slaves were counted as "3/5 of person." Rather than merely summarizing the events of each story, the FQR form encouraged students like Joanne to think further and seek additional information.

Moving Toward Independence

Nell, Susan, and Dave hadn't anticipated the lively discussions that would ensue as the students read through the picture books together. Thinking that the process of reading through the books and discussing each page at length would become tedious, the teachers tried to persuade the students to read independently. The students, however, objected. They valued the opportunity to discuss ideas in the book with each other. Judging by discussions like the following, most groups had little need for adult guidance as they worked.

This gave the teachers an opportunity to move about the room, observe the groups, and take notes on their conversations. These notes allowed them

Title: Aunt Harriet's Underground RR. **Name:** Nicole

Author: Faith Ringgold

Facts	Questions	Response
(I know) the underground RR was a path the slaves took to get away. Slaves lived + worked in the South not in the North. Slaves would go North to be free. Harriet Tubman carried hundreds of people to freedom on the underground RR. Never lost a passenger. Slaves traveled on cramped boats. They were sold in auctions. They were seperated from families. They couldn't get married or learn.	Are BeBe + Cassie dreaming? What's the train in the sky? How can a train be in the sky? Can the conductor be Aunt Harriet? What does "Go North or die" mean? Why North? When does the story take place? Why are they flying? Is the whole story a memory? Could this be heaven? Why were people so mean to black people? Why didn't they pay the slaves? How cramped were they? In one boat, about how many slaves were in them?	I think the whole book is just half fantasy and half true. I think it's just a book that puts facts in a fantasy book. It could mean most of the people died on the ships than on the slave grounds. I think that it is just horrible to have a slave to do your work for you or your family. I think that they were mean.

Figure 11.2 Fifth-Grade Students' Facts/Questions/Response Sheet on *Aunt Harriet and the Underground Railroad in the Sky*

to assess whether the students were using the comprehension strategies effectively, providing evidence that the kids were questioning and determining important information independently.

Following is an excerpt from a book discussion about *Now Let Me Fly*, the story of an African named Dongo who betrays his people, capturing children and taking them in shackles to a slave ship. It illustrates how the students discussed each story in depth.

Rachel: Dongo didn't disappear, he came back to the village and hid and grabbed the chief's daughter. Why would he do it if he knows he's already in trouble for capturing his own people?

Zack: He's working for the white people. He must want the money.

Joanne: But if he's in the same tribe, why would he do it if he's in their tribe?

Zack: Like the book said, they tried to banish him, but he came back.

Sarah: And now he's really angry. He went back to the white people and said I'll work for you. Some people have no feelings for other people. Dongo's like that.

As their book discussion continues, they notice an illustration of children being taken in shackles to the coast.

Rachel: But why did they take the children? That seems really cruel.

Joanne: Maybe they were easier to capture than adults; they couldn't fight like grown-ups.
John: That's what they did. So they'd grow up to be good slaves.

The teachers had not anticipated that the children would respond in such depth to these texts, elaborating on the ideas in each story. From the excerpt about *Now Let Me Fly*, it is clear that the students' discussion of Dongo's betrayal and motives for capturing his own people goes well beyond the information contained in the book. Although some of the children's thinking about slavery was supposition on their part, they were generally careful not to jump to unwarranted conclusions.

When Nell, Susan, and Dave reviewed their notes and observations from the small-group discussions, they agreed that students were well on their way to internalizing strategies such as questioning, inferring, and determining importance. Most important, they were using the strategies not simply to gain information but to try to achieve insight.

Application

As the students worked their way through the picture books, Dave noticed that some questions came up again and again. During one class discussion, Dave asked his students to put an asterisk next to questions that they found themselves still thinking about or were unable to answer even after reading several books. Sharing and listing these lingering questions piqued students' interest, and several brought their questions into the library to search for further information. Some of these research questions follow:

> Why were slaves considered 3/5 of a person? Does the Constitution say this? How was this decided?
> When families were split apart or sold at slave auctions, did they ever see each other again?
> Why would a slave have tried to escape if he knew he might have his hands or feet cut off if caught?
> How did slaves know where to go once they escaped their plantation? Was Harriet Tubman or someone there to lead them? Did they ever just leave and try to make it all alone?

Students sometimes found the answers to their questions in other picture books. The student who asked how slaves would know where to go once they escaped was amazed to read in Deborah Hopkinson's *Sweet Clara and the Freedom Quilt* that slaves made quilts that were really maps guiding them to safety. Another student, researching what happened to slave families when they were sold apart from each other, read a heartbreaking letter from a woman to her husband telling him that their son had been sold and begging him to ask his master to buy her so she wouldn't be sold, too. The immediacy of the letter brought home a horrifying realization: it wasn't unusual for family members to be sold and never see each other again.

When the students began their more formal study of the Civil War, Nell, Dave, and Susan noted that the background knowledge and understanding of the issues that students had gained from the picture book study helped focus classroom discussions on more substantive issues. In addition, students chose to continue the three-column FQR format with their historical novels and even their textbooks. When the time came to pursue their own research questions, most students were already curious about some issue or topic encountered in the picture books and had little trouble finding a topic. Similar to the research questions just listed, the students' later questions were quite focused, grounded in issues that had arisen from the picture books. Exactly what Nell, Susan, and Dave had hoped for.

CLASSROOM

PORTRAIT

Using Picture Books to Introduce the Topic of Immigration

Grade 7

Strategies: Making text-to-self, text-to-text, and text-to-world connections

Duration: One week

Responses: Two- and three-column note forms and charts for sorting sticky notes

Resources: Immigration text set
Dia's Story Cloth, by Dia Cha
How Many Days to America?, by Eve Bunting
Journey to Ellis Island: How My Father Came to America, by Carol Bierman
My Freedom Trip: A Child's Escape from North Korea, by Frances Park and Ginger Park
One More Border, by William Kaplan with Shelley Tanaka
Our Journey from Tibet, by Laurie Dolphin

As Anne watched her own middle school–aged children wend their way through long, complicated novels, she felt a tinge of regret at their aversion to the picture books they had loved as children. One day she asked her son, Kai, why he never picked up a picture book anymore. "Too short," he replied, effectively cutting off further discussion. Kai may no longer read picture books, but he does have to live with them. A confirmed bibliophile, Anne long ago ran out of room in her house for book storage, so Kai's room contained the overflow, right next to his bed. When Anne went to his room one evening to say good night, she found him reading DuBose Heyward's *The Country Bunny and the Little Gold Shoes.* The secret was out. Middle school kids still love picture books; it's just that they don't have opportunities to read them.

Soon after this incident, Anne introduced a small group of seventh graders to reading comprehension strategies. The students, generally enthusiastic about reading, were struggling to keep up with their long novels and accompanying questions and had willingly signed up to work with her. A few minutes of conversation told Anne that these seventh graders were unfamiliar with the language of reading comprehension strategies discussed in this book. Perhaps they used comprehension strategies in their own reading, but they didn't appear to be used to talking about them.

Anne began with the strategy of making connections for two reasons. First, connection making is one of the most accessible strategies and encourages kids to bring their personal experiences to their reading. Second, to prepare for an upcoming study of immigration, it made sense to search for connections among picture books on this topic. Anne and the kids scoured the school library to put together an immigration text set. The students searched for and found books about immigration from a variety of cultures and time periods. Each student selected two or three books for in-depth study.

Modeling and Anchor Texts

Before turning students loose to read their own books, Anne modeled making connections with Carol Bierman's *Journey to Ellis Island: How My Father Came to America*. This is the true story of the author's father, Yehuda Weinstein, who as a young boy journeyed to America from Russia (via Holland). Before Anne could even model her own personal connections to the story, Kylie interrupted. She explained that one of the illustrations in the book, a postcard of the ship *SS Rotterdam*, which Yehuda took from Amsterdam to New York, reminded her of a family story. Her great-grandfather's ship, she told the group, had been torpedoed by a German submarine during World War I as he left Holland to emigrate to New York. Amazingly enough, the ship limped to New York to safely deliver its passengers.

Anne asked Kylie to jot her connection on a chart, suggesting that the students keep track of their personal connections using this format (see Figure 11.3). Kylie filled in the first two columns of the chart, headed Text and My Personal Connection. She didn't understand the third column, headed How This Connection Helped Me Better Understand the Text, so she drew a big ? in the column. As Kylie finished writing, Tamding, whose family had recently come to the United States from Tibet, looked up from Laurie Dolphin's *Our Journey from Tibet*, which he had picked out as the group searched the school library for an immigration text set. Incredulous at finding a book written about his own experiences and still struggling with English, he looked at the group and said, "This book is about me." Anne asked Tamding to add this thought to the chart, too.

After students were well into their respective books, Anne explained the third column on the chart, saying "When we make personal connections to books, we usually understand the book a little better. Maybe we had some of the same experiences as characters in the book, so we know how they felt. Tamding, for instance, knows exactly what the people in his book experienced, because he went through a similar ordeal. Does anyone else have a thought about how connections helped them better understand their picture book?"

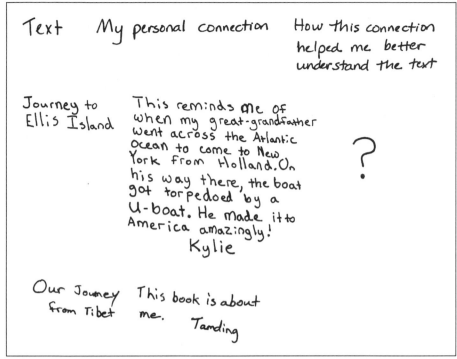

Figure 11.3 Seventh-Grade Students' Personal Connections to Picture Books on Immigration

Anne's question was met with silence. Although the students' personal connections clearly heightened their engagement with the books, they seemed unsure of how their connections enhanced their understanding. Anne considered stopping the class then and there to model how connections enhance understanding, but she decided against it. She sensed that asking the students to articulate how connections enhanced their understanding might be premature. At this point, asking the students to "think about their thinking" didn't make much sense. Instead, Anne decided to continue to work with the students on personal and text-to-text connections. Metacognitive understanding could come later.

Guided Practice

The next day, Anne explained the idea of text-to-text connections as she read aloud Frances Park and Ginger Park's *My Freedom Trip*. Based on the experience of the authors' mother, the book is the story of a little Korean girl, Soo. At the beginning of the Korean War, Soo leaves her mother (who plans to follow later) in North Korea and escapes to South Korea to be reunited with her father. At the point in the book when Soo and her guide are stopped at the border between North and South Korea, the students interrupted.

Tyler remarked that there was a war going on in his book, too. John commented that he was reading about a family struggling to get to Poland from Russia in William Kaplan's *One More Border.* The students noticed that, like Soo, the people in these books risked their lives to leave their homelands. As Anne listened to these students' text-to-text connections, she decided it was time to encourage connections in their own books.

Later that period, as Anne conferred with the kids about their own books, she realized that the students were not writing down many text-to-text connections. Puzzled, she looked more closely at their responses. Rather than making text-to-text connections, they were jotting significant events from each book on sticky notes. Anne reasoned that the kids were having difficulty focusing on the themes in their books, not to mention linking similar ideas and themes across texts.

Deciding that the students needed explicit instruction to help them infer themes using evidence from text, Anne gathered them together. She explained they were going to reread the beginning of *My Freedom Trip* out loud. "Listen to the beginning and watch how I think about the events in the story. I'll be looking for big ideas or themes that are central to the story."

The students listened to the words "Many years ago, when I was a little schoolgirl in Korea, soldiers invaded my country. The soldiers divided Korea into two countries, North Korea and South Korea. In North Korea we could no longer speak our minds, or come and go as we pleased. We lost our freedom. Many of us secretly escaped to South Korea, the freedom land."

Anne demonstrated how she used words from the text as evidence of two themes: that people leave their country because of conflict and that they may flee to a new country hoping they will find freedom there. She wrote her thoughts on a two-column chart:

What's Happening in the Text?	What's the Theme Here?
Soo had to flee to South Korea from North Korea because soldiers invaded and her family had lost their freedom.	People leave their country because of conflicts and wars. People go to a new country because they want to be free.

As she wrote words from the text in the left-hand column, Anne explained how she inferred from Soo's experiences why people leave a beloved homeland for a strange, new country. Before the students returned to their reading, Anne asked them to find events or reasons that provided evidence for why people have to leave their homes. She also suggested they note problems encountered as the immigrants were leaving or coming into a new country. She hoped that reading with a more clearly defined purpose would encourage the students to identify themes their books had in common.

Moving Toward Independence

The next day, the students sorted their sticky notes on a large chart (see Figure 11.4), discussing how specific events and circumstances supported

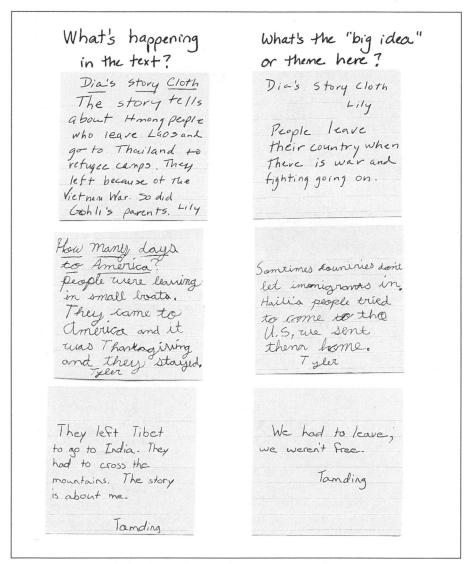

Figure 11.4 Seventh-Grade Students Infer Immigration Themes

one theme or another. As the students discussed their evidence for immigration themes common to several texts, Anne observed that they were able to generalize about the predicaments immigrants often found themselves in, regardless of their country or culture.

"I was able to read about something that happened to my family. My whole family could not believe that this story was in a book," noted Tamding. "We had to leave our country just like Soo did."

Lily noted that she had never realized what her classmate Gohli's parents and grandparents had experienced. "I read *Dia's Story Cloth* because my friend Gohli is Hmong. I know that her parents were born in Laos, but I had never realized why they had to leave. I had no idea they came here because the Hmong people helped us fight in Vietnam. They had to escape right away when we lost the war. It's amazing to think that this happened to people I know."

Tyler described his surprise that the people in *How Many Days to America?* were able to stay in America. Tyler was well informed about the plight of Haitian refugees trying to flee their country. He had learned about the situation from news stories aired during the Haitian crisis several years earlier. "I thought that the people in this book must have been trying to leave Haiti. In the pictures, it looked like they lived on an island. And I thought our soldiers or someone made the boats turn around, or took them back to their country. In the book the people got to America and were allowed to stay. It seems like the ending in the book isn't exactly what really happened. From what I remember from television, we didn't let the people stay here."

Anne chimed in here, labeling Tyler's comments as a text-to-world connection. To make sure the kids understood how Tyler was connecting events in the book to his knowledge of recent events in Haiti, Anne reiterated his connection: "It sounds to me like Tyler just made a text-to-world connection. He connected the story of people leaving because of the soldiers in *How Many Days to America?* with what he remembered from news reports about people fleeing Haiti. And he also remembered that unlike the people in *How Many Days to America?* the Haitian refugees had been forced to return to Haiti."

Natalie pointed out that she remembered another time when a ship carrying refugees had been turned away, too. "When I visited the Holocaust Museum, there was a display talking about that ship that brought Jews trying to escape from Europe to the United States. And it [the display] said the boat had to turn around. I couldn't believe we wouldn't let those people in."

Impressed with the personal, text-to-text, and text-to-world connections these books had elicited, Anne encouraged the kids to remember these themes as they began a more formal study of immigration. Wondering if students might have a better sense of the power of connections to enhance understanding, she reiterated her original question, saying, "So, how did these connections help you understand the books better?"

This time the kids were ready with answers.

"We thought about some of the books more because the stories happened to Gohli's family and Tamding's family, people we know," replied Lily.

"When I read about the bad experiences people had leaving, like having to escape and almost getting caught by soldiers, I thought they were brave to try to leave. I guess they thought it couldn't be any worse in a new place," added Tyler.

"I used to think immigration was about coming to Ellis Island, just like my great-grandfather did. He came to this country for a better job," added

Kylie. "But some people have to leave because it is so dangerous. And I didn't know kids' families in our school had to leave their homes because of wars."

Anne listened to this conversation, realizing that the kids had taken the idea of connections far beyond what she had anticipated. Impressed with the kids' thoughtful responses, she summarized their work. "You've not only made interesting connections to these books, you've made connections to each other, too," she said. "I don't know about you, but when I learn about Gohli's family, or Tamding's experiences, or Kylie's great-grandfather, those are the connections that really make me think. Maybe we've learned a lot from the stories in these books, but we'll really remember the stories of people we know."

In *How Reading Changed My Life,* Anna Quindlen writes, "Part of the great wonder of reading is that it has the ability to make human beings feel more connected to one another." We couldn't say it any better.

These three classroom portraits illustrate how comprehension strategy instruction can strengthen content instruction. In the classroom, if we do a good job with strategy instruction, we enhance students' understanding of content. But as we've said before in this book, process is crucial, too. For these students, reading comprehension strategies were a means to an end. Some students used the strategies to acquire knowledge about space, others to enhance their understanding of the Civil War. The seventh graders gained insight into the topic of immigration and a deeper understanding of the lives and cultures of their classmates. All three portraits show how using comprehension strategies over time can deepen understanding.

Chapter

12 Assessing Comprehension
How Do We Know?

Steph's two kids couldn't be more different. Her son, Alex, wears his heart on his sleeve. He makes his thinking public, by telling anyone within earshot exactly what's on his mind at all times, even when they'd rather not know! Her daughter, Jessica, on the other hand, keeps things to herself. She's hard to figure out, and there are times when Steph has no clue what Jess is up to. She has to listen carefully to what Jessica says and watch closely for signs of her thinking. It's tough sometimes, unless your name is Houdini.

Readers are no different. Lots of them are like Jessica. They keep their thinking to themselves as they read. This is as tough on teachers as it is on moms and dads. We aren't telepathic; we simply can't know what readers are thinking if they don't tell us in one way or another. And if we don't know what they are thinking, we might as well call it quits. What a reader is thinking before, during, and after reading is the only measure of what he is understanding and learning.

Finding Out What Students Are Thinking

Throughout this book, we have shown how we assess and respond to kids' thinking about their reading. When we lead a discussion, we notice and evaluate children's responses. When we look over students' written responses after class, as Anne did after reading *Rebel* out loud, we learn what we have to teach or reteach the next day. Small-group sessions such as book groups or study groups provide opportunities for students to practice the strategies on their own. And we can stand back to observe what happens. For an example of how we assess children's thinking and strategy use, see Appendix G, "Assessment Interview with Fourth Graders."

The only way we can confidently assess our students' comprehension is when they share their thinking with us. Readers reveal their comprehension by responding to text, not by answering a litany of literal questions at the end of the chapter on rocks and minerals. Personal responses to reading give us a window into students' minds. We connect with their thinking when we know what's going on for them as they read.

Enhancing understanding, acquiring knowledge, and constructing meaning are the goals of reading comprehension. All the lessons, discussions, responses, and study groups described in this book have one purpose: to move kids toward independence as readers. What ultimately matters is that students internalize comprehension strategies that promote understanding. When we listen to kids, ask them questions, and watch them closely, we learn not only what they understand but also what they don't understand. We can begin to see which comprehension strategies they activate to help themselves make meaning and which ones lag behind. We find out if readers are using comprehension strategies in the following ways.

Listening to kids We can't stress enough how much we learn about kids' reading and thinking by simply listening closely to what they say. If we listen, they will talk. Sometimes kids might say, "I made a connection" or "I'm synthesizing." Using the language isn't enough, however. We check to see that there is substance underlying their statements.

Listening in on conversations Even though we were both taught that eavesdropping is rude, we know that it's invaluable when trying to find out what kids are thinking about their reading. Listening in on conversations kids have with one another during reading workshop is a surefire way to get at their honest thinking. We hear what kids are really saying when we listen in on them.

Observing expressions and body language A scrunched-up nose, a raised eyebrow, or a quizzical look lets us know what a reader is thinking. We watch kids carefully and notice their expressions while they read to give us a glimpse into their thinking.

Charting responses and conversations in group discussions We record what kids say in class discussions on charts, which makes their thinking visible, public, and permanent. Students can refer to the charts during discussions or use them as guides when crafting their own responses. See Appendix F, "Response Options for Each Strategy."

Conferring with children The reading conference continues to be the ideal venue for talking one-on-one with students and helping them sort out the thinking they do when they read. Sometimes, discovering what readers are thinking only takes asking them. Those natural talkers are only too happy to fill you in on their thinking, and those more reticent kids may surprise you and open up, too, if you only ask.

Keeping anecdotal records of conferences and conversations In classrooms where we work, teachers keep track of student thinking by taking notes of interactions they have with students and reviewing them regularly. Many teachers have three-ringed binders with a tab for each student. Behind the tabs, teachers mark the date and record notes about individual students' reading, writing, and thinking.

Scripting what kids say, recording their comments and questions Teachers we work with move about the classroom with clipboards, keeping track of kids' comments by scripting what they say, just as Nell, Dave, and Susan did in the Civil War book club classroom portrait. Later, when things have settled down, teachers take a look at these transcripts and reflect on them to determine if students are using the strategies independently.

Examining and evaluating written work samples to determine if kids are making meaning We read student-written responses very closely to find signs that the reader is constructing meaning. We also study and reflect on students' work to plan future instruction.

How Do We Know Students Are Understanding?

When we ask children to use one of the dozens of ideas for oral and written responses mentioned in this book, we're asking them to keep track of their thinking about reading. It's important for us to know when they get it and when they don't. But more important, *they* need to realize when they make meaning or when meaning breaks down. As readers come to understand the strategies, they learn to apply them on their own. When Anne first asked the seventh graders in the immigration group the question How does this connection help you better understand the text? they didn't understand what she meant. After the students gained practice in using comprehension strategies to discern themes in their books, they had a clearer sense of how connections between books aided understanding.

We know our kids are understanding when they provide us with specific evidence of their thinking. Our students show us their strategy knowledge in the following ways.

Using a variety of response options to ground their thinking in the text, answer questions, and support their interpretations Text codes, response forms, and charts encourage kids to use evidence and examples that build meaning and limit irrelevant responses. These structured response options keep kids' thinking and our discussions focused on what's essential. Going back and citing evidence from the text clarifies thinking and keeps readers on track.

Answering questions during reading conferences to illustrate their thinking while reading We often begin reading conferences with a question. We ask kids to page through the text they are reading and share their connections, questions, inferences, and so on. The goal is to capture a child's evolving thinking during reading. Rather than waiting until a child has finished reading a piece of text, we want to observe them using strategies that help them make meaning as well as clear up any misconceptions, confusion, and questions they may have while reading.

Some generic questions for each strategy, adapted from Keene and Zimmermann (1997), include the following:

- *Connections.* Is there a part of this story or piece that reminds you of something in your own life? of something that's happened to you?
- *Questions.* Can you show me a part of the text where you have a question? What were you wondering about as you read this part? Can you show me a part where you were confused? What was confusing about it?
- *Visualizing.* Were there places in the text where you made a picture in your mind? What images or pictures did you see? What specific words helped you create that picture in your mind?
- *Inferring.* What do you predict will happen in this piece? Can you show me a place in the text where you found yourself making an inference? What do you think were the big ideas in the story?
- *Determining importance in text.* What is this story or piece mostly about? Can you tell me about some of the important ideas that struck you? Any important themes you noticed? What do you think is most important to remember about this story/topic?
- *Synthesizing.* Can you tell me what the piece is about in just a few sentences? Can you show me a place in the piece where your thinking changed? How did your thinking change? Do you have some new ideas or information?

Articulating how and why a given strategy enhances understanding Discussing their reasons for using a particular strategy with their teachers and peers hones kids' ability to choose the most appropriate strategy for any given situation. When reading becomes more difficult, students need to think about which strategy makes sense and choose accordingly. To help them articulate their reasons for choosing a particular strategy, we ask them to tell us. In addition, as we pose some of the reading conference questions mentioned previously, we might stop and ask them to think out loud about how a particular strategy helps their understanding. For example, if they mention a picture they created in their mind, we might ask them how this picture helped them better understand what they read.

Out of the Pens of Kids

Who knows better than the kids if and how these comprehension strategies help them? Students love to share their ideas and talk about their thinking. Fifth-grade teacher Eleanor Wright sees merit in having her students write about how strategies help them comprehend text.

Eleanor's students spent the entire year engaged in comprehension instruction. Prior to that, they had never been in a classroom where teachers and students studied comprehension strategies and responded to reading in ways we discuss in this book. After a year of writing back and forth to her students about their reading, Eleanor asked them how comprehension strategies helped them better understand what they read.

She suspected that teaching these strategies was making a difference in her kids' comprehension, but she never dreamed how much. Her students' responses provided Eleanor with evidence that they were using reading comprehension strategies to enhance their understanding. What is more, these fifth graders made the jump from using strategies to understand text to reflecting on their own process as readers.

In her response, Amy writes about how visualizing helps her "get it" when she reads:

> I had lots of trouble with reading. I mean I can read but I didn't *get* the book. Now, I have a film through my head like I am actually there in the book.

Skilynn shows how she stops and thinks about her reading for a minute or two before going on—synthesizing, if you will:

> This year I have been going home and reading for at least 30 minutes and I *love* it! Ever since we started the sticky notes, it has really been making me think a minute or two to understand what the book is about. When I go home, I always go back and look at my questions to see if I can answer them yet. I usually can.

And Cassie, finally, has an outlet for those pent-up thoughts and feelings (see Figure 12.1). Eleanor was amazed by these responses. She was delighted that her students were so engaged in reading. The strategies helped them move between their lives and books in meaningful ways.

The writer Jean Fritz says, "As human beings, we thrive on astonishment. Whatever is unknown quickens us, delivers us from ourselves, impels us to investigate, and inspires us to imagine" (Hearne 1993). When readers read deeply, and use strategies to enhance their understanding, their imaginations soar. We only have to show them how and let them read.

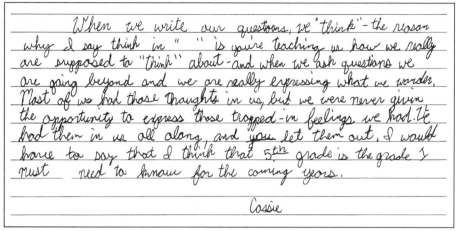

When we write our questions, we "think" - the reason why I say think in " " is you're teaching us how we really are supposed to "think" about - and when we ask questions we are going beyond and we are really expressing what we wonder. Most of us had those thoughts in us, but we were never given the opportunity to express those trapped-in feelings we had. We had them in us all along, and you let them out. I would have to say that I think that 5th grade is the grade I must need to know for the coming years.

Cassie

Figure 12.1 Cassie's Thoughts on How Reading Comprehension Instruction Helped Her

PART III

Resources That Support Strategy Instruction

K ids need books they can sink their teeth into. If students are to acquire knowledge, enhance their understanding, and gain insight, they need books full of substantive and engaging information. The information woven through these books, both fiction and nonfiction, builds students' knowledge and heightens their curiosity so they want to find out more. The books described here encourage students to use of one or more of the comprehension strategies to enhance their understanding of a topic.

In Appendixes A, B, and C we list these books alphabetically by title with the author's name next to each title. The bibliography at the end of the book, arranged alphabetically by author, includes all of the necessary publication information.

For years we have resisted making lists of books for comprehension instruction. We understand that all lists fall short in one way or another. You may wonder why your favorite book for teaching questioning or for investigating the Underground Railroad is not listed. Out of the many thousands of great books out there, we chose a few we love. Consider this a starter list. Lists are for cutting or adding to. Have at it!

Three types of book lists are included. The Appendix A list is designed to help teachers choose books for the purpose of reading comprehension strategy instruction. This list is composed of books that support teachers in teaching the strategies of making connections, questioning, visualizing, and inferring. We recognize that all books require readers to flexibly apply all of the strategies we have discussed in this book when they read. But we have found that the books listed here lend themselves to introducing and practicing a particular strategy. They weren't easy to classify. Many good books fit into multiple categories. Some teachers may find that a certain book or author is better for teaching inferring than for teaching questioning, or vice versa. Use the books according to your best judgment, and don't forget to add your own personal favorites. No book works better than a book you love.

We've also included an extensive list of content area text sets in Appendix B. We developed these lists based on the curriculum topics we encounter most frequently in schools. We can't imagine teaching science, history, social studies, and the arts without picture books and short text. We launch a discussion of issues, build background knowledge, and capture our students' interests with these riveting books. These lists are lengthy and are probably most useful when you are preparing to teach a specific curriculum topic.

Appendix C lists several categories of some of our favorite books for adults. Teachers more than any other professionals must be readers first. We've found these books essential to build our own background knowledge in science, history, and literacy, so we've included them here for reference.

Appendix D presents a list of magazines especially selected for young people, and Appendix E, a list of professional journals that review books for classroom use.

Appendix F, "Response Options for Each Strategy," provides a variety of forms that support strategy instruction and practice. Strategy charts, replicas of charts that teachers and kids create for some books during strategy lessons, are also included. These charts become visible, permanent classroom reminders of the strategy and how to use it. They were created by teachers and students together in context after instruction in a particular strategy.

Finally, in Appendix G, we include an authentic interchange between Anne and some students at Columbine Elementary in Boulder, Colorado. Anne uses the book *My Freedom Trip* to assess how effectively these students were using comprehension strategies to better understand text.

Great Books and Author Sets to Launch Strategy Instruction and Practice

Making Connections

Books that contain common themes universal to childhood, such as friendship, fear, jealousy, family relationships, feeling different, and other issues of growing up.

Amazing Grace by Mary Hoffman
Grace learns that she can be anything she wants to be.

Amos and Boris by William Steig
Friendship between a whale and a mouse prompts endless human parallels.

Going Home by Eve Bunting
A family returns to its original home in Mexico and is greeted with much warmth and celebration.

Hey World, Here I Am by Jean Little
Vignettes that trace the thoughts and feelings of preadolescent Kate Bloomfield.

I Hate English by Ellen Levine
Life in a New York school is difficult for a child who has just emigrated from China.

Ira Sleeps Over by Bernard Waber
A child's first night away from home, with predictable anxieties.

Mirette on the High Wire by Emily Arnold McCully
A young girl helps an older man overcome his fear of heights.

Near the Window Tree: Poems and Notes by Karla Kuskin
A collection of poems all kids can relate to.

The Pain and the Great One by Judy Blume
The story of a classic sibling relationship told from each point of view.

Rondo in C by Paul Fleischman
Everyone listens to a piano recital, and while listening, each person thinks back and remembers his or her own experiences.

Snippets by Charlotte Zolotow
>   Little pieces of life and experience prompt young children to write their own "snippets."

The Snowy Day by Ezra Jack Keats
>   All kids who have ever played in snow can relate to the first snowfall of the season.

Sol a Sol by Lori Marie Carlson
>   Poems in English and Spanish about everyday events, including riding bikes, looking at the stars, and making tortillas. The perfect companion to Charlotte Zolotow's *Snippets*.

Three Brave Women by C. L. G. Martin
>   Three generations pass their fear of insects on to the next and discover hilarious ways to conquer it.

Up North at the Cabin by Marsha Chall
>   Memories of a summer on a Minnesota lake.

Wilfrid Gordon McDonald Partridge by Mem Fox
>   An old woman who has supposedly lost her memory shares important thoughts, experiences, and memories with a young neighbor.

William's Doll by Charlotte Zolotow
>   A boy wants a doll and is teased unmercifully because of it.

Author Sets

Tomie de Paola

The Art Lesson
>   A young boy couldn't wait for art classes in school until he found out his picture had to look like everyone else's.

Nana Upstairs, Nana Downstairs
>   A young boy's great-grandmother dies, and he learns to cope.

Now One Foot, Now the Other
>   Grandfather Tom helped Tommy learn to walk, and when the grandfather has a stroke, Tommy comes to his aid.

Oliver Button Is a Sissy
>   Oliver loves to tap dance until kids start to make fun of him.

Kevin Henkes

Chrysanthemum
>   Her name is a big problem until she finds out the first name of her favorite teacher.

Julius, the Baby of the World
>   Lily has no interest in the baby and turns into a nightmare of a big sister until she has to come to Julius's defense.

Owen

> Owen's family thinks he's too old to drag around a tattered blanket, but Owen disagrees.

Sheila Ray the Brave

> Sheila is brave, almost arrogant, until her little sister has to help her out of a jam.

Arnold Lobel

Frog and Toad Are Friends
Frog and Toad Together
Days with Frog and Toad
Frog and Toad All Year

> Short stories about the famous amphibians, one shy and one outgoing, who understand the value of friendship and make us laugh as we peek into their lives. All readers relate to their trials and tribulations.

Patricia Polacco

Chicken Sunday

> As a little girl, Patricia and her friends Stewart and Winston idolize the boys' grandmother, Miss Eula, and are determined to buy an Easter hat for her.

The Keeping Quilt

> The story of Polacco's ancestors, and the importance of carrying on traditions.

Mrs. Katz and Tush

> Staving off loneliness through friendship is the theme of this story of neighbors who come together in times of need.

Mrs. Mack

> This horsewoman helps Patricia conquer her fears.

My Rotten Red-Headed Older Brother
> Sibling rivalry, of course.

Some Birthday!

> Patricia spends summers with her father in Michigan and something hilarious is always happening.

Thank You, Mr. Falker

> Learning to read wasn't easy for Polacco, but this story is a testament to Mr. Falker's gift for teaching (and the importance of good teachers everywhere).

Cynthia Rylant

Birthday Presents

> A family remembers their little boy's early birthdays.

Every Living Thing
> Short stories about people who love animals never fail to get kids thinking about their own experiences with these four-legged creatures.

Miss Maggie
> A relationship between a reclusive old woman and a little boy bridges the gap between generations.

The Relatives Came
> Hilarious adventures on the family vacation that all kids can relate to.

When I Was Young in the Mountains
> Cynthia Rylant's recollections of her childhood in Appalachia.

Judith Viorst

Alexander and the Terrible, Horrible, No Good, Very Bad Day
> Every one has a bad day now and then, which all readers can relate to.

Earrings
> Every child can relate to a child who desperately wants something that her parents won't allow, in this case, pierced ears.

Rosie and Michael
> The ups and downs of childhood friendships.

The Tenth Good Thing About Barney
> A family tries to adjust to life without a beloved cat.

Questioning

Books that prompt questions before, during, and after reading.

Amelia's Road by Linda Altman
> A little girl, the child of migrant workers, wants a place she can call home. Because many children lack background for this kind of life, they have many questions about it.

Charlie Anderson by Barbara Abercrombie
> The story of a cat who has two families, unbeknownst to his owners. When he doesn't show up one night, everyone wonders what's going on.

The Day of Ahmed's Secret by Florence Parry Heide and J. D. Gilliland
> Throughout the day, Ahmed reminds the reader of his secret, only revealed at the end of the day and the end of the book.

Elizabeth by Claire Nivola
> The true story of a little girl who has to leave her beloved doll behind when she is forced to flee Nazi Germany. Thoughtful questions about families leaving and their destinations abound.

How Come? by Kathy Wollard
> This book with common scientific questions on many topics inspires kids to ask their own as well as answer some in the process.

The Librarian Who Measured the Earth by Kathryn Lasky
> Eratosthenes asks lots of questions, which leads to his doing something that no one had ever done before. Encourages kids to keep thinking and wondering.

Pink and Say by Patricia Polacco
> Two soldiers, one white and one black, are captured and treated harshly by the Confederates. Readers can't help but wonder why one lives and the other perishes.

The Potato Man by Megan McDonald
> The touching story of a potato vender who is teased unmercifully by the neighborhood kids. Readers are filled with questions about the kids' behavior.

Something Permanent by Cynthia Rylant
> The beautiful poetry inspired by Walker Evans's Depression-era photographs spurs questions about the pictures and the text.

Storm Boy by Paul Owen Lewis
> When a young boy falls out of his canoe and finds himself in a land beneath the sea, kids have many questions about what's real and what's mythical.

UFO Diary by Satoshi Kitamura
> A UFO lands, and many questions emerge as to its origins. The alien, whom we never see, befriends a little boy.

The Van Gogh Cafe by Cynthia Rylant
> The odd goings-on at the magical Van Gogh Cafe spur multiple questions.

Why Is the Sky Blue? by Sally Grindley
> The theme of teachers as learners comes through in this story of an old donkey and a young, very curious rabbit.

Author Sets

Eve Bunting

Readers wonder about the themes in Bunting's books. Her books often end without clear resolution, resulting in lingering questions on the part of the reader. These are also great books for inferential thinking.

A Day's Work
> A day laborer and his grandson are reminded of the importance of honesty and hard work.

Fly Away Home
> This story of a little boy and his father struggling to survive homelessness by living in an airport spurs many questions.

How Many Days to America?
> This story of what appears to be Haitian boat people prompts many questions about why they are leaving and where they will go.

The Wall
> A son and grandson visit the Vietnam Veterans Memorial. Questions abound about the nature of this monument and the war in general.

The Wednesday Surprise
> Children are initially misled and later incredulous at this story of adult illiteracy.

William Steig

Steig's characters find themselves in unusual predicaments from which they need to extricate themselves. Kids wonder all the way through how they are going to solve their problems.

The Amazing Bone
> The pig turns into a bone and frightens all who come near as the reader wonders about the outcome.

Brave Irene
> Irene struggles through a blizzard, and the reader wonders whether she will survive.

Dr. DeSoto
> Threatened by a fox with a toothache, the dentist outwits the sly fox.

Gorky Rises
> Gorky goes aloft with a magic potion and can't figure out how to get down.

Solomon and the Rusty Nail
> Turning into a nail is a big problem!

Sylvester and the Magic Pebble
> Sylvester's parents are heartbroken when their dearest donkey disappears. Will he ever return?

Visualizing

Books whose vivid language create images in the mind of the reader.

Abuela by Arthur Dorros
> A little girl and her grandmother imagine what they would see if they flew high above the park and over the city. A glossary of Spanish terms completes the text.

All the Small Poems by Valerie Worth
> The poet writes about everyday things like hoses, paper clips, and crickets in vivid, striking language that stimulates pictures in the mind.

Festival in My Heart: Poems by Japanese Children edited by Bruno Navasky
> Poems written by children spark visual images. Includes beautiful Japanese paintings and sketches.

Fireflies by Julie Brinkloe
Striking language describes firefly hunting in the early summer evening. The author paints pictures with her words, creating wonderful images.

Good Dog Carl by Alexandra Day
One of a series of wordless picture books about a dog who takes care of a baby. The reader must visualize the pictures between the book's illustrations. Other titles include *Carl's Masquerade* and *Carl Goes Shopping*.

I'm in Charge of Celebrations by Byrd Baylor
A young girl writes about natural events such as Coyote Day, Green Cloud Day, and other special occurrences in poetic language that spurs visualizing.

A Lucky Thing by Alice Schertle
An especially vivid collection of poems that provide insight into the natural world as well as the creative process.

Painted Words/Spoken Memories: Marianthe's Story by Aliki
When Marianthe enters school without speaking any English, she speaks with her paints, illustrating for children how to tell a story without words.

Sailboat Lost by Leonard Everett Fisher
A wordless picture book about two boys who are carried away on a wayward sailboat. The reader must visualize to fill in the gaps.

The Sailor Dog by Margaret Wise Brown
"Born at sea in the teeth of a gale, the sailor was a dog." So begins Margaret Wise Brown's enchanting story of a dog who sails the globe. Garth Williams's compelling illustrations create a movie in the reader's mind.

The Seashore Book by Charlotte Zolotow
A little boy who lives in the mountains asks his mother what the seashore is like. She uses vivid language to describe it and encourages him to imagine the seashore.

Shadow Ball: The History of the Negro Leagues by Geoffrey Ward, Ken Burns, with Jim O'Connor
This riveting account of the Negro Leagues begins with a stunning lead depicting the team playing baseball in pantomime. The reader never suspects that there is no ball, because the words create such strong visual images.

Twilight Comes Twice by Ralph Fletcher
Summer evenings described in rich language that prompts readers to make their own pictures in their minds of twilight at dawn and dusk.

Author Set

Jonathan London

Baby Whale's Journey
> The author's simple, poetic narrative describes the early years of the endangered sperm whale from birth through weaning to joining the pod.

The Condor's Egg
> A pair of California condors struggle to survive. Realistic paintings bring this book to life.

Dream Weaver
> We see the behavior of one tiny spider through the eyes of a young boy in this poetic bedtime story.

At the Edge of the Forest
> While snow shoeing in the forest, a young boy discovers a coyote. Later when the boy's father finds a dead lamb, he sets out to eliminate the coyote.

Hurricane
> When a hurricane hits a Puerto Rican neighborhood, two boys head for a shelter. Filled with vivid language to describe the raging storm.

Into This Night We Are Rising
> The author's fantastic explanation of what happens when children fall asleep. They take flight and fill the sky, using clouds for pillows and the moon for a gong.

Like Butter on Pancakes
> In lyrical language the author describes a little boy's morning that begins with luscious breakfast smells and sunlight streaming through the window.

Puddles
> The author's vivid language captures the joy of wading and stomping in mud puddles after a fresh rainstorm.

Inferring

Books that stimulate inferential thinking.

Bull Run by Paul Fleischman
> In this collection of vignettes about different characters connected to the first battle of the Civil War, the reader must infer who they are, where they are, what they are doing and why.

Dateline: Troy by Paul Fleischman
> Contemporary newspaper articles are linked with ancient historical events, and the reader needs to infer the connection between the two.

Dandelion by Eve Bunting
> Because the woman and her daughter in this pioneer family are so

stoic, the reader must infer how the characters really feel about their increasing isolation.

Encounter by Jane Yolen

The fictionalized account of Columbus's arrival in the New World, from a Taino boy's perspective, nudges readers to try to understand his culture's plight.

Fables by Arnold Lobel

Twenty original tongue-in-cheek animal fables that poke a little subtle fun at the human condition. Great for inferring the moral.

June 29, 1999 by David Wiesner

A wordless picture book that requires the reader to infer the meaning behind the pictures. *Free Fall*, another wordless book by Wiesner, also requires readers to use inferential thinking skills.

The Rag Coat by Lauren Mills

This book about a young girl who loses her father at an early age prompts readers to draw inferences about her feelings as well as about the outcome of the story.

Rose Blanche by Roberto Innocenti

This story of a young German girl who passes a concentration camp on the way to school each day leaves lots of gaps that the reader must fill in, particularly in regard to the ambiguous ending.

See the Ocean by Estelle Condra

Clues abound that something is wrong with Nellie, but what could it be?

The Table Where Rich People Sit by Byrd Baylor

A young girl asks her parents why they say they're rich when they obviously have very little money. Readers have to infer another meaning of the word *rich* to fully understand this story.

Teammates by Peter Golenbock

This moving story of teammates Pee Wee Reese and Jackie Robinson brings up multiple themes, from racism to friendship, that readers must infer.

Tight Times by Barbara Shook Hazen

A boy desperately wants a pet, but times are rough in his house. Even the title requires inferential thinking.

Author Sets

Alexandra Day

Frank and Ernest
Frank and Ernest Play Ball
Frank and Ernest on the Road

The charming stories of two fast friends, a bear and an elephant, who take temporary work in a diner, for a baseball team, and as truck drivers. They use the jargon that matches each profession. The reader must infer the meaning of the job-specific terms such as "in the cellar" to describe the dwelling place of the local baseball team. Kids have a blast inferring the meaning of the unique vocabulary.

James Marshall

George and Martha
George and Martha Encore
George and Martha Rise and Shine

> Short short stories about the antics of two lovable hippos. The writing leaves enough out to require readers to infer on practically every page. Great books to introduce inferring.

Chris Van Allsburg

Throughout these books, the author leaves clues to lead the reader to make inferences to better understand as the author's white dog pops up in every story.

The Garden of Abdul Gasazi

> A young boy accidentally lets a dog into a magician's yard and is shocked when a duck appears from the yard, no dog in sight.

Jumanji

> A brother and sister play a jungle board game, which becomes frighteningly real.

The Mysteries of Harris Burdick

> The reader must infer the mystery behind a series of illustrations.

The Stranger

> A stranger appears, and the weather gets cooler and the leaves begin to change. Could it be Jack Frost?

The Wreck of the Zephyr

> The story of a flying sailboat is told by an old man who may have in fact been the young boy he talks about.

Great Books for Teaching Content in History, Social Studies, Science, Music, Art, and Literacy

World Exploration

Historical Fiction

Encounter by Jane Yolen

A Taino Indian child watches Columbus's ships arrive. Although the little boy is suspicious of the men and their motives, his elders do not listen until it is too late. Presents issues of discovery from the perspective of indigenous peoples; puzzling narrative and language encourage questioning and inferring.

Nonfiction

Around the World in 100 Years: From Henry the Navigator to Magellan by Jean Fritz

Fritz examines the travels of ten explorers, emphasizing their forays into what map makers in the 1400s called the unknown. Sophisticated language and ideas, appropriate for older students. Her book *Where Do You Think You're Going, Christopher Columbus?* may be a better choice for elementary students. Students invariably ask lots of questions and learn that history can be funny and fascinating.

Explorers by Carlotta Hacker

Women explorers featured in this book include explorer Isabella Bird, Amelia Earhart, Mary Kingsley, Annie Peck, founder of the American Alpine Club, and Soviet astronaut Valentina Tereshlova. Chapters on each woman describe their early years, formative years, and finally their accomplishments. Short profiles of ten additional female explorers are included.

The History News: Explorers by Michael Johnstone

Written in newspaper format with a bit of glib humor, the book begins with the Polynesians and the Phoenicians. Includes maps, interesting information, and even "letters to the editor" from the likes of Columbus.

Lewis and Clark: Explorers of the New American West by Steven Kroll
Excellent for questioning, focusing on important ideas, and developing research questions based on the events of the journey. Introduces Native American tribes along the way, and famous personalities including Sacajawea. The afterword contains additional information about what happened to the members of the expedition in later years.

Locks, Crocs, and Skeeters: The Story of the Panama Canal by Nancy Winslow Parker
Appealing informational text about the diplomats, engineers, and poets who explored, built, and wrote about the Panama Canal. A poem written in 1866 and illustrated by Parker introduces the Canal and the obstacles those who built it faced. Pages on colorful characters, historical events, and a variety of disease-carrying mosquitoes and insects.

Lost Treasure of the Inca by Peter Lourie
The author/adventurer takes the reader along on an edge-of-your-seat hunt for Inca treasure in Peru.

Talking with Adventurers by Pat Cummings and Linda Cummings
This book characterizes eleven contemporary explorers from the fields of oceanography, ecology, anthropology, archaeology, etc. Each portrait begins with a personal narrative written by the adventurer and concludes with a follow-up interview.

U.S. History

Colonial Times

Historical Fiction

Samuel Eaton's Day: A Day in the Life of a Pilgrim Boy by Kate Waters
Sarah Morton's Day: A Day in the Life of a Pilgrim Girl by Kate Waters
Tapenum's Day: A Wampanoag Indian Boy in Pilgrim Times by Kate Waters
Photographs from Massachusetts' Plimoth Plantation portray many aspects of colonial and Native American life. Children's work, clothing, school, and play are illustrated with simple, easy-to-read text. Great for research on the people of the times.

Stranded at Plimoth Plantation: 1626 by Gary Bowen
The fictional journal of one Christopher Sears, who, indentured by his unscrupulous uncle on a ship journeying west, finds himself stranded in Plimoth when his ship founders on the rocks.
Facts/Questions/Response three-column note form (see Part III, Appendix F) works well for kids to pull out information about daily life, diseases, meeting with the Native Americans. An excellent model for kids who may write a journal from a colonist's perspective.

Nonfiction

The Colonial Mosaic: American Women 1600–1760 by Jane Kamensky

A sourcebook appropriate for older, more sophisticated readers about women during colonial times. Stories of women as heroes, rebels, captives, witches, and of course, wives and mothers. The book chronicles the working lives of women regardless of their roles, using historical sources, especially journals, letters, and poems. Part of the Young Oxford History of Women in the U.S. series, edited by Nancy F. Cott.

Molly Bannaky by Alice McGill

An exiled English dairy maid is sent to America as an indentured servant. Molly stakes her own land and, although she deplores the institution of slavery, buys a slave to help start her farm. She eventually marries this former African prince, and they become successful landowners, despite the unusual circumstances of their marriage. Their grandson, Benjamin Banneker, a self-taught scientist and astronomer, was the first black man to publish an almanac. A wonderful story of determination and overcoming obstacles, not to mention fascinating historical details.

The New Americans: Colonial Times 1620–1689 by Betsy Maestro and Giulio Maestro

Begins with the Native Americans who first peopled the North American continent, putting the arrival of the Pilgrims in perspective. The history of Native American tribes and individuals is woven throughout colonial history, with helpful maps and illustrations detailing home life as well as historical events.

Poetry

Hand in Hand: An American History Through Poetry collected by Lee Bennett Hopkins

Beginning with the Pilgrims and continuing through Neil Armstrong's moon walk, this collection shares American history through poetry.

American Independence

Historical Fiction

Crossing the Delaware by Louise Peacock

A crucial turning point in the Revolutionary War, when Washington crossed the Delaware and fought the Battle of Trenton, is described from several perspectives. Fictional letters from a soldier in the heat of battle, a modern-day young man visiting Washington Crossing, and authentic diaries provide readers with an understanding of the dilemmas Washington faced and the desperate situation of the Continental Army. An excellent way to introduce different points of view as historical sources.

Emma's Journal: The Story of a Colonial Girl by Marissa Moss

Written by ten-year-old Emma in journal form with entries spanning a two-year period from May 1774 until July 1776, this clever book describes life and times in the colonial period and tells Emma's story of overhearing enemy battle plans and sneaking information out to the Colonial Army. Emma is a terrific role model for girls everywhere.

Katie's Trunk by Ann Turner

As Tories, Katie's relatives run away to the woods when the rebels come to their house looking for valuables. When she returns and hides, one of the patriots searching the house, a friend of her family's, keeps her secret and calls off his companions, illustrating compassion in the midst of war. Children's questions and inferences stimulate a thoughtful discussion of the meaning of themes such as loyalty and allegiance.

Redcoats and Petticoats by Katherine Kirkpatrick

A story of a boy who lives near a Redcoat encampment on Long Island who, without knowing it, becomes part of a Setauket spy ring. Thomas's mother seems to act peculiarly as she washes laundry, when she is in fact signaling the patriots about the comings and goings of the Redcoats. Excellent background information about patriots, loyalists, how the British kept prisoners on prison ships, and other aspects of the Revolutionary War. Recording notes on a three-column Facts/Questions/Response form (see Part III, Appendix F) brings out important information contained in the text.

Sleds on Boston Common: A Story from the American Revolution by Louise Borden

A nine-year-old colonial boy convinces British General Thomas Gage to allow him and his friends to go sledding on Boston Common even though it is occupied by British troops.

Nonfiction

The Boston Tea Party by Steven Kroll

A blow-by-blow account of events leading up to the Boston Tea Party, in particular, the meetings of the Long Room Club, which included luminaries such as Sam Adams, John Hancock, and Paul Revere. The Tea Party itself is described in detail with striking illustrations. Strategy emphasis can include inferring and questioning as the events unfold.

Charlotte by Janet Lunn

This picture book, based Charlotte Haines Peters's life, tells the story of a family torn apart by the Revolution. Charlotte, the daughter of a determined patriot, pays a high price for going to say good-bye to her loyalist cousins as they are about to leave for Canada and a new life. Themes that emerge include the high personal price people may be willing to pay to stand by their beliefs and prejudices.

Dear Benjamin Banneker by Brian Pinkney

Unlike many black people of his time Benjamin Banneker grew up free. A brilliant student, he never forgot how his brothers suffered under slavery, and he spoke out about it throughout his life. A great book for questioning, since Benjamin Banneker asked many questions himself.

Can't You Make Them Behave, King George? by Jean Fritz
A hilarious description of King George and his difficulties with the rebellious colonies tells the story of America moving toward independence. The author's remarkable sense of interesting detail and humorous style make this and the following titles a great set for introducing Revolutionary War themes and ideas.

And Then What Happened, Paul Revere? by Jean Fritz
This book about Paul Revere's adventurous life includes information about colonial Boston and the beginning of the American Revolution.

Shh, We're Writing the Constitution by Jean Fritz
The story, complete with the full cast of founding fathers, describes the ins and outs of drafting the Constitution.

Will You Sign Here, John Hancock? by Jean Fritz
The story of the writing and signing of the Declaration of Independence and the interesting personalities who played a part.

The American West—Native Americans

Historical Fiction

The Ledgerbook of Thomas Blue Eagle by Jewel Grutman and Gay Matthai
Written as a facsimile of a ledgerbook by the fictional boy Thomas Blue Eagle, the story recounts his early years with his family on the plains. Sent to an Indian school in Carlisle, Pennsylvania, he recalls life among white people and his eventual return to his people. The illustrations are traditional pictograph drawings, similar to those in the real ledgerbooks of the late nineteenth century. Reading this beautiful volume, written in longhand, is like studying an authentic historical document.

The Long March by Marie-Louise Fitzpatrick
The story of a group of Choctaw Indians who aided the victims of the Irish potato famine by donating $170 to this cause in the 1840s. Choona, a young Choctaw, speaks out against helping the *Nahullo,* or Europeans, but gradually changes his mind as he listens to his grandmother's story of his tribe's long and tragic march west. Encourages students to infer important ideas, including overcoming bitterness and resentment.

Red Hawk's Account of Custer's Last Battle by Paul Goble
A sophisticated but gripping account of this battle, written from the Native American perspective. Paul Goble's purpose in writing this book was to illustrate an uncommon perspective. Pictograph illustrations add to the authentic tone.

Nonfiction

A Boy Called Slow by Joseph Bruchac
A Lakota Sioux boy, named Slow at birth because of his careful and deliberate actions, became a hero in battle when he was fourteen. The

boy earned the name Sitting Bull, and because of his bravery and determination became one of the greatest Lakota warriors.

Buffalo Hunt by Russell Freedman
Told through the story of the buffalo, "a gift from the great spirit," this history of the Plains Indians describes the importance of the buffalo in all aspects of life, especially buffalo magic, the hunt, and its eventual disappearance. Paintings by George Catlin, Karl Bodmer, and others who documented the life of the Plains Indians add to the book's authenticity.

In a Sacred Manner I Live: Native American Wisdom edited by Neil Philip
Native Americans write about historical and twentieth-century themes, past and present. Poems, essays, and speeches include Chief Joseph's speech "I Will Fight No More Forever" and Tecumseh's words at a treaty signing: "My heart is a stone, heavy with sadness for my people." Traditions and beliefs about the power of Native American cultures come through in these original writings.

The Life and Death of Crazy Horse by Russell Freedman
An extensive history of the famous Teton Sioux warrior, detailing his childhood and later his continued resistance to giving up traditional ways. Illustrations from a famous ledgerbook by Amos Bad Heart Bull describe the Oglala Sioux's final struggles against Indian and white enemies and portray the tribe's dances, ceremonies, and hunting practices.

Shadow Catcher: The Life and Work of Edward S. Curtis by Laurie Lawlor
Edward Curtis, a famous photographer, traveled the country and worked tirelessly to capture Native American life in the late 1800s and early 1900s. Curtis endured a lifetime of personal and financial problems to complete *The North American Indian,* an exhaustive portfolio of Indian life.

The Trail of Tears by R. Conrad Stein
Thoughtfully written information about the Cherokee and their forced journey westward from their native lands in the southeast. Portraits of Cherokee and white leaders, period paintings of Cherokee on their journey, and engravings supplement the story of the outrageous treatment these people endured.

The Unbreakable Code by Sara Hunter
The story of brave Navajos who risked their lives to encode secret messages into the Navajo language during World War II. Told from the perspective of a grandfather telling his grandson about his role in the war, the story adds an important dimension to a study of World War II.

Series

Native American Series by Virginia Driving Hawk Sneve
Beginning with creation myths from each tribe—Cherokee, Iroquois, Navajo, and Hopi—short chapters include traditional roles of men, women, and children, the coming of the white man and disputed treaties, arts and religious ceremonies, and more recent information.

Clear headings and interesting illustrations make this series useful for intermediate-grade research projects.

Poetry and Legends

Between Earth and Sky by Joseph Bruchac
> Paintings by Thomas Locker illustrate nature poems by Seneca, Wampanoag, Navajo, and other Native Americans. Creation poems by Cherokee, Cheyenne, and Hopi people describe how the sacred permeates all aspects of life.

The Circle of Thanks: North American Poems and Songs of Thanksgiving by Joseph Bruchac
> Excellent short poems illustrating different ways of life among tribes in different regions of North America. The poems and songs depict ceremonies, beliefs, hunting practices, and other aspects of daily life. Excellent for introducing important themes in different tribal cultures.

Dancing Teepees selected by Virginia Driving Hawk Sneve
> Short poems include songs to the blue elk, the stars in the sky, poems and prayers about children, and the importance of the natural world. This easily read collection stimulates discussion of Native American values, traditions, and beliefs.

Storm Boy by Paul Owen Lewis
> A tale about a young Haida boy who falls overboard as he fishes in his canoe in a storm. The transformation that takes place as the boy moves between his Haida village and the world of the killer whale people under the sea requires students to infer and ask questions. *Frog Girl,* by the same author, provides additional information in another story about the Haida culture. Notes at the end of the story explain Haida beliefs and themes that are helpful in answering kids' questions.

The American West—Pioneers and Cowboys

Historical Fiction

Cassie's Journey: Going West in the 1860s by Brett Harvey
> In this story of the journey west, Cassie describes fellow travelers sick with fever, hoisting the wagon over high mountains, losing their cow while crossing a river, and celebrating the Fourth of July at Independence Rock, among other adventures. Interesting, thoughtful details are packed into Cassie's words.

Dandelion by Eve Bunting
> A story of a family's journey west from the perspective of a pioneer mother and her daughter who experience loneliness and isolation. Great for inferring and visualizing. Several beautifully descriptive scenes of nature as well as of people's feelings provide an in-depth understanding of how difficult life was for pioneers.

Going West by Jean Van Leeuwen

> Told from the point of view of seven-year-old Hannah, the simple but descriptive text tells the story of hardships and building a new life on the plains. Harsh weather and loneliness challenge the family, but springtime brings hope.

New Hope by Henri Sorensen

> How the settlement of New Hope, Minnesota, came to be when Lars Jensen's wagon axle broke on his way west in 1885. A great story of how serendipitous history can be. Easy text and beautiful illustrations make this a good choice for a read-aloud for younger readers/listeners.

Nothing Here But Trees by Jean Van Leeuwen

> A family journeys from New York to the Ohio wilderness. Dismayed at the dense forest, calling the trees "dark, long-legged beasts, blocking out the sun," the family begins to clear the land and make its home. Told from the point of view of a young boy, the story describes a family struggling to make a new life.

Rachel's Journal: The Story of a Pioneer Girl by Marissa Moss

> Written in journal form over a seven-month span in 1850, this book traces the family's covered wagon crossing from Illinois to California. The journal form is great for modeling writing.

Nonfiction

Bill Pickett: Rodeo-Ridin' Cowboy by Andrea Pinkney

> The true story of an extraordinary young man who grew up to become a famous black rodeo performer. The author's note gives extensive information on the black American cowboy.

Black Women of the Old West by William Katz

> The author features black women who played central roles in the settling of the West. The chapters describe women who were members of the Seminole tribes, nurses for Buffalo soldiers, mail-order brides, homesteaders, and agitators who fought for social justice. Authentic photographs and vignettes of individual women add to the book's interest and provide opportunities for students to infer from photographs and historical journals.

Children of the Gold Rush by Claire Murphy and Jane Haigh

> Historical photos, memorabilia, and narratives of life in Alaska during the Gold Rush portray the lives of children in mining camps and boomtowns. Journal entries and photographs complement the stories of the children's lives.

Children of the Wild West by Russell Freedman

> The lives of pioneer and Native American children are portrayed as families journey west and settle down. Pioneer schools, celebrations, and games are described in detail with numerous photographs. A sepa-

rate chapter describes the life of children in several different Indian tribes and how it changed as they were forced to give up their lands.

Daily Life in Covered Wagon by Paul Erickson
Pages with photographs and illustrations of everything a covered wagon could carry. Journal entries describe a family's trip west. Excellent for research and finding answers to questions about going west and pioneer life on the trail. An enormous amount of information can be gained by simply studying the pictures, which include photographs of real artifacts.

It Happened in Colorado by James Crutchfield
This book covers a number of events that took place in Colorado from prehistoric times until today. The richly written stories lend themselves to text-lifting mini-lessons for demonstrating how readers determine importance and synthesize information.

Plains Women by Paula Bartley and Cathy Loxton
Excerpts from the journals of homesteaders, independent women, and famous personalities like Calamity Jane. Includes an entry from the journal of General Custer's wife, Elizabeth, who commented on a surprise attack he led on an Indian camp in 1868 that killed 103 Indians: "It confused my sense of justice. Doubtless the white men were right but were the Indians entirely wrong? After all, these broad prairies had belonged to them." Excellent as a source for sharing short excerpts with students.

The Civil War

Historical Fiction

A. Lincoln and Me by Louise Borden
A young, gawky boy who shares a birthday with the sixteenth president learns that Lincoln too was teased in childhood. A great story about a boy who studies Lincoln and learns of the many possibilities for his own future.

Aunt Harriet's Underground Railroad in the Sky by Faith Ringgold
Harriet Tubman meets up with two modern-day children, and the story flashes back to the time of the Underground Railroad. Filled with information about slavery and the Underground Railroad. The puzzling narrative invites questions; the factual information about slavery is helpful for building background knowledge.

Bull Run by Paul Fleischman
Vignettes from the perspective of people who experience or are related to those at the Battle of Bull Run. Each person's story unfolds as the battle begins. Of particular interest is how each person's feelings about the war change once they experience it. The vignettes prompt lots of questions and require inferences; written in the language of the 1860s.

Follow the Drinking Gourd by Jeanette Winter
> The story, including the words to the song, of how the slaves journeyed North, following the Big Dipper.

Journey to Freedom: A Story of the Underground Railroad by Courtni Wright
> The story of one family's escape north, and the hardships they endured on the way. Told from the perspective of a young slave girl who travels with Harriet Tubman.

Moon Over Tennessee by Craig Crist-Evans
> A thirteen-year-old boy and his father, a Confederate soldier, journey to war together. The boy helps take care of the horses and does other chores but, most important, he keeps a journal. The journal entries are a series of poems capturing the sights, smells, sounds, and feelings of war. Poetic descriptions of the countryside, snapshots of camp life, and the horrors of the Battle of Gettysburg enable students to experience the events of 1863 through the eyes of a child not much older than themselves. Superb short text and striking black-and-white woodcuts prompt questions, inferences, and heartfelt responses.

Nettie's Trip South by Ann Turner
> A little girl journeys south and sees a slave auction, which outrages her. Told in the form of letters to a friend, Nettie's experiences strongly affect her sense of decency and justice.

Now Let Me Fly by Dolores Johnson
> Beginning in Africa, this realistic story tells how Africans were captured and taken forcibly to slave ships bound for America. The story of one slave family continues through the Civil War as family members struggle to remain close to each other despite harsh and brutal treatment. Excellent for determining important ideas and issues with respect to slavery.

Pink and Say by Patricia Polacco
> A poignant book about two boys, one black and one white, bravely fighting for the Union. The tragic story, told through the eyes of one of Patricia Polacco's ancestors, is eloquent testimony to the humanity that exists in the midst of the horrors of war. Questions and inferences abound as this story unfolds. Lest anyone have romantic ideas about bravery, courage, and sacrifice, this book dispels them.

Secret Signs by Anita Riggio
> A deaf child helps pass information along the Underground Railroad using his paintbrush and a panoramic egg. Kids brim with questions about the outcomes of this compelling story.

Seminole Diary: Remembrances of a Slave by Dolores Johnson
> In the 1820s a number slaves in Florida escaped tyrannical plantation owners and joined the Seminole Indians. The Seminoles called these people slaves but allowed them to live freely among them. Readers are filled with questions about what happened to these slave families and to their Seminole hosts during and after the Seminole Wars.

Sweet Clara and the Freedom Quilt by Deborah Hopkinson
>   Clara is a quilter and realizes how much she can help escaping slaves
>   once she begins sewing a quilt that is a map to guide their escape.

The Wagon by Tony Johnston
>   A slave boy recounts the story of his life, centered on the wagon his
>   father built for his master. The story, told in the boy's own words,
>   encourages readers to infer from his words. Themes of enslavement
>   and freedom are woven throughout the narrative.

Nonfiction

Abraham Lincoln: Great Speeches edited by John Grafton
>   A compilation of Lincoln's sixteen greatest speeches with historical
>   notes that explain the context for each. A terrific book for looking at
>   primary source documents and reading authentic writing from the
>   time.

Bound for America: The Forced Migration of Africans to the New World by James
Haskins and Kathleen Benson
>   Between 1500 and 1850, millions of Africans were captured and sent
>   across the Atlantic in one of the greatest tragedies in history. The
>   authors examine every aspect of the Middle Passage and attempt to
>   find meaning in this crime against humanity.

The Boys' War by Jim Murphy
>   The story of boys who fought, often lying about their youth, in the
>   Civil War. Sad stories of young boys eager to enlist who find out all too
>   soon about the horrors of war.

A Civil War Journal compiled by Albert A. Nofi
>   A compilation of over five hundred surprising episodes, anecdotes,
>   and little known facts of the Civil War. The compelling short text
>   makes it accessible to all kinds of readers.

For Home and Country: A Civil War Scrapbook by Norman Bolotin and Angela
Herb
>   Old photographs, newspaper clippings, and pictures of artifacts sup-
>   port chapters on food ("feast or famine"), day-by-day accounts of living
>   with the infantry, original photographs, and other interesting topics. A
>   time line of "four long years" presents a helpful overview.

Frederick Douglass: The Last Day of Slavery by William Miller
>   When a white overseer tries to break Frederick's spirit, he fights back,
>   "an act of courage that frees his spirit forever." This vividly sad story of
>   the early life of Frederick Douglass illustrates his determination to fight
>   against overwhelming cruelty and injustice.

From Slave Ship to Freedom Road by Julius Lester
>   Lester's hard-hitting prose and no-nonsense style complement Rod
>   Brown's graphic, contemporary paintings of escape, punishment, and
>   life as a slave. Lester challenges readers to imagine themselves as

slaves by including pointed, thoughtful questions throughout the text. The nature of the pictures and words make this most appropriate for middle school and up.

John Brown: One Man Against Slavery by Gwen Everett
Written from the perspective of his daughter, this books traces the great abolitionist John Brown's raid on the U.S. government arsenal at Harper's Ferry. In the 1940s the renowned African American artist Jacob Lawrence created a series of paintings chronicling this event. A book that sparks discussion about violence and whether it is ever justified.

Lincoln: A Photobiography by Russell Freedman
The Newbery Award–winning story of the sixteenth president. Superb for lifting short excerpts and reasoning through them together to determine important information and ideas.

Minty: A Story of Young Harriet Tubman by Alan Schroeder
A revealing account of the early life of this heroic figure. She was spunky and individualistic even as a young slave girl, so the reader is not surprised about who she went on to become.

Mr. Lincoln's Whiskers by Karen Winnick
The true story of the young girl Grace Bedell, who wrote Abraham Lincoln to suggest that he grow a beard. Readers can't help but infer how Mr. Lincoln will react to this suggestion. Will he take her advice?

A Separate Battle: Women and the Civil War by Ina Chang
Women's experiences during the Civil War include portraits of Harriet Beecher Stowe, nurse Clara Barton, and Dorothea Dix. One of the most interesting chapters describes women who successfully posed as male soldiers and spies.

World History

The First Great War, the 1920s, and the Depression

Historical Fiction

Angels in the Dust by Margot Theis Raven
Based on a true story, this book tells a tale of hardship and survival during the 1930s Oklahoma Dust Bowl. A good companion to Karen Hesse's *Out of the Dust* (see Short Text Collections).

The Babe and I by David Adler
Babe Ruth's hitting streak comes just in time for a needy family in the midst of the Great Depression. A young boy has no trouble selling papers thanks to the great baseball player.

Ballot Box Battle by Emily Arnold McCully
Poor Elizabeth Cady Stanton. Every time she was successful as a child, her father couldn't resist saying how she should have been born a boy. Eventually the story finds Stanton's young neighbor Cordelia at the

voting booth with Ms. Stanton, who points out to those present (all men, of course) that someday Cordelia will vote. Excellent short biography of Elizabeth Cady Stanton in the afterword.

Casey Over There by Straton Rabin

Casey sails away to France to fight in the Great War. When his seven-year-old brother doesn't hear from him, he writes to President Woodrow Wilson, who responds personally. The reader wonders throughout about the fate of brave Casey.

Good-bye, Charles Lindbergh by Louise Borden

Based on a true story, this book tells the tale of a young boy who meets the great hero when Lindbergh lands on a neighbor's field. A great story for inferential thinking.

Leah's Pony by Elizabeth Friedrich

During the 1930s Depression and in the midst of the Dust Bowl era, young Leah saves her family's farm. The book centers on Leah's love for her pony and describes her family's dilemmas as they almost lose their farm in a penny auction. Their neighbors refused to bid seriously when their friends were forced to auction off land and belongings.

Paperboy by Mary Kay Kroeger and Louise Borden

A compelling account of the 1927 fight between Jack Dempsey and Gene Tunney, when Tunney stunned the world and the neighborhood by unexpectedly winning the fight. Selling papers is tough, but young Willie Brinkman hangs in there and gets the break he needs.

The Potato Man by Megan McDonald

The touching story of a potato vender and the neighborhood kids who make fun of him because he has only one eye. Readers are filled with questions while reading this and can hardly wait to finish reading to discover the ending.

The Rag Coat by Lauren Mills

Minna is desperate to go to school, but first she needs a coat. The quilting mothers make one for her, but she is quite unprepared for the reaction of the kids at school. The author leaves many clues along the way, and readers can practice their inferring skills.

True Heart by Marissa Moss

The story of a sixteen-year-old girl who dreams of becoming an engineer. A good example of a story that places a girl in an unusual role. A thoughtful book about someone who had the determination to live out her dream.

Nonfiction

Children of the Dust Bowl by Jerry Stanley

Okie children who have moved to California are treated with disdain until one courageous soul from the town school board encourages the community to create its own wonderful school. A heartwarming story about how innovative educational experiences can transform lives. Superb photographs of life in the Depression era provide documentation of a truly remarkable project.

Restless Spirit: The Life and Work of Dorothea Lange by Elizabeth Partridge
Dorothea Lange was famous for photographing migrant workers during the Depression and Japanese Americans interned during World War II. This biography recounts her life and work. Once again, the photographs offer great opportunities for inferential thinking.

Something Permanent by Cynthia Rylant
Walker Evans's Depression-era photographs tell the stories of everyday Americans during those very tough times. Cynthia Rylant's text takes off from these photographs and brings them to life. It encourages kids to look at photographs and imagine the stories behind them.

World War II

Historical Fiction

All the Secrets of the World Jane Yolen
The story tells what war is like from a child's point of view when her father is sent overseas. When he returns several years later only an older cousin has any recollection of the dad who left.

The Bracelet by Yoshiko Uchida
When a Japanese American family leaves San Francisco for an internment camp, two little girls learn a great deal about the meaning of friendship. When seven-year-old Emi loses her best friend's bracelet, she learns that it is the memory of her friend that matters most.

The Lily Cupboard by Shulamith Oppenheim
When the Nazis invaded Holland during World War II, many Dutch families living in the country hid Jewish children. In this story, the Dutch family who keeps and hides a little Jewish girl on their farm takes a considerable risk, especially when soldiers come to search the house.

The Little Ships: The Heroic Rescue at Dunkirk in World War II by Louise Borden
In 1940 half a million British and French soldiers were trapped by Germans in a corner of northern France. The only way out was the sea. This book describes a heroic rescue effort by British civilians as well as military personnel.

Rose Blanche by Roberto Innocenti
This book recounts the story of a young German girl who passes a concentration camp on the way to school each day. Her daily journey leads her down the path from curiosity to sympathy to action. An extraordinary book for inferring and questioning, particularly because the ending remains unresolved.

Star of Fear, Star of Hope by Jo Hoestlandt
> Nine-year-old Helen lives to regret her parting words to her friend Lydia, who leaves Helen's birthday party to warn her family that Jews are being arrested. Helen only later understands why Lydia fled, but it is too late, and she never sees her again. She can only hope that Lydia survived, and she tells her story for others to learn from.

Nonfiction

Anne Frank: Beyond the Diary by Ruud van der Rol and Rian Verhoeven
> Pictures from Anne Frank's family photo albums illustrate what her life was like before and during the war, providing mesmerizing reading for anyone interested in Anne's diary and her fate as a Jewish child during World War II. Photographs and cutaway drawings of the secret annex explain the Franks' life in hiding.

Baseball Saved Us by Ken Mochizuki
> Based on the author's own experience, the story describes how Japanese Americans interned during World War II organized a baseball team and built a baseball diamond, which provided a diversion during this sad period in their lives. To understand the story, readers need to infer some of the characters' thoughts and feelings.

The Children of Topaz: the Story of a Japanese-American Internment Camp by Michael O. Tunnell and George W. Chilcoat
> The diary kept by a third-grade class taught by Anne Yamauchi in 1943 at the Topaz internment camp. The book describes, from a child's point of view, how Miss Yamauchi and her students tried to continue with normal school life despite difficult conditions. Archival photographs provide a detailed look at life in Topaz.

Elizabeth by Claire Nivola
> A moving story of a little girl who leaves her beloved doll behind as her Jewish family flees Germany. Years later she is reunited with her doll in an amazing story, one based on the experience of the author's mother. Thoughtful questions are prompted by the ambiguities and amazing end to the story.

Faithful Elephants by Yukio Tsuchiya
> The true story of the elephants at the Ueno Zoo in Tokyo at the height of World War II and their zookeepers, who were torn about whether to kill them or save them. Questions and inferences come fast and furiously. The text sparks deep discussion about how war takes a toll on the innocent.

Passage to Freedom: The Sugihara Story by Ken Mochizuki
> Told from the point of view of Hiroki Sugihara, the son of the Japanese consul to Lithuania during World War II. Hiroki describes how his father disobeyed orders from his government and granted visas to as many as ten thousand Jewish refugees from Poland, enabling them to escape the Nazis threatening Lithuania. Important ideas and themes

that arise during a discussion of the book include mustering the courage to do what's right and following one's conscience even if it means disobeying rules or laws.

Red-Tail Angels: The Tuskegee Airmen of World War II by Patricia McKissack and Fredrick McKissack

Until the end of World War II, African Americans could not serve in the U.S. Air Force. Finally, an all-black fighter squadron was formed, and the men distinguished themselves by their bravery, being awarded large numbers of medals and commendations.

Rosie the Riveter by Penny Colman

The women who filled the civilian and defense jobs during World War II deserve to have their stories told. Their determination and hard work resulted in a phenomenal rate of production of necessary goods that helped to win the war. Builds background for what life was like on the home front during World War II.

Sadako by Eleanor Coerr

A picture book version of the famous short chapter book *Sadako and the Thousand Paper Cranes.* This quiet story tells how Sadako bravely fought leukemia, the "atom bomb disease." Working to fold one thousand paper cranes so that the gods would grant her wish to get well, Sadako never gave up hope for a peaceful world.

Shin's Tricycle by Tatsuharu Kodama

This true story of a three year old who finally gets a tricycle and then dies an agonizing death while learning to ride it as the atom bomb falls on Hiroshima. This sad and disturbing picture book is not for small children but rather for middle schoolers to read with an adult for discussion purposes.

Tell Them We Remember by Susan Bachrach

A complete history of the Holocaust, from its beginnings in Nazi Germany, with descriptions of the ghettos and concentration camps, and reports of the resistance movements and rescue operations. Personal stories of courage, and photographs and descriptions of individual children and their fates, remind us never to forget.

The Unbreakable Code by Sara Hunter

Navajos encoding secret messages during World War II. See description in the preceding section "The American West—Native Americans."

V Is for Victory: The American Home Front During World War II by Sylvia Whitman

Recounts what happened in the United States as women found new roles in the workforce, shouldered family responsibilities, and joined other citizens of all ages to support the war effort. Important themes include strife between races and ethnic groups, and hardships such as rationing. War posters, photographs, and excerpts from personal letters and memoirs are useful to study as historical documents.

War Boy by Michael Foreman
> The author looks back on his own wartime childhood on the Suffolk coast in the shadow of a large navy base that was under frequent attack. A compelling story told with tenderness and humor from the perspective of the boy who lived it.

Poetry

I Never Saw Another Butterfly: Children's Drawings and Poems from Terezin Concentration Camp, 1942–44 edited by Hana Volavkova
> Poetry written in Terezin concentration camp is both tragic and hopeful. The children's sad but generous and thoughtful spirits come through despite their horrendous situations.

General History Series

Dear America series
> These diaries, written from the perspective of children growing up in virtually every period of American history, provide an authentic picture of life long ago. Written by a variety of authors, these books are excellent for lifting short text excerpts and reasoning through the text to build background knowledge of a particular time period. Favorites include *I Thought My Soul Would Rise and Fly: The Diary of Patsy, a Freed Girl* by Joyce Hansen, the story of a girl at the end of the Civil War; *Standing in the Light: The Captive Diary of Catharine Carey Logan* by Mary Pope Osborne, the story of a young girl captured by Indians in 1763; *The Girl Who Chased Away Sorrow: The Diary of Sarah Nita, a Navajo Girl* by Ann Turner, the tale of a Navajo girl in New Mexico in the 1860s.

A History of U.S.: The Story of America by Joy Hakim
> This series of ten volumes of U.S. history begins with *The First Americans* and concludes with *All the People,* covering over two hundred years of American history. Great photographs and primary source documents along with compelling writing make this series a must for upper elementary and middle school kids.

The History News by Michael Johnstone
> Written in newspaper format, the series includes volumes on Aztecs, Egyptians, explorers, Greeks, Romans, and medicine. Feature articles about interesting historic figures, events, and common people present interesting information in an unusual front-page form. Extremely useful for teaching nonfiction conventions such as titles, headings, reading charts, and maps, and paying attention to different ways of organizing content.

Perspectives on History series
> This series, published by Discovery Enterprises Ltd. of Carlisle, Massachusetts, includes over two dozen short books on a variety of pertinent topics in American history, including the Manhattan Project,

the Great Depression, and several on each of the great wars. These books are packed with authentic examples that give kids an opportunity to practice reading primary source documents.

Social Studies

Civil Rights and the African American Experience

Historical or Realistic Fiction

Aunt Flossie's Hats (and Crab Cakes Later) by Elizabeth Fitzgerald Howard
Based on the author's feisty great-aunt, the story of two girls who visit their great-great-aunt on Sunday afternoons and hear her stories of long ago.

Dear Willie Rudd by Libba Moore Gray
A woman late in life thinks back to the things she would have liked to have done with her beloved black housekeeper: go to the movies, have dinner, and ride the bus. Segregation prevented all of this. A great way to build background knowledge through questioning.

Dinner at Aunt Connie's House by Faith Ringgold
Two kids discover twelve portraits of famous African American women in the attic. The women come to life and explain their accomplishments.

Li'l Sis and Uncle Willie: The Life of the Painter William H. Johnson by Gwen Everett
Based on the life of the painter William H. Johnson, this fictional story tells about Uncle Willie's visits with Ernestine Brown, the real Li'l Sis. Brown's vivid paintings illustrate the text and tell the story of a little girl learning about the world from her amazing uncle.

More Than Anything Else by Marie Bradby
Written in the first person, the story concerns nine-year-old Booker T. Washington, who is determined to learn to read. Because he wanted to read "more than anything else," Booker won't rest until he finds an adult to help him. Themes include perseverance and determination to overcome obstacles.

Nonfiction

The Day Martin Luther King, Jr. Was Shot: A Photo History of the Civil Rights Movement by Jim Haskins
This account begins on the day Dr. King was assassinated and looks back over the history of the American Civil Rights movement through realistic illustrations, photographs, and primary sources.

Free at Last by Sara Bullard
A history of the civil rights movement, including the Little Rock Nine, freedom riders, and individual portraits of people who gave their lives

for the cause. A time line from 1954 to 1968 and archive photographs bring this era to life.

Freedom Rides: Journey for Justice by James Haskins
"My family and I could not try on shoes in the white-owned stores downtown. We had to select what we wanted and hope they fit. We were served in the back of the store." Jim Haskins's childhood experiences strengthened his determination to tell the truth about school segregation, the Montgomery bus boycott, and the freedom riders' nonviolent protests.

The Great Migration by Jacob Lawrence
Paintings by the artist of African Americans who forsook the South for what they hoped would be a better life in the northern industrial cities.

I Have a Dream by Dr. Martin Luther King, Jr.
Stunning pictures illustrate Dr. King's most famous speech. This book deserves an honored place in every classroom and library in America.

Richard Wright and the Library Card by William Miller
This story is based on a scene from Wright's book *Black Boy.* In the South, Richard could only use the library by saying the books he checked out were for a white co-worker. Determined to learn, Richard experienced derision and insult to borrow and read books, learning about people and places that would change his life.

Shadow Ball: The History of the Negro Leagues by Geoffrey Ward, Ken Burns, with Jim O'Connor
A richly written account of the baseball leagues for black Americans in the 1930s, 1940s, and 1950s. Kids will be amazed at this part of our history when black baseball players, no matter how talented, could not play in the major leagues.

The Story of Ruby Bridges by Robert Coles
Ruby Bridges bravely went to school in New Orleans each day, one of the first children to attend an all-white school. But Ruby ended up being the only child in her class, because the white children stayed home to protest. Ruby stood her ground, her teacher supported her, and gradually the other children returned to school, now an integrated school.

Wilma Unlimited by Kathleen Krull
Wilma Rudolph overcame childhood polio to become the first woman to win three gold medals in a single Olympics. Her childhood struggles and determination are described in clear language that enables young readers to understand and applaud Wilma's courage and persistence. Excellent model for blending interesting facts with vivid language if students write their own biographies.

Zora Hurston and the Chinaberry Tree by William Miller
The childhood story of the great writer Zora Neale Hurston, whose mother died when she was young and whose father couldn't under-

stand her daydreaming and adventurous spirit. She promises her mother that she will always reach high.

Poetry

Brown Honey in Broomwheat Tea by Joyce Carol Thomas
> Poems about the African American experience, many of which are from the perspective of children.

Honey I Love by Eloise Greenfield
> A collection of rhythmic poems from around a city neighborhood. Great for snapping fingers, dancing, and choral reading.

Soul Looks Back in Wonder compiled by Tom Feelings
> A collection of poems by famous African American poets, including Maya Angelou, Langston Hughes, and Lucille Clifton.

Rulers, Tyrants, Traitors, Heroes, and Heroines

Nonfiction

The Bobbin Girl by Emily Arnold McCully
> A story of the heroic mill girls working in Lowell, Massachusetts, who, in the 1830s, worked hard to become independent wage earners. When the mill owners try to lower their wages, the girls protest, and although they were replaced by new workers, they set a precedent for workers' strikes and encouraged other women to rebel when treated unfairly. Excellent afterword provides additional information.

Chingis Khan by Demi
> The story of the twelfth-century Mongol ruler who conquered much of China and united the feuding Mongol tribes. By age nine, he was already in command of the largest Mongol tribe. His military genius led him to rule China for nearly sixty years.

Eleanor by Barbara Cooney
> "From the beginning the baby was a disappointment to her mother." So begins this account of Eleanor Roosevelt's childhood. Inspires much discussion about how this lonely child went on to become such an impressive woman in light of her sad early years.

Good Queen Bess by Diane Stanley
> The story of Elizabeth I of England, whose strong will and love of her people won their favor. The text and finely detailed paintings build background for life in Elizabethan times.

The Great Wall of China by Leonard Everett Fisher
> The tyrant emperor orders tens of thousands of Chinese to build a wall "wide enough to hold ten soldiers side by side." The black-and-white illustrations and strong words make the reader feel as if he were there, joining the masses for ten years of hard labor but ultimately victorious in keeping the hated Mongols out of China.

Heroes: Great Men Through the Ages by Rebecca Hazell
Rather than fighting battles or ruling kingdoms, these men changed the world by their good deeds and vision (Gandhi and Sequoyah), their brilliance and talent (Ben Franklin, Mozart, and Shakespeare) or their courage and wisdom (Socrates). Appealing paintings bring the men and their accomplishments to life.

Heroines: Great Women Through the Ages by Rebecca Hazell
Women who were queens (Elizabeth I), saints (Joan of Arc), and explorers (Sacajawea) fit Hazell's definition of a heroine. Women who fought for justice as well as artists and scientists are included in this lively volume. Maps with accompanying time lines provide excellent information on the women's lives and times.

The King's Day by Aliki
The life, times, and antics of King Louis XIV of France. Every page holds yet another wacky piece of information about this historic ruler. Readers revel in the pomp of the French court, made accessible by Aliki's wonderful drawings and captions.

The Librarian Who Measured the Earth by Kathryn Lasky
Eratosthenes, who lived two thousand years ago, asked lots of questions. All those questions led to his figuring out how to measure the earth, something no one had ever done before. A great story for encouraging us all to keep thinking and wondering.

Lou Gehrig: The Luckiest Man by David Adler
Courageous and self-effacing, Lou Gehrig met challenges throughout his life. But he faced his greatest challenge with a positive attitude and a quiet dignity that is his legacy today.

Outrageous Women of Ancient Times by Vicki Leon
Fifteen stories of ancient women from about 1500 B.C. until the second century A.D. who had an impact on the world in which they lived. They are called outrageous because powerful women were such a rarity in those days. A great book as a role model for girls.

The Tower of London by Leonard Everett Fisher
Within this bastion of history, children were murdered, queens beheaded, and famous soldiers imprisoned. Fisher's haunting black-and-white paintings complement these dramatic stories of Henry III, the Richards, Henry the VII and, of course, Anne Boleyn and Elizabeth I. From palace to prison, the story of the tower of London is a great introduction to some of the most exciting moments in English history.

Series

Notorious Americans and Their Times series
This series includes biographies of infamous individuals who took part in events that have come to shape American history. Titles include

Benedict Arnold and the American Revolution, John Wilkes Booth and the Civil War, Al Capone and the Roaring Twenties, and *Joseph McCarthy and the Cold War.*

Immigration: Past and Present

Historical or Realistic Fiction

American, Too by Elisa Bartone
> Rosina, just arrived from Italy, is anxious to drop her Italian ways and become a real American. Based on the author's own experiences, the story tells how Rosie surprises everyone during the traditional feast of San Genaro by dressing as the Statue of Liberty. In a real-life fairy tale ending, Rosie meets a young man dressed up as Uncle Sam that night and later marries him.

Grandfather's Journey by Allen Say
> Like his grandfather, Allen Say feels that "the moment I am in one country, I am homesick for the other." The story moves between two cultures, describing his grandfather's life in Japan and adventures in the United States.

How Many Days to America? by Eve Bunting
> A compelling story of leaving what appears to be a Caribbean land full of soldiers to find safety in the United States. The story invites comparisons to more recent situations in Cuba and Haiti. The ambiguity encourages inferring and questioning, since it is not clear where the family comes from and what will happen to them in America.

The Lotus Seed by Sherry Garland
> The story of a young woman who flees Vietnam, taking a lotus seed as a remembrance of the emperor and her country. The dangerous journey, life in a new land with her family, and eventually being able to honor her past and native country illustrate the importance of memories and traditions. The sparse text and a complicated narrative encourage inferring and especially questioning.

My Freedom Trip by Frances Park and Ginger Park
> The story of a little girl, Soo, who has to brave crossing the border alone to escape during the Korean War. Soo's mother, who promises to follow her to South Korea, encourages her to be brave, and themes like waiting, courage, and the price of freedom are woven into the story. The dilemma of leaving one's home to find freedom prompts questions and inferences.

Painted Words/Spoken Memories by Aliki
> A little girl from Greece first tells her story in paintings before she knows enough English to talk with her classmates, and then tells her story in words. The book is two books in one. Begin by reading *Painted Words*, then flip it over and read *Spoken Memories*.

A Picnic in October by Eve Bunting
> Tony doesn't understand why the whole family is taking the ferry out to the Statue of Liberty for a picnic until he sees how much it means to his grandmother. Kids have no idea why the grandmother is so insistent on going out on this blustery October day. The author drops gentle clues along the way, which demand inferential thinking.

When Jessie Came Across the Sea by Amy Hest
> The rabbi in Jessie's village chooses her to travel to America to start a new life. Jessie's letters back to her beloved grandmother tell about her new life on New York's Lower East Side. Letters from Jessie are interspersed throughout the text.

The Whispering Cloth by Pegi Deitz Shea
> A little girl and her grandmother who remain in a refugee camp tell their memories in a beautifully embroidered p'andau. Children ask lots of questions and must infer to find out what's really happening in the story and what is part of the character's imagination.

Nonfiction

Dia's Story Cloth by Dia Cha
> The story of Dia Cha's family and their journey from Laos to a refugee camp in Thailand and finally to the United States. This family story is told in a large, exquisite story cloth sewn by Dia's aunt and uncle. It preserves important memories and the history of the Hmong people's journey.

I Was Dreaming to Come to America by Veronica Lawlor
> Memories from the oral history project at Ellis Island capture the recollections of people who arrived in America during the heyday of immigration. In their own words, people remember coming over on ships, their days living at Ellis Island, and the excitement of coming to a new land to start a new life.

Immigrant Kids by Russell Freedman
> Photographs of children coming to this country and then at home, school, and work in the early decades of the twentieth century illustrate hardships they experienced in leaving their countries and cultures. Using the photographs of kids working, playing, and going to school provides kids an opportunity to think like historians, inferring and determining important information from historical documents.

Journey to Ellis Island by Carol Bierman
> Because of Yehuda Weinstein's injured hand, he and his mother and sister are almost sent back to Europe. Yehuda proves himself able to run around Ellis Island and shows the immigration inspectors that his hand is healing. Actual photos of the family, documents, and journal recollections add to the authenticity of the story.

One More Border by William Kaplan with Shelley Tanaka
> The story of the Kaplan family's journey across Russia, through Japan, and finally to Canada during World War II. Photographs of people, places, and original documents fill the text.

Global Culture and Geography

Realistic Fiction

Aunty Dot's Incredible Adventure Atlas by Eljay Yildirim
> Aunt Dorothy and Uncle Frank go on a world tour and send letters home from all over the globe, including the Taj Mahal, New Zealand, Jamaica, and even Lapland. Kids will love pulling the letters out of authentic airmail envelopes and reading about the next adventure on the itinerary.

The Day Gogo Went to Vote by Elinor Sisulu
> In South Africa in 1994 great-grandmother Gogo, who is one hundred years old, takes her great-granddaughter Thembi with her to vote. Gogo's relatives say she is too old to go, but she insists. This story is about the South African election that elected Nelson Mandela as president.

Erandi's Braids by Antonio Hernandez Madrigal
> A moving story about a seven-year-old Mexican girl's willingness to sell her hair to help her financially strapped mother. The story is based on the hair-selling practice of the 1940s and 1950s. The practice of hair selling will spur questions from many kids who have never heard of this.

Rebel by Allan Baillie
> The story of how one school child and the peasants in a small Burmese village band together to stand up to a newly installed military dictator. A great story to discuss civil disobedience.

Sammy and the Time of Troubles by Florence Parry Heide and J. D. Gilliland
> Sammy lives in war-torn twentieth-century Beirut, a life riddled with fear, uncertainty, and violence. The story describes how his family attempts to have a future amid civil chaos.

Nonfiction

Barrio—Jose's Neighborhood by George Ancona
> Jose lives in San Francisco's mission district, El Barrio. The homes, food, daily life, celebrations such as fiesta and the Day of the Dead, and family activities in this culturally rich neighborhood are depicted. Excellent photos and definition of Spanish terms.

Clambake: A Wampanoag Tradition by Russell M. Peters
> A present-day story of young Steven Peters, a Wampanoag Indian who lives in Plymouth, Massachusetts, illustrates the contemporary world of this tribe. One of an award-winning series called We Are Still Here:

Native Americans of Today. Another title in the series is *Songs from the Loom: A Navajo Girl Learns to Weave* by Monty Roessel.

Day of the Dead by Kathryn Lasky

Photographs and an information-filled text explain this important day in Latino cultures. The customs and traditions honoring family members in Mexico are vividly portrayed.

I Am Mexican American by Isobel Seymour

The story of one family's coming to America also includes excellent information about Mexico, mestizos, the Spanish, and Mexican food, arts, and celebrations. Additional titles in the Our American Family series describe the following cultures: Chinese American, Indian American, Irish American, Italian American, Japanese American, Jewish American, Korean American, Native American, Polish American, and Vietnamese American.

No More Strangers Now: Young Voices from a New South Africa by Tim McKee and Anne Blackshaw

Personal stories of adolescents in South Africa explain what the country and their lives are like after the end of apartheid. Young people from many walks of life tell of their experiences in recent years. What stands out are the economic disparities that remain despite changing laws and attitudes.

Oasis of Peace by Laurie Dolphin

The surprising story of a community in Israel known as Oasis of Peace, which is a cooperative village of Jews and Arabs. People remain loyal to their own cultures and religious identities but are committed to living together and engaging in a dialogue to more fully understand one another.

One Day We Had to Run by Sybella Wilkes

Refugee children tell their stories in words and paintings, explaining war in Africa and other cultures where children and their families are the victims of political disputes and economic problems. Paintings and drawings by the children themselves bring their stories to life.

Our Journey from Tibet by Laurie Dolphin

This is a true story of how three sisters escape over the Himalayas to the Tibetan refuge and school at Dharmsala in India. Their parents, who remain in Tibet, want their daughters to grow up and become educated in their own culture. A powerful statement about the Tibetans' determination to preserve their culture despite Chinese efforts to destroy it.

Talking Walls by Margy Burns Knight

Walls around the world, the Lascaux caves in France, the granite walls in Zimbabwe, Nelson Mandela's prison walls, and Diego Rivera's murals, among others, introduce children to the art, sculpture, and architecture of different cultures. Contains a map locating all of the sites. Great for visualizing.

Tea with Milk by Allen Say

May, raised in San Francisco, struggles upon her family's return to Japan with Japanese customs and expectations much different from what she was used to in America. This is the story of how the author's parents met and what home means to them. Young readers may have further questions about the Japanese culture and will infer well beyond the point of the story.

Tibet: Through the Red Box by Peter Sis

Peter Sis recounts the story of his father, who spent much time away from home when Peter was a child in the far-off country of Tibet. His father kept a diary of his time there, and when Peter grew up, he read it and recounts his father's tale here.

We Are All Related by George Littlechild

Mr. Littlechild, an artist in residence at Cunningham Elementary School in Vancouver, British Columbia, led his students in a multicultural project in which they explored their own heritage, interviewed an older relative, and created a collage of their family and culture. This is described in small vignettes on every page.

Series

Journey Between Two Worlds series
A Guatemalan Family by Michael Malone
A Hmong Family by Nora Murphy
A Kurdish Family by Karen O'Connor

This series portrays families from different parts of the world, some of whom have emigrated to the United States.

Contemporary Social Issues

Realistic Fiction

Amelia's Road by Linda Altman

The story of a migrant child who wishes for one thing—a home. Amelia's aversion to roads stems from her family's constant moving around. Teachers may want to encourage kids to discuss what they are wondering about Amelia's life and her hope about "someday."

A Day's Work by Eve Bunting

A grandfather teaches his grandson about honesty when things go awry with their landscaping work. Understanding the characters and inferring from their actions encourage students to draw conclusions about integrity and the importance of hard work.

Fly Away Home by Eve Bunting

Tough times have forced a boy and his father to take up residence in the airport to stay off the street while the father tries to get work. An anchor text for questioning. Kids can't stop wondering why they are in the airport, will they get a home, how does one become homeless, etc.

Good Luck, Mrs. K by Louise Borden

Everyone's favorite third-grade teacher, Mrs. Kempczinski, gets cancer and must leave school for treatment. This touching story from the perspective of one of her students delves into how kids deal with this. Hopeful in the end, Mrs. K comes back for a visit.

La Mariposa by Francisco Jimenez

A picture book adaptation of a chapter from Jimenez's *The Circuit*, illustrating a migrant boy's struggle to learn English and survive in school. Teachers may want to encourage children to draw inferences, thinking about how it feels to attend school and feel alienated from the dominant culture. Issues of acceptance and determination to succeed are central to the story.

A Name on the Quilt by Jeannine Atkins

Lauren and her family make a panel for the NAMES Project AIDS Memorial Quilt in memory of her uncle, who died of AIDS. As they sew, they reminisce and celebrate experiences with Uncle Ron. This book will provoke questions regarding the disease as well as death. Readers who have experienced death will identify closely with Lauren's feelings.

Smoky Night by Eve Bunting

A story set during the Los Angeles riots in the 1980s. Two lost cats go a long way toward bringing people together who couldn't get along. Kids brim with literal questions as well as deeper, more thoughtful questions.

Some Frog by Eve Bunting

An all too familiar story of twelve-year-old Billy, who waits patiently week after week for his dad to come. The frog-jumping contest is just around the corner. Once again dad doesn't show up, but Billy's got one special mom!

Sunshine Home by Eve Bunting

A family goes to visit their grandmother after putting her in a nursing home. Many kids who have experienced the angst in their family around this issue can relate to this difficult decision.

Uncle James by Marc Harshman

Uncle James keeps promising that he is going to send money to help out the family and that he is coming to visit soon, but when he finally arrives after many broken promises, he brings his own problems. He's an alcoholic. A hopeful ending to a realistic and all too often ignored social problem shared by many kids in our classrooms.

The Wall by Eve Bunting

A boy visits the Vietnam Veterans Memorial with his father and finds the name of his grandfather. Observing other people as they remember loved ones brings home both the tragedy of the war and this remarkable way of remembering those who died.

Your Move by Eve Bunting

Ten-year-old James thinks that the K-Bones are the cool group to hang with until he, along with his six-year-old brother, begins his initiation and realizes the reality and danger of gang life. Readers may identify with being dared, trying to be cool, and the adult life many young kids live. Those without background for this will learn about the harsh reality of gangs and will realize the importance of taking a stand.

Nonfiction

One April Morning by Nancy Lamb

The book, written in collaboration with teachers, therapists, clergy, and the children of Oklahoma City, tells the story of that dreadful day in April 1995 when a bomb destroyed the Murrah Federal Building in Oklahoma City, killing 169 people.

Voices from the Fields by S. Beth Atkin

Vignettes of migrant children and young adults who tell about their experiences living and moving around as the children of farm workers. The ties and values of Hispanic families come through in poems and interviews, as does the strain of moving constantly to new places and being poor in an affluent culture.

Science

Space

Fiction

Dogs in Space by Nancy Coffelt

Dogs visit the different planets, deciding it's too hot on one or too cold on another, but sharing what they learn with young readers. An afterword, "The Great Solar System Tour," provides interesting information and statistics on each planet.

Postcards from Pluto by Loreen Leedy

Postcards from the planets provide interesting information when a class visits the solar system and write home to their families. Great as a model for writing one's own book of postcards from the planets.

Nonfiction

First on the Moon: What It Was Like When Man Landed on the Moon by Barbara Hehner

Told from astronaut Buzz Aldrin's perspective, the book chronicles each part of the journey, including liftoff, the rockets and launchers, landing on the moon, and coming home. Superb photos and the first-person perspective keep the readers' interest. A time line of Milestones in Space is extremely useful for research projects and gaining a big picture of the U.S. space program over the years.

One Giant Leap by Don Brown

The story of Neil Armstrong, who as a child dreamed of floating in space, flying, and exploring. He was the first person to set foot on the moon, on July 20, 1969. Armstrong's life is portrayed in simple language and illustrations appropriate for primary-age space fans.

The Space Shuttle by Peter Murray

"Imagine that you are on the flight deck of the space shuttle, waiting for lift-off." So begins this first person perspective as the space shuttle blasts off and you hurl into space. A brief history of the space program follows, with amazing photographs and simple, well-written text. An index makes this book useful for researchers.

Series

Explore Space series by Gregory L. Vogt

Clear photographs and simple, concise text explain space topics kids are most interested in, including space stations, rockets, space shuttles, and space robots.

Mission to Mars series by John Hamilton

This series explores many aspects of Mars, scientific and mythical. Recent NASA photos and careful documentation of scientific observations as well as a description of some of the more far-fetched theories about the possibility of life on Mars make for interesting reading.

Series on the planets and stars by Seymour Simon

Books on the Sun, Saturn, and Jupiter include extraordinary photographs helpful for research as well as clear explanations of planetary phenomena.

Poetry

Star Walk edited by Seymour Simon

Sophisticated poems about space that will prompt lots of questions. Amazing photographs bring the poems to life.

Space Songs by Myra Livingston and Leonard Everett Fisher

Superb poetry about galaxies, planets, and messages from outer space informs and inspires kids to write their own space poems.

Weather

Nonfiction

Hottest, Coldest, Highest, Deepest by Steve Jenkins

The coldest, snowiest, hottest, highest, deepest places on earth are portrayed in this book, with collage illustrations of Mount Everest, the

Sahara Desert, Antarctica, and the Marianas Trench, among others. Visually fascinating pages are models for student projects.

Lightning by Stephen Kramer

Organized around questions like What is lightning?, What happens during a lightning strike?, and What is thunder?, the book tells all about lightning. A superb writer, Kramer includes a "fascinating facts" section full of amazing information.

The Reasons for Seasons by Gail Gibbons

Gail Gibbons, famous for her well-written and clearly illustrated nonfiction for younger children, explains everything one would want to know about the seasons. Diagrams of the Sun and Earth, explanations of equinoxes and each season, all with the author's careful wording and thoughtful pictures, provide an excellent introduction to this topic.

Series

Extreme Weather series by Liza Burby

A series organized around questions about various kinds of storms and natural weather disasters. Books include *Hail, Electrical Storms, Tropical Storms and Hurricanes, Tornadoes, Heat Waves and Droughts,* and *Blizzards.* Clear writing, photographs, and interesting questions such as How does hail start?, How does hail behave?, and Why is hail dangerous? motivate young researchers.

Weather Report series by Ann Merk and Jim Merk

Complicated weather terms are described in *Rain, Snow, and Ice* with superb photographs and simple, clear explanations that distinguish among rain, snow, falling ice, frost, dew, and other forms of precipitation. Other books in the series are *Clouds* and *Studying Weather.*

Environmental Issues and Nature

Fiction

And Still the Turtle Watched by Sheila MacGill-Callahan

Kids with spray paint deface a Native American rock carving of an ancient turtle. Community members come together to restore the turtle and move it to a safe place. Sparks discussion of community responsibility and respect for traditions and beliefs.

The People Who Hugged the Trees by Deborah Lee Rose

In long ago India, there was a beautiful forest located in the middle of a vast desert. When the maharajah wanted timber for his fortress, the people banded together and hugged the trees in protest. There is still a "hug the tree" movement in India.

A River Dream by Allen Say

A boy's imaginary fishing trip leads to the realization of beauty of all living things. Proud of catching a fish, Mark decides it's better to release the fish than to kill it in order to "keep" it.

She's Wearing a Dead Bird on Her Head by Kathryn Lasky

Based on the turn-of-the-century founding of the Audubon Society, this book mixes fact and fiction as two sisters begin the crusade to end the use of birds and their feathers for decorating ladies' hats.

Stellaluna by Janell Cannon

Gorgeous authentic illustrations complement the story of a fruit bat who gets separated from her mother. Great for inferring themes.

Washing the Willow Tree Loon by Jacqueline Briggs Martin

An oil slick coats the birds in Turtle Bay, and all sorts of concerned folks rush to the rescue. Finally catching an elusive loon in a net, the team goes to work cleaning the bird's wings, feeding it medicine, and watching it until it is ready for release. An informative note about bird rehabilitation will answer children's many questions about the intricacies of cleaning and caring for damaged wildlife.

Nonfiction

An American Safari: Adventures on the North American Prairie by Jim Brandenburg

This first-person account of photographing and working to save endangered North American prairies contains information about wildlife, prairie fires, and other aspects of this unique ecosystem. Twenty years of studying the prairie allowed Brandenburg to observe many changes, including the growth of American bison herds in their natural habitat.

Animals Eat the Weirdest Things by Diane Swanson

The author gives us a sampling of the strange dinners that animals consume. She throws in some rather bizarre meals for humans, too!

Dangerous Animals

This Nature Company book has huge realistic illustrations of dangerous animals of every shape and size. Kids love this one!

A Desert Scrapbook by Virginia Wright-Frierson

This book, the scrapbook of painter-author Wright-Frierson, allows us a peek into her observations, sketches, and paintings of all that goes on in the Sonoran Desert. A superb model for notebook writing with kids, especially young observers who love to study and write about the natural world. Wright-Frierson also wrote *An Island Scrapbook* about nature on a barrier island.

Elephants by Eric S. Grace

Everything you ever wanted to know about these amazing creatures, written in an interesting way. Great model for nonfiction writing.

Letting Swift River Go by Jane Yolen

The all too common story of wild rivers being dammed to create reservoirs across America, particularly during the 1920s, 1930s, and 1940s. Rooted in the author's own experience, this book laments the loss of these vital rivers.

Monarchs by Kathryn Lasky
> The story of the monarch butterfly's migration from Canada to Michoacán, Mexico, each winter. The monarchs roost in trees that the locals had been clear-cutting for years. But the advent of the monarchs brought tourists, and now both the trees and the monarchs are out of harm's way. A great win-win story!

Rattlesnake Dance by Jennifer Owings Dewey
> At age nine, the author was bitten by a rattler, and she has been fascinated with them ever since. She weaves her own personal accounts with factual information about the legends and truth of rattlesnakes.

Rio Grande: From the Rocky Mountains to the Gulf of Mexico by Peter Lourie
> Peter Lourie explores the Rio Grande to find out what makes the great river great. As with his other books on rivers, the author/adventurer follows the river by canoe and learns the history of the surrounding areas. Other river titles by Peter Lourie include *Amazon: A Young Reader's Look at the Last Frontier; Hudson River: An Adventure from the Mountains to the Sea; Yukon River: An Adventure to the Gold Fields of the Klondike; Erie Canal: Canoeing America's Great Waterway;* and *Everglades: Buffalo Tiger and the River of Grass*.

A River Ran Wild by Lynne Cherry
> The history of the Nashua River in Massachusetts and New Hampshire is a long and stormy one. First inhabited by Indians, the river was spoiled by years of development. In the 1960s environmentalists, led by activist Marion Stoddart, fought to restore the river to its former pristine state. Today it remains a refuge for birds, fish, and people.

Safari by Caren Barzelay Stelson
> A photographic safari in Tanzania. Wonderful photographs and vivid language make this a wonderful text to practice visualizing.

Sanctuary: The Story of Three Arch Rocks by Mary Anne Fraser
> Herman Bohlman and William Finley were naturalists who fought to save sea lions and nesting birds that came to Three Arch Rocks off the coast of Oregon. Their determined actions in the early 1900s resulted in the creation of the West Coast's first wildlife sanctuary. The naturalists' notes, wildlife sketches, and information about the men's heroic efforts result in a beautifully crafted work of nonfiction.

Spotlight on Spiders by Densey Clyne
> Great photographs and writing about these eight-legged creatures. A must for kids who can't get enough about spiders.

Spots: Counting Creatures from Sky to Sea by Carolyn Lesser
> A great book for primary kids for learning about animals and counting. Award-winning illustrations complement the poetic text.

Survivors in the Shadows by Gary Turbak
> Beautifully crafted short pieces about animals who are not easy to find. Great for text-lifting mini-lessons on synthesizing.

The Unhuggables

A terrific book, published by the National Wildlife Federation, about animals you wouldn't want to cuddle up to: tarantulas, cockroaches, sharks, etc. Short text entries on over twenty of these creepy creatures. Great for text-lifting mini-lessons on distilling important information from interesting details.

Will We Miss Them? by Alexandra Wright

This book, written by a middle school student, describes the plight of disappearing and endangered animals and asks the title question.

Poetry

Creatures of the Earth, Sea, and Sky by Georgia Heard

Poems about endangered animals and the importance of nature in our lives. Heard's carefully crafted yet accessible poems are wonderful models for children as they learn to write poetry themselves.

Safe, Snug, and Warm by Stephen Swinburn

Lovely poems about how each animal species protects its babies from predators. Accurate information presented in a compelling way.

Scientists, Inventors, and a Collection of Quirky Topics

Nonfiction

The Brooklyn Bridge by Elizabeth Mann

The story of John Roebling's dream, carried on by his family after he died as the result of an accident on the bridge, describes this engineering feat as well as the determination of John's family to continue the work he had begun. Superb drawings of the bridge, historical prints, and old photographs complement the text and provide an interesting perspective on New York as well as on the monumental task of building the bridge.

A Drop of Water by Walter Wick

A creative way of looking at the physics of water. Close-up photographs of water drops and water in all forms. The text explains the physics of water by suggesting some experiments you can do at home.

How Come? by Kathy Wollard

This book answers common questions that kids ask and often no one knows the answers to, such as Why is space black? Great for text-lifting mini-lessons on finding answers to specific questions.

The Librarian Who Measured the Earth by Kathryn Lasky

Eratosthenes, who lived two thousand years ago, asked lots of questions. All those questions led to his figuring out how to measure the earth, something no one had ever done before. A great story for encouraging us all to keep thinking and wondering.

Mistakes That Worked by Charlotte Foltz Jones

A collection of accidents that resulted in surprising inventions such as

Velcro, potato chips, and Post-it Notes. Kids love these unusual twists of events. A sequel, *More Mistakes That Worked*, is also available.

Snowflake Bentley by Jacqueline Briggs Martin

The 1998 Caldecott winner and the story of Wilson Bentley's passion for photographing and studying snowflakes. He "loved snow more than anything else in the world" and developed the techniques of microphotography that allowed him to take thousands of photographs of exquisite snow crystals. A story of following one's passion and determination to document the wonders of nature. Look for W. A. Humphrey and A. J. Humphrey's reprinted book *Snow Crystals,* a collection of 2,453 illustrations of snowflakes to use as a companion piece.

Starry Messenger by Peter Sis

The story of Galileo told with illustrations and text of extraordinary beauty. A wonderful book to build background about Renaissance times and introduce the themes of the power of knowledge.

Disasters: Man-made and Natural

Nonfiction

Avalanche by Stephen Kramer

A great nonfiction writer, Stephen Kramer gives the reader excellent content while at the same time painting vivid pictures with his words. Great for learning about avalanches as well as modeling strong nonfiction writing.

The Buried City of Pompeii by Shelley Tanaka

Well-written history of Pompeii. Visually interesting with photographs and drawings, the book answers many student questions about how people died, what really happened, and how the city, lost for so many years, was rediscovered. Good for visualizing in reading and showing not telling in writing.

Exploring the Titanic by Robert Ballard

Dr. Ballard, the marine scientist who located and explored the *Titanic,* gives us the full, accurate story of the doomed ocean liner. A compelling topic written in a rich, visual way makes this a book kids can't put down. Great for text-lifting mini-lessons on reading to answer a specific question and determining importance in text.

Eye of the Storm by Stephen Kramer

The life of a storm chaser–photographer is documented in this informative book about interesting weather and the equally interesting people who study violent storms.

Ghost Liners: Exploring the World's Greatest Lost Ships by Robert Ballard

Not just the *Titanic* but the *Andrea Doria,* the *Lusitania,* and others, all lost at sea. Real-life photos of the sinkings, tales from survivors, and the "on the bottom of the ocean" shots for which Ballard is famous. Exciting writing about a topic kids love.

The Great Fire by Jim Murphy
> The story of the great Chicago fire of 1871. The author includes personal accounts of survivors as well as an understanding of the history of the Chicago fire to tell a gripping story of the enormity of this event.

Hill of Fire by Thomas P. Lewis
> An I Can Read Book based on reports of the eruption of Paricutin volcano on February 20, 1943. This was one of only two eruptions in recorded history where the birth of a volcano has been seen by human eyes.

The Secrets of Vesuvius by Sara Bisel
> Riveting prose and pictures of this famous disaster.

Tornado by Stephen Kramer
> Once again the author does not disappoint. As much information as one could ever desire about tornadoes coupled with compelling nonfiction writing makes this a must-have for classroom libraries.

Extraordinary Children

Nonfiction

Cracking the Wall: The Struggles of the Little Rock Nine by Eileen Lucas
> An easy-to-read version of the story of the first black students to attend the all-white Central High School in Little Rock, Arkansas. The afterword provides background on what happened to the students when then-governor Faubus closed all the Little Rock public high schools rather than integrate the schools.

Kids at Work: Lewis Hine and the Crusade Against Child Labor by Russell Freedman
> Photographs of children at work in factories, on the streets, and living in squalor are the same ones Lewis Hine used in his actual crusade against child labor many years ago. Excellent original sources and interviews allow students to use documents to learn about Hine's work.

Kids Explore Kids Who Make a Difference by the Westridge Young Writers Workshop
> Kids who have helped to fight pollution, worked to ban Nazi video games, or overcome illnesses or difficulties in their own lives are featured in this book written by kids in Colorado's Jefferson County schools. Also featured is Iqbal Masih, who worked as a child slave in Pakistan making carpets and eventually became known to the world when he spoke out about the plight of children working as bonded laborers.

Only Opal: The Diary of a Young Girl by Barbara Cooney
> Taken in by a family who views her as a servant, Opal appears to be an extraordinarily literate orphan, who befriends the animals and gives them sophisticated names based on the stories she heard from her parents. The picture book is based on an amazing journal Opal kept when she was just five or six years old.

Orphan Train Rider: One Boy's True Story by Andrea Warren
> Beginning in 1854 trains carried orphaned children to new homes in

the West and South. The story of Lee and his brothers, all adopted by
different families, illustrates how the boys overcame grief and fear at
losing their parents and being separated during their early years.
Excellent information about this historical movement, tied together as
the brothers are reunited as adults.

Witnesses to Freedom: Young People Who Fought for Civil Rights by Belinda
Rochelle
Recollections by students who organized sit-ins, integrated their schools,
and participated in boycotts. The courageous behavior of these young
people encourages others to work toward ending discrimination and
injustice. In-depth information about the March on Washington, Freedom
Schools, and other nonviolent aspects of the civil rights movement.

Baseball

Fiction

The Babe and I by David Adler
Babe Ruth's hitting streak helps one boy sell lots of newspapers as he
tries to help his needy family during the Great Depression.

Ballpark by Elisha Cooper
Small watercolor and pencil figures detail the many people, objects,
and events a child might see on a visit to the ballpark.

Baseball Ballerina by Kathryn Cristaldi
Much to her embarrassment, a young baseball-loving girl is forced to take
up ballet. All ends well when her team cheers her on at the dance recital,
and she realizes that baseball and ballet are not mutually exclusive.

Baseball Bob by William Joyce
The author's familiar dinosaur is recruited by the worst team in history
and leads them to a hometown victory.

The Bat Boy and His Violin by Gavin Curtis
Reginald loves to practice his violin but his dad, the manager of one of
the worst teams in the Negro leagues, needs a batboy. During down-
time in the dugout, Reginald plays classical music and the team's luck
begins to change.

Frank and Ernest Play Ball by Alexandra Day
These bear and elephant friends take another temporary job and give
us a unique form of language, this time armed with a dictionary of
baseball terms to help them manage the Mudcats.

Hooray for Snail by John Stadler
Snail, the slowest member of the team, nails a home run that flies to the
moon and back. Kids relate to Snail and love the story's humor.

Play Ball Amelia Bedelia by Peggy Parish
Everyone's favorite literal thinker joins a baseball team and, to the
delight of young readers, takes the game's instructions literally.

Nonfiction

Baseball, the American Epic series by Geoffrey Ward, Ken Burns, and Jim O'Connor
> A series of three extremely well written books based on the PBS series of the same name. The titles include *Shadow Ball: The History of the Negro Leagues in America, 25 Great Moments,* and *Who Invented the Game?* Great models for visualizing in reading and showing-not-telling in writing.

Baseball's Best: Five True Stories by Andre Gutelle
> The author tells the story of five of the greatest Hall of Famers of all time, including Babe Ruth, Joe DiMaggio, Jackie Robinson, Roberto Clemente, and Hank Aaron.

Baseball's Greatest Hitters (Step into Reading) by Jim Campbell
> An account of the five greatest hitters of the twentieth century. Great for second- and third-grade readers.

Baseball's Greatest Pitchers (Step into Reading) by Jim Campbell
> Campbell introduces the reader to five of the greatest pitchers of all time. Solid second- and third-grade reading.

Baseball Saved Us by Ken Mochizuki
> Based on the author's own experience, Japanese Americans interned during World War II organize a team and build a baseball diamond which provides a diversion during this sad period in their lives.

Lou Gehrig: The Luckiest Man by David Adler
> A wonderful picture book that tells the story of one of baseball's greatest and his struggle with the disease that now bears his name.

Take Me Out to the Ball Game by Jack Norworth
> An account of the historic 1947 World Series game between the New York Yankees and the Brooklyn Dodgers is set to the words of the classic song. The book ends with a note detailing the famous game.

Teammates by Peter Golenbock
> The remarkable story of the friendship between Jackie Robinson and Pee Wee Reese during the period when Jackie broke the Major League color barrier. Thought provoking and rich in diverse themes.

Poetry

At The Crack of the Bat: Baseball Poems compiled by Lillian Morrison
> More than forty illustrated old and new poems for baseball fans everywhere.

Baseball, Snakes and Summer Squash: Poems About Growing Up by Donald Graves
> A collection of poems that describes the experiences and adventures of a young boy growing up.

Casey at the Bat by Ernest Lawrence Thayer
> A recent edition of the classic story with soft acrylic illustrations that will capture the heart of any baseball fan.

The Sweet Diamond: Baseball Poems by Paul Janeczko
A wonderful collection of baseball poems from Paul Janeczko, who obviously loves the game.

The Arts: Fine Art, Music, Drama

Fine Art

Fiction

All I See by Cynthia Rylant
Young Charlie sneaks down to the lake every afternoon to watch an older painter. A friendship ensues that opens Charlie up to the notion of passion and painting what you love. A great book to get kids thinking about what they really care about, their passions.

The Art Lesson by Tomie de Paola
Tomie de Paola's autobiographical story of a young boy who couldn't wait to start school and have real art lessons only to find that he had to draw what everyone else did. The story serves as an important reminder about individual differences.

Bonjour, Mr. Satie by Tomie de Paola
This clever story about a traveling cat in the 1920s Paris of Gertrude Stein addresses the notion that one person's art (Picasso's) is not necessarily better than another's (Matisse's), only different.

The Great Art Adventure by Bob Knox
Touring the wacky Museum of World Art, two kids wander through *New Yorker* artist Knox's fun-loving parodies of fine art and a certain big city museum. The writer includes reproductions of original pieces of art with informative captions combined with whimsical illustrations of what the kids see as they make their way around.

Linnea in Monet's Garden by Christina Bjork
Mr. Bloom takes Linnea to Paris and then on to Giverny to see the paintings and garden home of Monet. On the way, he teaches Linnea about Monet and his work.

Lucy's Picture by Nicola Moon
All the kids in class are painting pictures, but Lucy chooses to do a textured collage instead to give to her grandfather. The reader discovers that Lucy's grandpa is blind; he can feel the texture in Lucy's creation. The notion that it is all right to be different pervades this story.

The Squiggle by Carol Lexa Schaefer
Beautiful Chinese brush painting illustrations printed on stock that has the feel of rice paper. When the last little girl in line sees a red ribbon on the sidewalk, her imagination runs away with her. A true celebration of art and imagination that will ring true for kids everywhere.

Nonfiction

Artist in Overalls: The Life of Grant Wood by John Duggleb
The story of Grant Wood's life and art, described with photographs and his own paintings, is visually appealing, and his life as a farmer, teacher, interior decorator, and many other things makes fascinating reading.

Diego by Jeanette Winter
The story of the famous Mexican muralist Diego Rivera, which speaks to his wonderful art as well as his love of country. The text is written in Spanish as well as English.

Josefina by Jeanette Winter
The author discovers Josefina Aguilar and her painted clay sculptures in Ocotlán, Mexico. This story about a remarkable woman and her folk art portrays Josefina's life as one steeped in art and tradition.

Leonardo da Vinci by Diane Stanley
The inspiring story of a poor, illegitimate child who grew up to be one of the most extraordinary minds the world has ever known. Diane Stanley's exceptional illustrations perfectly capture the time period in which he lived. A great book for research into the Renaissance.

The Little Painter of Sabana Grande by Patricia Maloney Markun
Based on a factual story. Fernando's teacher shows him how to mix colors from native plants in his Panamanian village, but he has no paper at home. He paints the adobe walls of his home and soon is asked to paint all the houses in the village. He grows up to be a beloved art teacher.

Lives of the Artists by Kathleen Krull
One of a series of nonfiction books about writers, musicians, presidents, and athletes, containing interesting short biographies of visual artists.

My Name Is Georgia by Jeanette Winter
Written in the first person from the perspective of Georgia O'Keeffe, this book describes her individuality. She always saw the world differently and always knew she wanted to be an artist. Stunning illustrations fill the book, which lends itself to visualizing.

Talking with Artists (2 volumes) by Pat Cummings
Twenty-four well-known children's book illustrators tell their personal stories and answer questions about their artistic process. Each portrait includes photographs of the artist, a piece of art created by the artist as a child, and an example of the illustrations she does today.

When Clay Sings by Byrd Baylor
Baylor's homage to the early Native American art of pottery making and drawing. Terrific illustrations capture the early history and art of the Anasazi, Hohokam, and Mimbre. Kids love to draw these images and use them to visualize what life was like for these artistic people.

A Young Painter: The Life and Paintings of Wang Yani—China's Extraordinary Young Artist by Zheng Zhensun and Alice Low

The story of an Chinese artistic prodigy who had painted over ten thousand pictures by the time she turned sixteen. A terrific book to integrate art into a study of China.

Series

Famous Artists series by Antony Mason
> The series introduces young readers to the world's most celebrated painters and sculptors, including Cezanne, Leonardo, Michaelangelo, Monet, Picasso, and Van Gogh. Reproductions of famous works are included in each book.

Music

Fiction

Little Lil and the Swing-Singing Sax by Libba Moore Gray
> Lil finds a way to retrieve her uncle's cherished saxophone after he hocks it to help the family through some tough financial times. A touching story about a little girl's ingenuity and dedication.

Summertime from Porgy and Bess by Ira Gershwin, George Gershwin, DuBose Heyward and Dorothy Heyward
> Beautiful illustrations by Mike Wimmer depict the artist's interpretation of the famous Gershwin song "Summertime." Readers will enjoy comparing their summertime experiences with the artist's and each other's.

What a Wonderful World by George David Weiss and Bob Thiele
> The lyrics of Louis Armstrong's signature song are combined with illustrations of children from many different backgrounds in a celebration of diversity and unity.

Nonfiction

Charlie Parker Played Be Bop by Chris Raschka
> Great illustrations and words like *boomba, bippity, boppity* fill this book for primary readers that celebrates the music of the great saxophonist Charlie Bird Parker. The rhythmic text is great for sensory imaging.

Duke Ellington: The Piano Prince and His Orchestra by Andrea Davis Pinkney
> Beautiful illustrations by Brian Pinkney complement a stunning text that traces the career and life of Edward Kennedy "Duke" Ellington, the piano player and bandleader extraordinaire.

If I Only Had a Horn: Young Louis Armstrong by Roxane Orgill
> Based on a true event in the musician's life. Young Louis Armstrong's dream comes true when his neighbors pitch in to buy him a used cornet. A stunning lesson in community.

Lives of the Musicians by Kathleen Krull
> One of a series of nonfiction books about artists, musicians, presidents, and athletes, this one includes interesting short biographies of musicians.

Mozart: Scenes from the Childhood of the Great Composer by Catherine Brighton
Written from the perspective of Mozart's sister, this book traces Mozart's childhood travels through Europe with his sister and his father. An excellent informational book for research on Mozart.

Reach for the Moon by Samantha Abeel
The thirteen-year-old author, a student who struggles with a learning disability, composes beautiful poems and stories that complement Charles's Murphy's watercolors.

Sebastian: A Book About Bach by Jeanette Winter
"The first Voyager space craft was launched in 1977. On the spacecraft there is a recording of sounds from Earth. Should the spacecraft encounter any life beyond our galaxy, the first sound that will be heard is the music of Johann Sebastian Bach." So begins Jeanette Winter's stunning book about the life and work of Bach. Truly extraordinary illustrations make this one of her best.

Drama

Fiction

Illustrated Tales from Shakespeare by Charles Lamb and Mary Lamb
A recent adaptation of the Lambs' classic *Tales of Shakespeare*. Fifteen of the best known plays are retold in prose form to capture the imaginations of young readers. A great way to lure readers to the Bard.

Macbeth by Bruce Coville
A riveting rendition of one of Shakespeare's greatest plays. The eerie illustrations and the compelling text make this a story young readers will want to read over and over.

Nonfiction

The Bard of Avon by Diane Stanley
Although little is known about the Millennium Man's background, Diane Stanley fills the reader in on what likely happened in the life of the Western world's greatest playwright. The illustrations give an accurate picture of life in Shakespeare's day.

The World of Shakespeare by Anna Claybourne and Rebecca Treays
Great information on the prolific playwright. Filled with terrific photographs and illustrations and culminating with a short synopsis of each play.

Literacy

Fiction

Amber on the Mountain by Tony Johnston
Amber's life high on a mountain has precluded school and reading. A girl moves in nearby, bringing the gift of reading and books to Amber,

who returns the gift of a simple mountain life. Kids burst with questions when they read it, and the message that you can do anything you want to if you put your mind to it is a powerful one for children of all ages.

Amelia's Notebook by Marissa Moss
Hand-lettered journal written by nine-year-old Amelia. Great for promoting journal writing, jotting thoughts and feelings, as well as selecting topics. The same author wrote *Rachel's Journal* and *Emma's Journal.*

Aunt Chip and the Great Cripple Creek Dam Affair by Patricia Polacco
Aunt Chip, the librarian who understands the consequences of too much TV and not enough books, saves a town seduced by television from a terrible plight. An enjoyable book that inspires lots of questions as to the resolution.

Book by George Ella Lyon
Beautiful language and illustrations. This poem compares a book to a house, a treasure chest, a farm, and a tree. A book, it seems, is anything you make it. Writers and readers will enjoy savoring the metaphorical language.

The Chalk Doll by Charlotte Pomerantz
Rose, sick in bed, gets her mother to tell story after story about growing up in Jamaica. One story leads to another—a great model for telling and writing family stories.

The Conversation Club by Diane Stanley
Peter Fieldmouse's new neighbors invite him to join their Conversation Club, but he decides to start a listening club after the first meeting where everyone talks at once and no one listens. Often used to introduce book clubs, to get kids thinking about listening as well as talking.

The Day of Ahmed's Secret by Florence Parry Heide and J. D. Gilliland
This story, set in Egypt, shows a very different life for a six-year-old boy than most American kids are used to. Ahmed works rather than going to school. But at the end of the day, he reveals his most important secret: he has learned to write his name. This book is an anchor text for questioning. Kids wonder about the secret as well as the foreign life of young Ahmed.

Edward and the Pirates by David McPhail
Edward, who learned to read in McPhail's earlier *Santa's Book of Names,* now reads everything in sight. One night the pirates come to life in Edward's imagination, and after some harrowing moments he discovers that what they really want is to be read to. A great book for visualizing.

Emily by Michael Bedard
The author's fictional account of a young girl who lives next door to the mysterious, "crazy" Emily Dickinson. Her meeting with the recluse changes her perspective. The poetic quality and striking language make the book effective for teaching visualizing. And readers have to infer the nature of this mysterious character from start to finish.

How to Get Famous in Brooklyn by Amy Hest
> The focus here is on a young journal writer who carries her notebook with her at all times to jot notes about the neighborhood. She observes the hair salon, the bagel shop, and so on. This provides a great example of writer as observer, one who comments on everyday experiences.

I Hate to Read by Rita Marshall
> A good book to read to early readers, particularly those who are not that thrilled with reading, since Victor hates to read. The characters come to life and lure him into the adventure of reading.

I'm in Charge of Celebrations by Byrd Baylor
> The main character celebrates each day by keeping a notebook of natural occurrences and celebrating each one. A great model for showing how writers keep notebooks and write short descriptive entries.

The Library by Sarah Stewart
> This book is an homage to book-loving librarians everywhere. Elizabeth Brown liked reading so much that she ran out of room for her books and donated them all to the public library in her ripe old age.

My Great-Aunt Arizona by Gloria Houston
> Great-Aunt Arizona inspires her students to imagine by reading books about places far away, letting us in on one of the great joys of reading—that it can take you anywhere.

Read for Me, Mama by Vashanti Rahaman
> Joseph loves library day at school, but when he asks his mom to read him one of his library books, he discovers she can't. A powerful story about community literacy and a loving relationship between a boy and his mom.

Santa's Book of Names by David McPhail
> Edward is in first grade and struggling to read. His teacher suggests testing. His wise mom suggests waiting. Edward learns to read when he's ready and has a purpose. This book reminds us that readers learn to read at different times. Great for those kids who think they may never read.

Thank You, Mr. Falker by Patricia Polacco
> In this stirring account of her own learning disability in childhood, Patricia Polacco reminds all teachers of the importance of teaching and caring about students. Every child deserves a teacher like Mr. Falker. Great book to give kids an idea of how hard work and loving support make a difference in life.

A Weave of Words by Robert San Souci
> A powerful prince discovers that even though he's rich and handsome, a beautiful young and very clever woman will not marry him unless he learns to read. In the end, her courage and his ability to read save the day.

The Wednesday Surprise by Eve Bunting
> In this touching book about teaching, learning, and adult literacy, Anna teaches her grandmother to read, surprising not only her dad for his

birthday but also the reader. The reader bursts with questions and infers the surprise at the end from clues in the text.

Wolf! by Becky Bloom

A hungry wolf learns to read. His role models: a duck, a pig, and a cow who are pleased that he chooses reading over eating! A play on an old story, with an important message.

Nonfiction

The Brontës by Catherine Brighton

This book invites the reader into the early lives of the four Bronte children, three of whom became world-famous writers. They recorded their childhood escapades in tiny elaborate books, some of which still survive today as early indications of the great novelists they would become.

Coming Home: From the Life of Langston Hughes by Floyd Cooper

The story of the early life of the renowned poet Langston Hughes, who grew up in poverty with absentee parents. Fortunately Langston lived with a loving grandmother who believed that everyone needs heroes, so she read to him and told him stories.

Grass Sandals: The Travels of Basho by Dawnine Spivak

The story of Basho, the most loved poet in the history of Japan, who traveled around his homeland on foot, observing nature and writing haiku. Characters of the Japanese alphabet fill the text.

Lives of the Writers by Kathleen Krull

One of a series of nonfiction books about artists, musicians, presidents, and athletes, this one includes interesting short biographies of nineteen writers.

Speaking of Journals: Children's Book Writers Talk About Their Diaries, Notebooks, and Sketchbooks by Paula Graham

A must-have book that allows readers and writers of all ages to take a peek at the journals of several dozen writers. Through interviews and written samples, the reader can explore the nature of journal and notebook writing.

Tomas and the Library Lady by Pat Mora

This book was inspired by the life of Tomas Rivera, who spent his early life moving from town to town in a migrant family. Tomas was befriended by a librarian who introduced him to the world of reading and books. Rivera eventually became a successful educator and the chancellor of the University of California at Riverside. His story is a testament to the importance of educators and librarians everywhere.

A Writer's Notebook: Unlocking the Writer Within You by Ralph Fletcher

The author describes how to keep a record of "dreams, feelings, and thoughts" that might someday turn into a written piece.

Short Text Collections

Fiction

The Blue Hill Meadows by Cynthia Rylant
> Four short segments that each tell a story set in a different season about the simple adventures of Willie Meadow, a boy growing up in the Blue Hills of Virginia.

The Circuit: Stories from the Life of a Migrant Child by Francisco Jimenez
> Award-winning collection of short stories and vignettes written from the point of view of a child in a migrant family. A portrait of a difficult but loving and interesting family life. Themes include family closeness, feeling alienated and lonely in school, and childhood struggles adapting to a new language and culture.

Dateline: Troy by Paul Fleischman
> By juxtaposing newspaper clippings of modern day events with a retelling of the Trojan War story, the author points out many parallels between Homer's classic story and the present day.

Every Living Thing by Cynthia Rylant
> A group of stories with animals at the center. Kids often connect these stories to their own experiences, making this an anchor text for the connection strategy.

The Future Telling Lady and Other Stories by James Berry
> Stories from the Caribbean provide a picture of life there and an illustration of the tales people tell. One story that prompts a lot of questions tells of ghosts that inhabit the island, relics from colonial years who return each Sunday to picnic in their favorite spot and who are the ancestors of a young girl who discovers them one day.

Hey World, Here I Am! by Jean Little
> Vignettes that trace the thoughts and feelings of preadolescent Kate Bloomfield. Great for activating prior knowledge and making connections.

Leaving Home selected by Hazel Rochman and Darlene McCampbell
> Stories from authors as diverse as Amy Tan, Sandra Cisneros, Tim O'Brien, Gary Soto, and Norma Fox Mazer tell of the "perilous journeys" of leaving home. Each story is a glimpse into personal discoveries about growing up and away from childhood homes, wherever they may be. Excellent for middle school students.

Out of the Dust by Karen Hesse
> Written in free-verse poetry, this Newbery award-winning novel tells the story of Billie Joe, a strong heroine who confronts a life of misery during the Oklahoma Dust Bowl and begins to transcend it.

Owl at Home by Arnold Lobel
> Five endearing stories about an owl who lives at home and gets mixed up in all kinds of predicaments. With simple vocabulary that young readers can read on their own.

The Stories Julian Tells by Ann Cameron
> Julian is a heck of a storyteller and he can make everyone, especially his younger brother Huey, believe just about anything he says. But these tall tales sometimes get Julian, Huey, and their best friend Gloria into big trouble. The sequel, *More Stories Julian Tells,* doesn't disappoint.

The Van Gogh Cafe by Cynthia Rylant
> A girl and her father run a small cafe in Flowers, Kansas. Magic appears one day in the form of a possum, and things are never quite the same from that moment on. Each story stands alone but leads to the next with the last line of each chapter. This provides a great opportunity for readers to practice their inferential thinking skills.

Nonfiction

The Air Down Here: True Tales from a South Bronx Boyhood by Gil C. Alicea
> These stories of growing up in the South Bronx provide insight into the mind and emotions of a teenager. Family illness, school struggles, gang life and drugs, and Gil's relationship with his father are a part of his life.

A Summer Life by Gary Soto
> This series of short pieces and autobiographical vignettes explores life growing up in Fresno. Soto has recently written up some of these experiences in picture books like *Too Many Tamales.*

Poetry

The Music of What Happens: Poems that Tell Stories by Paul Janeczko
> Poetic narratives about people, events, issues, and ideas permeate this collection of poems that tell stories. Great for middle school kids.

Near the Window Tree: Poems and Notes by Karla Kuskin
> A collection of poems that all kids can relate to. The author inserts personal comments that explain how her poems emerge from her own experience.

Neighborhood Odes by Gary Soto
> Poems about growing up Latino in Fresno, California. Odes to sprinklers, tennis shoes, and raspados portray everyday life as seen through the eyes of a preadolescent boy.

The Place My Words Are Looking For selected by Paul Janeczko
> Thirty-nine of our leading poets share their poems as well as their thoughts and recollections about their inspirations and their lives.

Waiting to Waltz: A Childhood by Cynthia Rylant
> A collection of thirty poems about a girl growing up in a small Appalachian town.

Adult Text Sets

History and Current Issues

Bury My Heart at Wounded Knee: An Indian History of the American West by Dee Brown
A fully documented account of the systematic destruction of the American Indian culture during the end of the nineteenth century. Considered shocking and shameful when it was first published in 1971, the book brought considerable attention to the tragic history of Native Americans.

Certain Trumpets: The Call of Leaders by Garry Wills
A thoughtful examination from the Pulitzer Prize winner of what makes a good leader. The author describes sixteen categories of leadership and gives one exemplar of each and one ante-type who lacks leadership qualities.

Cold Mountain by Charles Frazier
The National Book Award winner tells the saga of a confederate soldier who journeys back to his home in the Blue Ridge Mountains at the end of the Civil War. The reader lives through Inman's long walk home and experiences the devastation of war.

From Beirut to Jerusalem by Thomas L. Friedman
An expansive look at the history of the Middle East beginning with the immigration of Jewish settlers from Russia to Palestine in the late 1800s and culminating with the peace process in the 1980s. Ten years later the author's insights still hold true.

Germs, Guns, and Steel: The Fates of Human Societies by Jared Diamond
In this book of broad scope, the author looks at "geography, demography and ecological happenstance" to explain the origins of western dominance in the world today.

The Killer Angels by Michael Shaara
A fictional account of the Battle of Gettysburg that changes the traditional textbook view of what actually happened in this battle.

Lincoln at Gettysburg: The Words That Remade America by Garry Wills
Garry Wills researches and interprets the Gettysburg Address as Abraham Lincoln meant it in this Pulitzer Prize winner. According to

the author, Lincoln used the 272 words of the Gettsyburg Address to change the course of history.

Night by Elie Wiesel

The account of Nobel Laureate Elie Wiesel's attempt to find meaning in the horror of the Holocaust is based closely on his own experiences in Nazi concentration camps.

A Night to Remember by Walter Lord

In this gripping, factual account of the tragedy of the *Titanic,* the author conveys the drama in human terms.

Seven Years in Tibet by Heinrich Harrer

Originally published in 1953, this book tells the story of Austrian mountaineer Heinrich Harrer's escape into the remote country of Tibet where he eventually became the tutor of the teenage Dalai Lama.

The Things They Carried: A Work of Fiction by Tim O'Brien

Described as novel, short story, and memoir all in one, this work of fiction weaves together the personal histories and experiences of a group of men who fought in the Vietnam War. Stories of growing up, the dilemma of going to Vietnam or leaving for Canada, and the war and its aftermath are told from different perspectives. The title, of course, is a metaphor for the courage, determination and frailties human beings bring to any dangerous journey.

Undaunted Courage: Meriwether Lewis, Thomas Jefferson, and the Opening of the American West by Stephen Ambrose

The history of the Lewis and Clark Expedition is described through the eyes of Meriwether Lewis with excerpts and sketches from his personal journal. Provides great background on the exploration of North America.

Science and Technology

Arctic Dreams by Barry Lopez

A look at the striking natural history of the Arctic, a place where icebergs are the "size of Cleveland" and "polar bears fly down out of the stars." The author explores the natural and human history of a part of the world that is not as desolate as we all assume.

Data Smog: Surviving the Information Glut by David Shenk

The author explains how the barrage of information we experience each day causes confusion and leads to problems such as "social fragmentation, the decline of educational standards and the breakdown of democracy." He proposes a number of solutions including suggestions on how to filter too much data.

Desert Solitaire by Edward Abbey

A deeply personal, poetic account of the author's three years in the Canyonlands of Utah. In this passionate tribute to the desert, the author laments the commercialization of this pristine environment.

The Double Helix by James D. Watson
> The story of the race to unravel the mysteries of genetic structure illustrates that science is about politics and intrigue as well as hard work and brilliance. Two young scientists, Watson and Crick, figured out the structure of DNA by experimenting with an erector set and beat Linus Pauling to the Nobel Prize.

The Great Bridge: The Epic Story of the Building of the Brooklyn Bridge by David McCullough
> The epic story of John Roebling and his family's determination to build a bridge connecting Manhattan and Brooklyn in the mid-1800s. Full of interesting personal, historical, and technical details about this remarkable feat of engineering.

How the Mind Works by Steven Pinker
> Written in an entertaining and compelling way, this book explains what the mind is, how it works, and how it allows us to think and feel.

The Illustrated Longitude: The True Story of a Lone Genius Who Solved the Greatest Scientific Problem of His Time by Dava Sobel and William J. H. Andrewes
> This book is as much a story of mystery as of science. While everyone else was trying to figure out how to calculate longitude from the stars, John Harrison took a different tack, saying, "Let's just make a better clock." Voila, it worked.

A Natural History of the Senses by Diane Ackerman
> In this book, divided into five sections according to each of the senses, Ackerman investigates a wide range of natural phenomena such as kissing, pain, and sneezing, and discusses them in novel ways.

Oranges by John McPhee
> In a compelling book written as only the great nonfiction writer John McPhee could, the author explores every aspect of the orange: its botany, history, and the nature of the orange industry. Full of interesting tidbits, this book reads like a novel.

The Quotable Einstein collected and edited by Alice Calaprice
> This is a collection of over 500 quotes from the great physicist. Einstein, a prolific and gifted writer, never disappoints when sharing his brilliant and sometimes quirky thinking.

Satellite Atlas of the World by Carl Mehler
> Gorgeous three-dimensional satellite photograph maps explore the mountains, the deserts, the oceans, and everything in between. The text describes how natural forces and humans affect life on earth.

Ship Fever by Andrea Barrett
> The author, a scientist by training, blends nineteenth-century history with science to give us eight short stories about the natural world. This book won the National Book Award.

"Surely You're Joking, Mr. Feynman!" by Richard Feynman
> The Nobel Laureate, Richard Feynman, shares his life story culminating

with his involvement in the Manhattan Project. The quirky physicist delights readers with his genius and sense of humor.

Refuge: An Unnatural History of Family and Place by Terry Tempest Williams
The writer interweaves the sad story of her mother's impending death from breast cancer with the tale of the rise of the Great Salt Lake that in turn threatened the wildlife refuge that she so dearly loved.

What Do You Care What Other People Think? Further Adventures of a Curious Character by Richard Feynman
Feynman continues his life story focusing on his tenure as a member of the space shuttle Challenger commission and his discovery of the cause of the disaster.

Literacy

Better than Life by Daniel Pennac
This book about the joys of reading sold over 300,000 copies when it was first published in France. Now translated into English, it describes how the love of reading begins, how it is sometimes lost, and how to retrieve it.

Bird by Bird: Some Instructions on Writing and Life by Anne Lamont
The author's father once told her ten-year-old brother who was struggling with a school report on birds to just take it "bird by bird, buddy." The author never loses her wonderful sense of humor as she encourages people to sit down in the chair and take a crack at writing.

Booknotes: America's Finest Authors on Reading, Writing, and the Power of Ideas by Brian Lamb
This book is a compilation of conversations about writing between Brian Lamb, the host of the CSPAN program, and a variety of famous authors.

Childtimes by Eloise Greenfield
Short vignettes from the writer and her extended family. Small and large events of childhood are especially useful as models for children's own personal narrative writing.

Dear Genius by Ursula Nordstrum, edited by Leonard S. Marcus
In a compelling look at children's book publishing, the editor presents years of correspondence between perhaps the finest children's book editor of all time and her beloved authors and illustrators, many of whom referred to her simply as Genius.

E. B. White: Some Writer! by Beverly Gherman
A glimpse into the life and mind of one of our greatest American writers.

Elements of Style by William Strunk and E. B. White
If you buy one book on how to write, this should be it!

The Friendly Shakespeare by Norrie Epstein
Epstein's book is full of interesting facts and details of each play, the

characters, and the most famous productions. This book brings Shakespeare into the twentieth century. Irresistible!

A Hope in the Unseen: An American Odyssey from the Inner City to the Ivy League by Ron Suskind
Based on a Pulitzer Prize–winning series in the *Wall Street Journal*, the story of Cedric Jennings' journey from an inner-city high school in Washington, DC, to Brown University points out our country's glaring educational inequities. Cedric's determined mother makes all the difference in his ability to bridge two worlds.

How Reading Changed My Life by Anna Quindlen
The Pulitzer Prize–winning writer offers her take on a life filled with books by sharing how much they have meant to her. She includes lists of her favorites at the end.

If You Want to Write by Brenda Ueland
When this book was first published in 1938, Carl Sandburg called it the best book ever written on writing. The author explains that whatever you write you must "be sure that your imagination and love are behind it."

Interview by Claudia Dreifus
The journalist Claudia Dreifus interviews people she categorizes as saints, philosophers, "media phreaks," and poets, including such varied personalities as the Dalai Lama, Kareem Abdul-Jabbar, and Cokie Roberts.

On Writing Well: An Informal Guide to Writing Nonfiction by William Zinsser
Written like a novel, one of the best books ever written on the art of nonfiction writing offers tips that bring the genre to life.

One Writer's Beginnings by Eudora Welty
The famous author shares her early love of reading and the impact a life of literacy has had on her writing.

Ruined by Reading by Lynn Sharon Schwartz
A passionate, personal essay on the significance of reading to the formation of the author's sense of self. Stories of the author's childhood are interspersed with her memories of well-loved books that made a difference in her life.

Talk: NPR's Susan Stamberg Considers All Things by Susan Stamberg
In this compilation, Susan Stamberg interviews anyone and everyone from John Ehrlichman to Alden Whitman, the *New York Times* obituary writer.

Wordstruck: A Memoir by Robert MacNeil
Robert MacNeil, retired anchor of the MacNeil Lehrer NewsHour, describes an early life steeped in wonderful language and literature. He attributes his way with words to those early experiences.

Writing Down the Bones by Natalie Goldberg
In short two- or three-page segments, the writer shows us how she uses

her experience in Zen meditation to help convey her own writing
process with humor and zest.

The Writing Life by Annie Dillard
  The Boston Globe calls this book "a kind of spiritual Strunk and
  White." If you want to know what it feels like to live as a writer, read
  this book.

Writing Toward Home by Georgia Heard
  Georgia Heard gently guides readers through the process of getting
  started on their own writing. Her own well-crafted vignettes serve as
  jumping off points to get writers going.

Magazines and Newspapers for Kids and Young Adults

Calliope: World History for Young People
Cobblestone Publishing, 30 Grove Street, Peterborough, NH 03458

Click
The Cricket Magazine Group, P.O. Box 7434, Red Oak, IA 51591-0434

Cobblestone: The History Magazine for Young People
Cobblestone Publishing, 30 Grove Street, Peterborough, NH 03458

Contact Kids
Children's Television Workshop, 1 Lincoln Plaza, New York, NY 10023

Cricket
The Cricket Magazine Group, P.O. Box 7434, Red Oak, IA 51591-0434

Dolphin Log
Cousteau Society, 870 Greenbrier Circle, Chesapeake, VA 23320

Dramatics: The Magazine for Students and Teachers of Theatre
Educational Theater Association, 3368 Central Parkway, Cincinnati, OH 45225

Faces: People, Places, Cultures
Cobblestone Publishing, 30 Grove Street, Peterborough, NH 03458

Highlights for Children
Box 269, Columbus, OH 43216-0269

Junior Scholastic
Scholastic Inc., 555 Broadway, New York, NY 10012-3999

Kids Discover
170 Fifth Avenue, New York, NY 10010

Literary Cavalcade
Scholastic Inc., 555 Broadway, New York, NY 10012-3999

Muse
The Cricket Magazine Group, P.O. Box 7434, Red Oak, IA 51591-0434

National Geographic
National Geographic Society, 17th and M Streets N.W., Washington, DC 20036

National Geographic World
National Geographic Society, 17th and M Streets N.W., Washington, DC 20036

Ranger Rick
National Wildlife Federation, 8925 Leesburg Pike, Vienna, VA 22184-0001

Scholastic News
Scholastic Inc., 555 Broadway, New York, NY 10012-3999

Smithsonian
Smithsonian Institute, 900 Jefferson Drive S.W., Washington, DC 20560

Sports Illustrated for Kids
Time Inc., Time-Life Building, 1271 Avenue of the Americas, New York, NY 10020-1393

Time for Kids
Time Inc., Time-Life Building, 1271 Avenue of the Americas, New York, NY 10020-1393

Tomorrow's Morning: News Stories for Kids
125 South Barrington Place, Los Angeles, CA 90049

Weekly Reader
Box 120023, Stamford, CT 06912-0023

Wild Outdoor World
Rocky Mountain Elk Foundation, Box 1249, Helena, MT 59624

Wildlife Conservation
Wildlife Conservation Park, Bronx, NY 10460

Zillions (Consumer Reports for Kids)
Consumers Union, 101 Truman Ave, Yonkers, NY 10703-1057

Zoobooks
Wildife Education Ltd., 9820 Willow Creek Road, San Diego, CA 92131-1112

Professional Journals for Selection of Children's Books

Book Links: Connecting Books, Libraries, and Classrooms

American Library Association, 50 East Huron Street, Chicago, IL 60611-2795

Intended for librarians and teachers, the articles contain information on children's books and ways to incorporate children's books into the curriculum. Articles include annotated bibliographies of picture books and fiction and nonfiction books with recommended grade level. *Book Links* recently began including Web sites related to children's interests. Online version, accessed through ALA's Web site, www.ala.org, has selected articles as well as archived listing of *Book Links* articles beginning with September 1998 issue. Six issues per year.

Booklist

American Library Association, 50 East Huron Street, Chicago, IL 60611-2795

Reviews more than 2,500 recommended fiction and nonfiction children's books and audiovisual materials a year. Feature articles include columns, author interviews, bibliographies, and book-related essays. "Editors' Choice," top picks of books and videos from the previous year, are published once a year. *Booklist* online includes a cumulative index not offered in print. Published semimonthly (twenty-four issues per year).

Bulletin, Center for Children's Books

Publications Office, Graduate School of Library and Information Science, University of Illinois at Urbana-Champaign, 501 East Daniel Street, Champaign, IL 61820-6211

Reviews feature critical annotations of selected new titles on content, reading level, strengths and weaknesses, and curricular uses. Titles are given one of four ratings, with outstanding books starred. Each issue is indexed by genre, subject, and curricular uses. "Bulletin Blue Ribbons," published annually, is a selection of the year's best books. The July issue includes annual index arranged by subject, title, and author. Published monthly except August.

The Horn Book Guide to Children's and Young Adult Books
> Horn Book Inc., 11 Beacon Street, Boston, MA 02108-3017
> Published by *Horn Book Magazine* in January and July, the *Guide* contains critical annotations of recently published children's hardcover books. Fiction books arranged by grade level and genre, nonfiction books arranged by Dewey classification. Annotated reviews are rated from 1 to 6, with 6 being the highest rating. Author, illustrator, subject, and series indexes make this a valuable resource for selection of children's books. Published twice a year.

Horn Book Magazine: Recommending Books for Children and Young Adults
> Horn Book Inc., 11 Beacon Street, Boston, MA 02108-3017
> Features literary articles about and by children's authors and about issues related to children's literature. Signed critical reviews are of recommended fiction and nonfiction titles; all are subject to the qualifications in the notes. Annotated titles include fiction, arranged by genre, and nonfiction, arranged by Dewey classification. Titles that a majority of the reviewers believe to be outstanding are starred. Published six times a year.

The New Advocate
> Christopher-Gordon Publishers, 1502 Providence Highway, Suite 12, Norwood, MA 02062-4643
> Through articles on thematic studies, teaching strategies, and research on current topics, *The New Advocate* demonstrates how literature is an integral part of the work with children. Bibliographies of recommended literature, both fiction and nonfiction, accompany each article. Published four times a year.

The Reading Teacher
> International Reading Association, 800 Barksdale Road, Box 8139, Newark, DE 19714-8139
> Professional journal with articles considering practices, issues, and trends in literacy education and related fields. Articles include bibliographies of children's books cited. Each issue features an annotated section on children's books, usually thematically selected. Published eight times a year.

School Library Journal: The Magazine of Children, Young Adults, and School Librarians
> Reed Elsevier Business Information, 249 West 17th Street, New York, NY 10011, subscriptions to Box 57559, Boulder, CO 80322-7559
> Feature articles on timely topics directed to public and school librarians. Numerous titles are reviewed in each issue. Reviewers are contracted by SLJ, and reviews are individual opinions subject to editor's approval. Titles are organized into preschool through fourth-grade fiction and nonfiction, and fifth-grade through eighth-grade fiction and nonfiction. Starred reviews are listed in each issue. The March issue

features "Notable Books for Children," selected from books published the previous year. Published eleven times a year.

Science and Children

National Science Teachers Association, 1840 Wilson Boulevard, Arlington, VA 22201

Well-written articles are useful for teachers of science and include bibliography of books used with students. The March issue features "Outstanding Trade Books" published the previous year. Annotated bibliography categories include biography, life science, and earth science with suggested grade levels for each title. Published eight times a year.

Response Options for Each Strategy

Making Connections

Oral Responses

Discussion

- ◆ Small-group or whole-class discussion about various types of connections we make when we read

Verbal Responses

- ◆ "That reminds me of…"
- ◆ "I have a connection…"
- ◆ "Remember when…"

Written Responses

Text Codes

- ◆ R, reminds me of (student writes a brief explanation on a sticky note)
- ◆ T-S, text-to-self connection
- ◆ T-T, text-to-text connection
- ◆ T-W, text-to-world connection
- ◆ BK, background knowledge (brief explanation on a sticky note)
- ◆ PE, prior experience (brief explanation on a sticky note)

Two-Column Note Forms

- ◆ Quote or Picture from Text/My Connection
- ◆ What the Text Is About/What It Reminds Me Of
- ◆ Words in the Text/My Personal Connection
- ◆ Words in the Text/My Connection to Another Text
- ◆ Words in the Text/My Connection to an Issue, Event, or Person

Other Response

- ◆ Response page with the top half left blank for an illustration of the connection and the bottom half lined for a short written explanation

Text-to-Self Connections

While reading, highlight or mark a sentence or two where you connect your own life to the text. Think about your past experiences and prior knowledge. In the space below, copy the words or explain or draw the picture, and write down your connection.

Quote or Picture from Text

This reminds me of…

Quote or Picture from Text

This reminds me of…

Adapted from Tovani (in press).

Text-to-Text Connections

While reading, highlight or mark a sentence or two where you connect one piece of text to another. It could be a book, an article, a movie, a script or song, or anything that is written down. In the space below, copy the words or explain or draw the picture, and write down your connection.

Quote or Picture from Text

This reminds me of…

Quote or Picture from Text

This reminds me of...

Adapted from Tovani (in press).

From *Strategies That Work: Teaching Comprehension to Enhance Understanding* by Stephanie Harvey and Anne Goudvis. Copyright © 2000. Stenhouse Publishers, York, Maine.

Text-to-World Connections

While reading, highlight or mark a sentence or two where you connect an event, person, or issue to the text. In the space below, copy the words or explain or draw the picture, and write down your connection.

Quote or Picture from Text

This reminds me of…

Quote or Picture from Text

This reminds me of…

Adapted from Tovani (in press).

From *Strategies That Work: Teaching Comprehension to Enhance Understanding* by Stephanie Harvey and Anne Goudvis. Copyright © 2000. Stenhouse Publishers, York, Maine.

MAKING CONNECTIONS

OLIVER BUTTON IS A SISSY by Tomie de Paola

When we read stories we make connections to our own experiences = TEXT-TO-SELF CONNECTIONS (t-s) = and to other books we've read = TEXT-TO-TEXT CONNECTIONS (t-t) = These are some connections we made while reading Oliver Button is a Sissy:

(t-t) Oliver Button is a Sissy reminds me of Amazing Grace because they both liked to dress up. (Rosa)

(t-t) Oliver Button reminds me of when I tried out for Little League and couldn't hit the ball and kids teased me. (Ann)

(t-s) It reminds me of playing soccer because there are only two girls on our team. (Claire)

(t-s) In preschool there were some 5th graders who would pick on a little boy, just like the boys who picked on Oliver. (Lucas)

(t-s) It reminds me of when this boy took my sweater and ran away with it and passed it to his friends and wouldn't give it back to me. (Jacob)

(t-t) Oliver keeps practicing dance even though the boys teased him, just like in Amazing Grace when Grace kept practicing to be Peter Pan even though kids told her she couldn't. (McKenna)

(t-s) Kids teased me when I was little. (Jonathan)

(t-s) In my sister's dance class there is only one boy and he gets to be the main character in her recitals. (Claire)

Questioning

Oral Responses

Discussions
- Discussion that focuses on searching for an answer to a specific question
- A "what do you wonder?" discussion

Verbal Responses
- "I wonder…"
- "How come…"
- "Why…"
- "I'm confused…"
- "I don't get it…"

Written Responses

Text Codes
- ?, question that reader has (noted briefly on a sticky note)
- C, confused
- Huh?, confused

Two-Column Note Forms
- Quote or Picture from Text/My Question
- What the Text Is About/What It Makes Me Wonder About
- What I Know/What I Wonder
- What I Learned/What I Wonder
- Questions/Facts

Three-Column Note Forms
- What I Know/What I Wonder/What I Want to Know
- Facts/Questions/Response
- Questions Before Reading/Questions After a First Reading/Questions After a Second Reading

Other Responses
- Question of the Day. Each day, challenge a different student to come up with a sincere question about a topic under study. Class members and teachers work together to answer it.
- Question Webs (see Chapter 7)
- Ongoing list of burning questions for the class to ponder

Asking Questions

While reading, highlight or mark a part of the text or picture where you have a question. Write down the part that surfaces your question and then record your question below. If you think you are headed toward an answer, share that too.

Quote or Picture from Text

My Question

Possible Answers

Quote or Picture from Text

My Question

Possible Answers

Asking Questions Throughout the Reading Process

Readers ask questions before, during, and after reading. Look at the cover and read the title, record any questions you might have before you start to read. While reading, highlight or mark a part of the text or picture where you have a question and record your question below. When you finish reading, write down any remaining questions. If you have answered any questions, record your answers in the space below.

Questions Before Reading

Questions During Reading

Questions After Reading

Possible Answers

Questioning

We read the story
ELISABETH, by Claire Nivola.

As we listened, we wondered about things that were happening in the story and asked lots of questions.

Is that turtle real?
Why did the soldiers watch their house?
Why did they have to leave everything behind?
Couldn't she have grabbed her doll?
Why did they have to leave so fast?
Did this really happen?
Was the doll really Elisabeth?
Why couldn't they ever go back?
Why, if the family was German, did they have to leave Germany?

NEXT, we checked to see if we had answered some of our questions. We could answer some of them, but we needed more information to answer others.

Question   <u>Yes</u>   <u>No</u>   <u>We need more information</u>

• Why did they have to leave so fast?
   The story didn't tell us — maybe
   because of a war because there were   ✓
   soldiers.

• Did this really happen?
   We noticed on the front flap that
   there was a photograph of Ruth (the   ✓
   author's mother) with Elisabeth. That
   means it <u>did</u> happen.

• Was that doll really Elisabeth?
   The teeth marks from where the dog   ✓
   dragged it told us it was the same doll.

Visualizing

Oral Responses

Discussion
- Discussion about how words in the text make pictures in the mind
- Discussion about showing not telling in writing and how it links to visualizing

Verbal Responses
- "I get a picture in my mind..."
- "I can see it..."
- "It's like a movie in my head..."
- "I visualized..."

Written Responses

Text Codes
- V, visualized (reader writes a few words or draws briefly on a sticky note the pictures she visualizes)
- P (or drawing of an eye), picture
- T (or drawing of a tongue), taste
- Sm (or drawing of a nose), smell
- Tch (or drawing of a hand), touch

Two-Column Note Forms
- Quote or Picture from Text/My Mental Image
- What the Text Is About/What I See
- Words on the Page/Picture in My Mind
- Words on the Page/My Mental Map of What Happened

Three-Column Note Form
- Words on the Page/Picture in My Mind/My Personal Response

Other Responses
- Listening to a recording of sounds that stimulate certain images—slapping ocean waves and chirping sea gulls or honking horns and noisy cars on city streets—and then fixing the image in the mind to recall the concept at a later time
- Drawing what is visualized after hearing a tape as described above
- Drawing what is visualized when reading
- Listening to music and describing what is visualized
- Drawing the movie in the reader's mind—a sequence of drawings that convey the mental images the reader creates from text
- "Sketch to stretch." Kids fold a paper into four parts. As the teacher reads aloud, kids draw the movie in their mind, a different frame in each quadrant.

Visualizing

While reading, highlight or mark a sentence or two where you get a clear picture in your mind that enhances your understanding of the text. In the space below, copy the words from the text and write down or draw what you visualize.

Quote from Text

What I Visualize

Quote from Text

What I Visualize

Adapted from Tovani (in press).

VISUALIZING

We read poetry out loud together. We listened to the words and created pictures in our minds to go with the words. Then we drew our pictures — and some of us wrote our own poem!

The white clouds and dark clouds are coming together. They <u>all</u> rain.

by Brayden

A shooting star
Flies through
The sky.
Over the world.
And it's gone
In a minute.

by McKenna

Inferring

Oral Responses

Discussion
◆ Discussion about themes

Verbal responses
◆ "I think…"
◆ "Maybe it means…"
◆ "I'm guessing that…"
◆ "I predict…"

Written Responses

Text Codes
◆ I, inference (student writes a brief explanation on a sticky note)
◆ P, prediction
◆ +, inference or prediction is confirmed by the text
◆ –, inference or prediction is contradicted by the text
◆ TH, theme

Two-Column Note Forms
◆ Quote or Picture from Text/Inference
◆ Facts/Inferences
◆ Questions/Inferences
◆ What I Think/ Support for That Idea
◆ Words in the Text/Theme(s)
◆ Plot/Theme(s)
◆ Theme(s)/Response
◆ Words in the Text/Prediction of What Will Happen

Three-Column Note Forms
◆ Picture or Quote from the Text/Inference/My Personal Response
◆ Facts/Questions/Inferences
◆ An Unfamiliar Word/My Inference/Confirmation
◆ Words in the Text/Prediction/Confirmed or Contradicted

Other Responses
◆ "Charades" requires more inferential thinking than just about any game we can think of, and kids love it.
◆ Taking turns reading faces and body language. We make inferences about a person's feelings based on their body language and facial expressions. When a teacher feigns crying, kids are likely to infer sadness.
◆ Drawing inferences about unusual items (such as in the kitchen utensil lesson in Chapter 3).

Inferential Thinking

While reading, highlight or mark a sentence or picture with I when you make an inference. Write down the sentence or describe the picture that surfaces your inference, and then record your inference below.

Quote or Picture from Text

My Inference

Quote or Picture from Text

My Inference

Adapted from Tovani (in press).

Inferring Themes

While reading, highlight or mark a sentence or picture with TH for theme when you come upon one of the bigger ideas in the story. Themes stir emotions. Write down the sentence or describe the picture that makes you infer a theme, write the theme below, and explain how it makes you feel and why.

Quote or Picture from Text

The Bigger Idea or Theme

How It Makes Me Feel and Why

Predicting

While reading, highlight or mark a sentence or picture with P when you find yourself making a prediction. Write down the sentence or describe the picture that spurs your prediction, and then record your prediction below. After finishing reading, note whether your prediction was confirmed or contradicted by checking the box. Explain what finally happened at the bottom of the page.

Quote or Picture from Text

Prediction

Prediction Confirmed ☐
Prediction Contradicted ☐

What Happened

Inferring

REDCOATS AND PETTICOATS
by Katherine Kirkpatrick

Facts	Questions	Inferences
• The mother is acting funny — washing laundry all the time.	• Why? What's going on?	• Maybe the laundry
• Father in prison		
• The mother went to her parents with a letter.	• What did the letter say? What was it for?	• Maybe the letter was a message to the British.
• Mother took a letter to the prison ship.	• Was father still OK?	
• The father was let go from the prison ship.	• Did they really trade vegetables for the father?	• At the end of the story we thought the letter from the mother's parents (Tories) probably helped save the father from prison.
	• What would happen to a spy if she was caught?	

Important things we learned from this book...
- Some families were Loyalist and Patriots.
- Spies had to be careful — mother kept the signals a secret.
- Kids like Thomas could help win the Revolutionary War.
- The British had prison ships for keeping prisoners.
- The father had to hide, even though he got out of prison.

Determining Importance

Oral Responses

Discussion

◆ Discussion about content

Verbal Response

◆ "This is really important…"

Written Responses

Text Codes

◆ I, important
◆ L, learned something new
◆ *, interesting or important information or fact
◆ Aha!, big idea surfaces
◆ S, surprising
◆ S!!!, shocking
◆ !!!, exciting

Two-Column Note Forms

◆ Topic/Details
◆ Words from the Text/Important Information
◆ Words from the Text/Important Ideas
◆ What's Interesting/What's Important
◆ Opinion/Proof from the Text
◆ Theme/Evidence for Theme
◆ Important Event/Evidence from the Text
◆ Characters' Motivation/Evidence from the Text

Three-Column Note Forms

◆ Facts/Questions/Response
◆ Topic/Details/Response
◆ Evidence For/Evidence Against/Personal Opinion

Determining Important Information

While reading, highlight or mark a picture or part of the text with * when you come to an important part you want to remember. Write down the piece of the text or describe or draw the picture that gives you this important information and note it under important information. Describe why it's important for you to remember and how you might help yourself remember it.

Quote or Picture from Text

Important Information

Why It Is Important

How Can I Remember It?

Determining Important Ideas

While reading, highlight or mark a picture or part of the text with ∗ when you come to an important idea you want to remember. Write down the piece of the text or describe or draw the picture that gives you this important idea and note it under important ideas. Describe why it's important for you to remember and how you might help yourself remember it.

Quote or Picture from Text

Important Idea

Why It Is Important

How Can I Remember It?

Text Cues

Some common signal words and their corresponding text structures. These words signal the nature of the text structure. Readers need to be aware of these text cues and understand what they signal.

Cause/Effect	Comparison/Contrast	Problem/Solution
since	in like manner	one reason for that
because	likewise	a solution
this led to	similarly	a problem
on account of	the difference between	
due to	as opposed to	
may be due to	after all	
for this reason	however	
consequently	and yet	
then, so	but	
therefore	nevertheless	
thus		

Question/Answer	Sequence
How	until
When	before
What	after
Where	next
Why	finally
Who	lastly
How many	first/last
The best estimate	then
It could be that	on (date)
One may conclude	at (time)

Adapted from Dole 1997.

DETERMINING   IMPORTANCE

As we read Dr. Robert Ballard's <u>Exploring the Titanic</u> we couldn't help but wonder what caused this "unsinkable" ship to sink. So we read to find an answer to that question. We had to pick out important information to help us understand.

Some things we noticed were:
- Iceberg warnings kept coming but they were ignored.

- The radio operators were tired and inexperienced.
- The sea was calm. It looked like clear sailing.
- The sky was clear and the sun was out.
- The captain was unconcerned.
- The captain knew that floating ice was not unusual at this time of year.
- "What danger could a few pieces of ice present to an unsinkable ship?"

★ All of this information combined can help us better understand why the ship sank. The people believed it was unsinkable and thus ignored all these danger signs.

Synthesizing

Oral Responses

Discussion
◆ Ongoing discussion of evolving thinking

Verbal Response
◆ "I get it…"
◆ "Aha!…"
◆ "Yes!!…"

Written Responses

Text Codes
◆ SZ, synthesize
◆ 2 + 2, put it all together (Chryse Hutchins suggests coding the text with this equation when a passage suddenly makes sense.)
◆ Drawing of a lightbulb, new idea surfaces or confusion clarified

Two-Column Note Forms
◆ What the Text Is About/What It Makes Me Think About
◆ Direct Quote/Personal Response
◆ Opinion Before Reading/New Ideas
◆ Quote or Picture from Text/New Idea
◆ Information from Text/New Insight
◆ Content/Process
◆ What's Interesting/What's Important

Three-Column Note Forms
◆ Content/Process/Craft
◆ Facts/Questions/Response
◆ Topic/Details/Response
◆ Thinking/New Information/New Thinking
◆ Compare and Contrast

Other Responses
◆ Venn diagram
◆ Time line of our thinking—recording on sticky notes the mini-syntheses readers make while reading and fixing them on a piece of posterboard for a graphic example of the evolution of thought
◆ Distilling the details of an article down to the six questions of the investigative reporter, Who? What? Where? When? Why? How?, to remember the information and make sense of it

Synthesizing Information

While reading, highlight or mark a picture or part of the text with SZ for synthesize when you have a new idea, when the lightbulb goes on! Write down the sentence or describe or draw the picture that gives you this new idea and then explain it under New Thinking.

Quote or Picture from Text

New Thinking

Quote or Picture from Text

New Thinking

Synthesizing

See the Ocean

When we finished reading **See the Ocean** by Estelle Condra we looked back at some of our post its. We put them in order (sort of) and we noticed that our thinking changed. It really changed when we finally figured out that Nellie was blind.

At first we asked questions...

(Josh)
Why does she spend so much time in the sand?

(Marnie)
Why didn't she complain that they got it first?

(Bobbie)
Why didn't she get car sick looking down?

Then we were confused...

(Silva)
When she asked, "What color is the ocean?" I thought why did she ask that question — couldn't she see for herself?

(Elisabeth)
In the pictures she covers her eyes. She does not look out the window She does not play the games. Why?

Then we understood... but still wondered...

(Patricio)
I think the mom and dad raised her on the beach so that she could feel and touch the things on the beach.

(Tod)
She's a good imaginer - maybe because her mom and dad and brother told her about the ocean and that's what it looks like to her.

(Meg)
Was she blind her whole life?

(Jon)
How did she become blind?

Assessment Interview with Fourth Graders

Why This Assessment Interview?

This assessment interview was conducted with three fourth graders—Tiffany, Rachel, and Stuart—during reading workshop in the classroom. The purpose of this small-group discussion was to assess the children's ongoing thinking rather than checking for understanding after they had finished a story. Asking the students to think out loud as they read through the text together enabled Anne to observe and document those strategies the children used to understand the first few pages of the picture book *My Freedom Trip: A Child's Escape from North Korea*, by Frances Park and Ginger Park. The book portrays a family who tries to flee from North Korea to South Korea just as the Korean War begins. One interesting aspect of the book is that a character from the Korean alphabet is written at the top of each page, representing the theme of that page. Kids are drawn to these symbols, determined to figure them out.

Children view the interview as an opportunity to discuss their thinking with their peers as they read a story together, each with a copy of the book. Teachers can observe kids in action, documenting their strategy use in an authentic situation. The goal is to assess ongoing comprehension, not comprehension after the fact.

Logistically, this kind of short interview is best conducted during a time when the rest of the class is reading or writing independently. The following interview took about twenty-five minutes. Teachers may want to meet with small groups of children for these short interviews about once a month because the format is easy to implement and manage.

To prepare for the interview, Anne selected a compelling picture book that required a lot of interpretation. She knew that these three students had been introduced to questioning and inferring, and thought that the ambiguity in the story would provide many opportunities for them to practice these and other comprehension strategies. The goal was for the students to reason through the text together as they encountered the text for the first time. Anne wanted them to lead the discussion, so she did not prepare specific comprehension questions. She was ready with prompts (see the list in Chapter 12) if the group conversation lagged. Anne scripted their conversation to reflect on it later and evaluate their use of strategies.

Introducing the Think-Aloud

Anne first asked the children to explain which comprehension strategies they found themselves using most frequently. Rachel jumped in, saying, "I infer."

"Can you explain what you mean by inferring?" Anne asked.

"I make pictures in my head about what will happen next, with all the clues from the story." Anne scripted her comment and polled the other kids for ideas.

Tiffany added, "I ask questions when something's going on and I wonder what will happen next."

"Or if it's puzzling, I ask a question to try to figure it out," Stuart chimed in.

Next, Anne directed the kids in this way: "What I'd like you to do today is think out loud about the story as you read it together. I'm interested in what's going on in your heads—what you're thinking about that helps you understand the story. You just mentioned that inferring and asking questions are two strategies that you use a lot. As you read the story together, you might use questioning, inferring, or other strategies to better understand it, especially if you come to a part that's confusing. I'm interested in learning about what you think, so I'll just listen and write down what you say. Okay?"

Reading the Story and Thinking Aloud

Tiffany, Rachel, and Stuart looked over the cover and title pages of the book, discovering a list of the Korean characters translated into English. The English list, they noted, included words like peace, fear, waiting, and love.

Tiffany glanced at the cover and said, "It's about a Chinese family."

"No, Korean," Rachel noted. "It says so right in the title, 'A Child's Escape from North Korea.'"

Stuart flipped to the page with the translations, and then pointed to the first Korean character. "Look! This means peace!" he said.

Rachel said, "I'm inferring—they ran away for freedom. The little girl is telling her life story about when she ran away."

"Or traveling back in time in her memory," Tiffany added. She began paging through the book, wondering out loud if the Korean characters described what each page was about.

"Maybe it's what the page means," suggested Stuart.

Anne's comments: Rachel labeled her thinking as inferring. She predicted what she thinks the story will be about: "The little girl is telling her life story about when she ran away." Tiffany also inferred that "She's traveling back in time in her memory." Stuart and Tiffany discussed the Korean characters at the top of each page, correctly inferring that they help to enhance the meaning of the story. These inferences provide evidence that the children are thinking ahead about what will happen in the story.

Tiffany, Rachel, and Stuart next read the Introduction, written years later.

> Many years have passed. I am no longer a little schoolgirl. But I still think about Mr. Han, my gentle guide, and about the soldier who set me free. Mostly, I think about my mother. When the evening is full of moon and warm winds, I can still hear her cry—Be Brave, Soo! Brave for the rest of my life!

"I wonder what 'brave for the rest of my life' means?" asked Stuart. "And who's the soldier?"

"So it is about her life story," Rachel added. Tiffany suggested that Soo (the little girl) may have some problems, wondering why she will have to "keep being brave."

Anne's comments: *Rachel noted that the Introduction confirmed her prediction. Stuart asked, "I wonder what 'brave for the rest of my life means?'" He wondered about the soldier. Tiffany also wondered why Soo will have to "keep being brave." It's surprising that the kids didn't discuss the confusing introduction a little more, although they noticed and questioned the ominous tone of the text.*

The children read Soo's words describing her home: "a peaceful sun shone down upon my village in North Korea, over rice paddies and pagoda roofs, on pink petals in ponds...and a soft breeze carried butterflies." Unfortunately, the peace and beauty were short-lived, because Soo's friends were leaving the country, and she found herself walking to school all alone. The next page in the story introduces the idea of leaving:

> Then one night my father came to my room and gently woke me. It was so dark that I could not see his face. He spoke softly.
>
> "Tonight I must go on a trip. A man named Mr. Han will guide me to South Korea. He knows of a secret passage where I will cross the border at the shallow end of a river."
>
> "Apa," I wailed, "do not go!"
>
> My father stroked my hair. His fingers were trembling. "Soon, very soon, Mr. Han will return for you, too, Soo. And he will take you on your freedom trip. Then it will be your mother's turn."

"Why is he only taking one person at a time?," wondered Tiffany.

No one seems to know, but Stuart is puzzled about how they leave.

"How do they leave? Do they go on a boat, a plane, walking, how?" he asked.

Rachel asked, "Will Soo really leave?"

Tiffany pointed to the Korean character at the top of the page. "I know why it says *whisper*," she commented. "It's because the dad spoke very softly."

They continued reading the story:

> "But why can't we go together?" I pleaded.

"Only one of us can go at a time, " he tried to explain. "Less people means less danger of being captured by soldiers."

What was danger? It sounded as deep and dark and cold as a river.

My father kissed my cheek, then left my side. He stood in the doorway for a long time.

"I will be waiting for you on the other side of the river," he promised.

Stuart was puzzled. "I don't get it. Why did she ask what danger was?"

Rachel commented that maybe nothing bad had ever happened to her before. Tiffany concurred, suggesting that up until now, Soo had had a peaceful life. The children wondered again if Soo was going to leave and why each person had to go alone. Ever attentive to the Korean characters, Tiffany explained the symbol for *promise* saying, "I think it's telling us that the dad promises to wait for her on the other side of the river."

Anne's comments: Stuart consistently asked questions about what he doesn't understand, and both Tiffany and Rachel responded with explanations that help clarify his confusions. Questions propelled the kids' thinking and kept them engaged. Rachel asked if Soo would leave, Tiffany wondered why only one person could go at a time. Tiffany continued to explain each Korean character and its relation to the events and emotions in the story.

On the next page, Tiffany pointed out the Korean character for *waiting*, telling the group that "she's waiting to go see her father." In the story, mother and daughter wait nervously for word that Soo's father has made it to the freedom land. When word finally comes, they are relieved, but now it is Soo's turn to leave.

My mother quietly rejoiced, then began packing my knapsack with jelly candy, fruit, and clothing.

"Tonight you go on your freedom trip, Soo," she carefully announced. "Now quickly, you must change your clothes."

"Oma," I begged, "come with me!"

She cupped my face and whispered, "Do not worry." Her breath was as warm and soothing as tea. "Mr. Han will return for me, and we will be reunited."

My mother hugged me. I could feel her heart beating against mine like a dying dove. "Be brave, Soo!" she cried.

"That's the symbol for *love*," Tiffany said, as she pointed to the character at the top of the page. "Because she's leaving her mom and she loves her very much."

Rachel added, "She's leaving, that's for sure. If you didn't know you could look at the picture and tell that."

"She's getting to freedom," added Tiffany. "Can you imagine how the mom would feel all alone in that house?"

"The family has to spread apart now, but someday they'll get to a new place together," said Rachel.

Stuart added, "They're moving like a little worm, first the dad, then the little girl, then the back part will go that is the mom."

Anne stopped the kids at this point and asked them to summarize what had happened so far, suggesting they try to tell what was going on in a few words.

Stuart mentioned that he thought there would be more soldiers, saying, "I'm wondering, is there a war, or what? And I still don't understand how they were leaving. Did they just walk all the way?"

Rachel summed up her version of the story, saying, "It's about a trip to the freedom land, they have to leave for freedom. But the little girl doesn't want to leave her mother, and I wonder if she meets her father. I wonder if something will happen."

Tiffany paged through the text, retelling the story according to the Korean character on each page, saying, "First there was peace, then the dad was whispering. On this page, Soo was afraid, and then there was love because the mother loves her, and she had to let her go away."

"They're like chapters," Stuart chimed in.

Tiffany added, "It's like the symbols tell what the people are thinking, or what's going to happen, through the whole story."

Anne's comments: *When asked to summarize the story thus far, Stuart seemed unclear about what Anne was asking him to do and, determined to figure out what was going on, posed additional questions. Rachel thoughtfully summed up the story, but still wondered about what would happen. Tiffany once again discussed the Korean characters, compelled to try to understand these symbols and their relationship to the text. She explained that they "tell what the people are thinking, or what's going to happen."*

Assessing the Children's Understanding

Hooked on the story and the fate of Soo and her family, Tiffany, Rachel, and Stuart raced off to read on their own. Anne jotted down comments about each child's thinking in an assessment notebook. It was clear that the children had used the strategies they mentioned—questioning and inferring—to reason through the text together. Based on the discussion, Anne realized that questioning and inferring enabled the kids to clarify confusions, better understand the characters, and anticipate story events and outcomes. Most important, however, inferences helped them think through and fill in gaps in the story, those things the authors left unsaid, or that would be resolved only at the end of the story.

Although all three children used the questioning and inferring strategies, Stuart primarily used questions to clarify what was going on or to ask his partners to explain something that confused him. He asked important questions, such as "What does 'brave for the rest of my life' mean?" but didn't stop to try to answer them.

Rachel asked lots of questions and was able to sum up the important ideas in the story. She continued to wonder whether Soo would meet her father after all and described how it must be hard for the mother to allow her to leave.

Tiffany, intent on deciphering the Korean symbols, demonstrated considerable insight as she linked them to the people, emotions, and events in the story. She seemed particularly attuned to the feelings of the characters in the story, empathizing with the mother, all alone in the house after Soo and her father have gone.

The next day, after the children had finished reading the story on their own, Anne introduced them to the idea of inferring themes. She pointed out that many of their questions and inferences had focused on story themes, especially having to leave one's home and loved ones for freedom and a new life. She wanted to give the kids language, such as the term *theme*, to describe their thinking. The children also discussed the story's ending, because they had assumed the family would all escape. They were surprised that Soo was able to escape, but incredulous that she never saw her mother again. Paging back through the text, they searched for hints and evidence that the story would end this way.

Although Tiffany, Rachel, and Stuart were engaged with the content of the story, the point of the interview was not to assess their understanding of story events. Assessment interviews like these can be done at any point in a story. In fact, we tend to conduct these interviews early on in the story because we gain a more accurate picture of kids' ongoing thinking. That's when they have to fill in the gaps and figure things out, before the issues and problems that drive the story have been resolved. If kids only discuss the story after finishing it, they usually focus on the ending, and we don't have any idea what they were thinking all the way through. At that point it's difficult to tell if and how kids kept track of their thinking as they read. We want to capture kids' thinking throughout their reading, to check if they are monitoring their ongoing understanding. That's the only way to find out if and how students are using strategies on their own, when it matters most.

Abbey, Edward. 1991. *Desert Solitaire.* New York: Ballantine Books.

Abeel, Samantha. 1993. *Reach for the Moon.* Duluth, MN: Pfeifer-Hamilton.

Abercrombie, Barbara. 1990. *Charlie Anderson.* New York: McElderry Books.

Ackerman, Diane. 1990. *A Natural History of the Senses.* New York: Vintage.

Adler, David. 1993. *A Picture Book of Anne Frank.* New York: Holiday House.

———. 1995. *A Picture Book of Ben Franklin.* New York: Holiday House.

———. 1997. *Lou Gehrig: The Luckiest Man.* San Diego: Harcourt Brace.

———. 1999. *The Babe and I.* San Diego: Harcourt Brace.

Alicea, Gil. 1995. *The Air Down Here.* San Francisco: Chronicle Books.

Aliki. 1989. *The King's Day.* New York: Crowell.

———. 1998. *Painted Words/Spoken Memories: Marianthe's Story.* New York: Greenwillow.

Allen, Janet, and Kyle Gonzalez. 1998. *There's Room for Me Here: Literacy Workshop in the Middle School.* York, ME: Stenhouse.

Allington, Richard. 1994. "The Schools We Have. The Schools We Need." *The Reading Teacher* 48, 1: 28+.

Altman, Linda. 1993. *Amelia's Road.* New York: Lee and Low.

Ambrose, Stephen. 1997. *Undaunted Courage: Meriwether Lewis, Thomas Jefferson and the Opening of the American West.* New York: Touchstone Books.

Ancona, George. 1998. *Barrio—Jose's Neighborhood.* San Diego: Harcourt Brace.

Anderson, R. C., C. Chinn, M. Commeyras, A. Stallman, M. Waggoner, and I. Wilkinson. 1992. The Reflective Thinking Project. In *Understanding and Enhancing Literature Discussion in Elementary Classrooms.* Symposium, 42nd Annual Meeting of the National Reading Conference, San Antonio, Texas.

Anderson, R. C., and P. D. Pearson. 1984. "A Schema-Theoretic View of Basic Processes in Reading." In *Handbook of Reading Research,* ed. P. D. Pearson. White Plains, NY: Longman.

Atkin, S. Beth. 1993. *Voices from the Fields.* Boston: Little, Brown.

Atkins, Jeannine. 1999. *A Name on the Quilt.* New York: Simon and Schuster.

Atwell, Nancie. 1987. *In the Middle: Writing, Reading, and Learning with Adolescents.* Portsmouth, NH: Boynton/Cook.

Bachrach, Susan D. 1994. *Tell Them We Remember.* Boston: Little, Brown.

Baillie, Allan. 1994. *Rebel.* New York: Tichnor and Fields.

Ballard, Robert. 1988. *Exploring the Titanic.* New York: Scholastic.

Ballard, Robert, and Rick Archbold. 1998. *Ghost Liners: Exploring the World's Greatest Lost Ships.* Boston: Little, Brown.

Barrett, Andrea. 1996. *Ship Fever.* New York: W. W. Norton.

Barry, Dave. 1991. *Best Travel Guide Ever.* New York: Fawcett.

Bartley, Paula, and Cathy Loxton. 1991. *Plains Women.* New York: Cambridge University Press.

Bartone, Elisa. 1996. *American, Too.* New York: Lothrop, Lee and Shepard.

Baylor, Byrd. 1972. *When Clay Sings.* New York: Aladdin Books.

———. 1986. *I'm in Charge of Celebrations.* New York: Charles Scribner.

———. 1994. *The Table Where Rich People Sit.* New York: Charles Scribner.

Beck, Isabel, Margaret McKeown, Rebecca Hamilton, and Linda Kucan. 1997. *Questioning the Author: An Approach for Enhancing Student Engagement with Text.* Newark, DE: International Reading Association.

Bedard, Michael. 1992. *Emily.* New York: Doubleday.

Berger, Barbara. 1984. *Grandfather Twilight.* New York: Putnam and Grosset.

Berger, Melvin, and Gilda Berger. 1997. *The Strength of These Arms: Life in the Slave Quarters.* Boston: Houghton Mifflin.

———. 1998. *Do Stars Have Points?* New York: Scholastic.

Berry, James. 1993. *The Future Telling Lady.* New York: HarperCollins.

Bierman, Carol. 1998. *Journey to Ellis Island: How My Father Came to America.* New York: Hyperion.

Bisel, Sara. 1990. *The Secrets of Vesuvius.* New York: Scholastic.

Bjork, Christina. 1987. *Linnea in Monet's Garden.* New York: Farrar, Straus, Giroux.

Bloom, Becky. 1999. *Wolf!* New York: Orchard Books.

Blume, Judy. 1984. *The Pain and the Great One.* New York: Bradbury Press.

Bolotin, Norman, and Angela Herb. 1995. *For Home and Country: A Civil War Scrapbook.* New York: Dutton.

Borden, Louise. 1997. *The Little Ships: The Heroic Rescue at Dunkirk in World War II.* New York: McElderry Books.

———. 1998. *Good-bye, Charles Lindbergh.* New York: McElderry Books.

———. 1999a. *A. Lincoln and Me.* New York: Scholastic.

———. 1999b. *Good Luck, Mrs. K.* New York: McElderry Books.

Bowen, Gary. 1994. *Stranded at Plimoth Plantation: 1626.* New York: HarperCollins.

Boyd, Robert S. 1999. "Moonstruck Scientists Count 63 and Rising." *Denver Post,* January 3.

Bradby, Marie. 1995. *More Than Anything Else.* New York: Orchard Books.

Brandenburg, Jim. 1995. *An American Safari: Adventures on the North American Prairie.* New York: Walker.

Brantley, Ben. 1996. "Flying Feet Electrify the Sweep of History." Review of *Bring in da Noise, Bring in da Funk. New York Times,* April 26.

Bridges, Ruby. 1999. *Through My Eyes.* New York: Scholastic.

Brighton, Catherine. 1990. *Mozart: Scenes from the Childhood of the Great Composer.* New York: Doubleday.

———. 1994. *The Brontes: Scenes from the Childhood of Charlotte, Branwell, Emily, and Anne.* San Francisco: Chronicle Books.

Brinkloe, Julie. 1985. *Fireflies.* New York: Aladdin Books.

Broad, William. 1997. "Misunderstood Sharks, Not Just Feeding Machines." *Denver Post,* December 7.

Brown, Dee. 1991. *Bury My Heart at Wounded Knee: An Indian History of the American West.* New York: Henry Holt.

Brown, Don. 1997. *One Giant Leap.* New York: Scholastic.

Brown, Margaret Wise. 1992. *The Sailor Dog.* Racine, WI: Western.

Bruchac, Joseph. 1994. *A Boy Called Slow: The True Story of Sitting Bull.* New York: Philomel.

———. 1996a. *Between Earth and Sky: Legends of Native American Sacred Places.* San Diego: Harcourt Brace.

———. 1996b. *The Circle of Thanks: North American Poems and Songs of Thanksgiving.* New York: BridgeWater Books.

Bullard, Sara. 1993. *Free at Last: A History of the Civil Rights Movement and Those Who Died in the Struggle.* New York: Oxford University Press.

Bunting, Eve. 1988. *How Many Days to America?* New York: Clarion.

———. 1989. *The Wednesday Surprise.* New York: Clarion.

———. 1990. *The Wall.* New York: Clarion.

———. 1991. *Fly Away Home.* New York: Clarion.

———. 1993. *Someday a Tree.* New York: Clarion.

———. 1994a. *A Day's Work.* New York: Clarion.

———. 1994b. *Smoky Night.* San Diego: Harcourt Brace.

———. 1994c. *Sunshine Home.* New York: Clarion.

———. 1995. *Dandelion.* San Diego: Harcourt Brace.

———. 1996. *Going Home.* New York: HarperCollins.

———. 1998a. *Some Frog.* San Diego: Harcourt Brace.

———. 1998b. *Your Move.* San Diego: Harcourt Brace.

———. 1999. *A Picnic in October.* San Diego: Harcourt Brace.

Burby, Liza. 1998. Extreme Weather Series. New York: Rosen.

Burnett, Frances. 1938. *The Secret Garden.* New York: Lippincott.

Caduto, Michael J., and Joseph Bruchac. 1988. *Keepers of the Earth: Native American Stories and Environmental Activities for Children.* Golden, CO: Fulcrum.

———. 1994. *Keepers of the Night: Native American Stories and Nocturnal Activities for Children.* Golden, CO: Fulcrum.

Calaprice, Alice. 1996. *The Quotable Einstein.* Princeton, NJ: Princeton University Press.

Campbell, Jim. 1992. *Baseball's Greatest Pitchers.* New York: Random House.

———. 1995. *Baseball's Greatest Hitters.* New York: Random House.

Cannon, Janell. 1993. *Stellaluna.* San Diego: Harcourt Brace.

Carlson, Lori Marie. 1998. *Sol a Sol.* New York: Henry Holt.

Carrick, Carol. 1988. *Left Behind.* New York: Clarion.

Cech, John. 1991. *My Grandmother's Journey.* New York: Bradbury Press.

Cha, Dia. 1996. *Dia's Story Cloth.* New York: Lee and Low.

Chall, Marsha Wilson. 1992. *Up North at the Cabin.* New York: Lothrop, Lee and Shepard.

Chang, Ina. 1996. *A Separate Battle: Women and the Civil War.* New York: Puffin.

Charlton, James. 1991. *The Writer's Quotation Book: A Literary Companion.* New York: Barnes and Noble Books.

Cherry, Lynne. 1992. *A River Ran Wild.* San Diego: Harcourt Brace.

Cisneros, Sandra. 1991. *Woman Hollering Creek and Other Stories.* New York: Vintage Contemporary Books.

Clyne, Densey. 1995. *Spotlight on Spiders.* St. Leonard's, Australia: Little Arc.

Coerr, Eleanor. 1993. *Sadako.* New York: Putnam.

Coffelt, Nancy. 1993. *Dogs in Space.* San Diego: Harcourt Brace.

Cole, Joanna. 1986. *Hungry, Hungry Sharks.* New York: Random House.

Coles, Robert. 1995. *The Story of Ruby Bridges.* New York: Scholastic.

Colman, Penny. 1995. *Rosie the Riveter.* New York: Crown.

Condra, Estelle. 1994. *See the Ocean.* Nashville, TN: Ideal Children's Books.

Conroy, Pat. 1994. *Prince of Tides.* New York: Bantam.

Cooney, Barbara. 1982. *Miss Rumphius.* New York: Viking Penguin.

———. 1994. *Only Opal: The Diary of a Young Girl.* New York: Scholastic.

———. 1996. *Eleanor.* New York: Viking.

Cooper, Elisha. 1998. *Ballpark.* New York: Greenwillow.

Cooper, Floyd. 1994. *Coming Home: From the Life of Langston Hughes.* New York: Philomel.

Coville, Bruce. 1997. *Macbeth.* New York: Dial.

Cowley, Joy. 1980. *Mrs. Wishy Washy.* Chicago: Wright Group.

Crist-Evans, Craig. 1999. *Moon Over Tennessee: A Boy's Civil War Journal.* Boston: Houghton Mifflin.

Cristaldi, Kathryn. 1992. *Baseball Ballerina.* New York: Random House.

Cristelow, Eileen. 1995. *What Do Authors Do?* New York: Clarion.

Cruise, Robin. 1999. Personal interview.

Crutchfield, James A. 1993. *It Happened in Colorado.* Helena, MT: Falcon Press.

Cullinan, Bernice E. 1981. *Literature and the Child.* San Diego: Harcourt Brace.

Cummings, Pat. 1992. *Talking with Artists.* 2 vols. New York: Simon and Schuster.

Cummings, Pat, and Linda Cummings. 1998. *Talking with Adventurers.* Washington, DC: National Geographic Society.

Curtis, Gavin. 1998. *The Bat Boy and His Violin.* New York: Simon and Schuster.

Dangerous Animals. 1995. Nature Company Discoveries Library. New York: Orchard Books.

Daniels, Harvey. 1994. *Literature Circles: Voice and Choice in the Student-Centered Classroom.* York, ME: Stenhouse.

Davey, Beth. 1983. "Think Aloud: Modeling the Cognitive Processes of Reading Comprehension." *Journal of Reading* 27: 44–47.

Day, Alexandra. 1985. *Good Dog Carl.* New York: Scholastic.

———. 1988. *Frank and Ernest.* New York: Scholastic.

———. 1989. *Carl Goes Shopping.* New York: Farrar, Straus, Giroux.

———. 1990. *Frank and Ernest Play Ball.* New York: Scholastic.

———. 1992. *Carl's Masquerade.* New York: Farrar, Straus, Giroux.

———. 1994. *Frank and Ernest on the Road.* New York: Scholastic.

de Paola, Tomie. 1978. *Nana Upstairs, Nana Downstairs.* New York: Puffin.

———. 1979. *Oliver Button Is a Sissy.* New York: Harcourt Brace.

———. 1981. *Now One Foot, Now the Other.* New York: Trumpet.

———. 1989. *The Art Lesson.* New York: Putnam.

———. 1991. *Bonjour, Mr. Satie.* New York: Putnam.

Dear America series. 1995+. New York: Scholastic.

Del Calzo, Nick. 1997. *The Triumphant Spirit: Portraits and Stories of Holocaust Survivors, Their Messages of Hope and Compassion.* Denver: Triumphant Spirit Publishing.

Demi. 1991. *Chingis Khan.* New York: Henry Holt.

Dewey, Jennifer Owings. 1997. *Rattlesnake Dance.* Honesdale, PA: Boyds Mills Press.

Diamond, Jared. 1999. *Germs, Guns, and Steel: The Fates of Human Societies.* New York: W. W. Norton.

Dillard, Annie. 1989. *The Writing Life.* New York: HarperCollins.

Dole, Jan. 1997. Public Education and Business Coalition Reading Comprehension Workshop. Denver, CO. April.

Dolphin, Laurie. 1993. *Oasis of Peace.* New York: Scholastic.

———. 1997. *Our Journey from Tibet.* New York: Dutton.

Dorros, Arthur. 1991. *Abuela.* New York: Dutton Children's Books.

Dreifus, Claudia. 1997. *Interview.* New York: Seven Stories Press.

Duggleb, John. 1995. *Artist in Overalls: The Life of Grant Wood.* San Francisco: Chronicle Books.

Duncan, Dayton. 1996. *People of the West.* Based on the public television series *The West.* Boston: Little, Brown.

Durkin, Dolores. 1979. "What Classroom Observations Reveal About Reading Instruction." *Reading Research Quarterly* 14: 481–533.

Edlin, John. 1992. "Rhino Dehorned by Rangers." *Denver Post,* January 10.

Edwards, James. 1998. "What Johnny Can't Read." *Time Magazine.* December.

Epstein, Norrie. 1993. *The Friendly Shakespeare.* New York: Penguin.

Erickson, Paul. 1994. *Daily Life in Covered Wagon.* New York: Puffin.

Esquibel, Curtis L. 1999. "Frigid Weather Teases State." *Denver Post,* March 13.

Everett, Gwen. 1991. *Li'l Sis and Uncle Willie.* New York: Rizzoli.

———. 1993. *John Brown: One Man Against Slavery.* New York: Rizzoli.

Feelings, Tom. Comp. 1993. *Soul Looks Back in Wonder.* New York: Dial.

Feynman, Richard. 1985. *"Surely You're Joking, Mr. Feynman!"* New York: Bantam.

———. 1988. *What Do You Care What Other People Think? Further Adventures of a Curious Character.* New York: Bantam.

Fielding, Linda, and P. David Pearson. 1994. "Reading Comprehension: What Works?" *Educational Leadership* 51, 5: 62–67.

Fisher, Leonard Everett. 1986. *The Great Wall of China.* New York: Simon and Schuster.

———. 1987. *The Tower of London.* New York: Macmillan.

———. 1991. *Sailboat Lost.* New York: Macmillan.

Fitzpatrick, Marie-Louise. 1998. *The Long March.* Hillsboro, OR: Beyond Words Publishing.

Fleischman, Paul. 1988. *Rondo in C.* New York: Harper and Row.

———. 1993. *Bull Run.* New York: Scholastic.

———. 1996. *Dateline: Troy.* Cambridge, MA: Candlewick Press.

Fletcher, Ralph. 1996. *A Writer's Notebook: Unlocking the Writer Within You.* New York: Avon Books.

———. 1997. *Twilight Comes Twice.* New York: Clarion.

Foreman, Michael. 1989. *War Boy.* New York: Little, Brown.

Fox, Mary Virginia. 1991. *The Story of Women Who Shaped the West.* Chicago: Children's Press.

Fox, Mem. 1985. *Wilfrid Gordon McDonald Partridge.* Brooklyn, NY: Kane/Miller.

——. 1988. *Koala Lou*. Orlando, FL: Harcourt Brace.

Fraser, Mary Ann. 1994. *Sanctuary: The Story of Three Arch Rocks*. New York: Henry Holt.

Frasier, Charles. *Cold Mountain*. 1997. New York: Atlantic Monthly Press.

Freedman, Russell. 1980. *Immigrant Kids*. New York: Scholastic.

——. 1983. *Children of the Wild West*. New York: Clarion.

——. 1988. *Buffalo Hunt*. New York: Scholastic.

——. 1994. *Kids at Work: Lewis Hine and the Crusade Against Child Labor*. New York: Scholastic.

——. 1996. *The Life and Death of Crazy Horse*. New York: Holiday House.

——. 1997. *Lincoln: A Photobiography*. New York: Clarion.

Friedrich, Elizabeth. 1996. *Leah's Pony*. Honesdale, PA: Boyds Mills Press.

Fritz, Jean. 1973. *And Then What Happened, Paul Revere?* New York: Putnam and Grosset.

——. 1976. *Will You Sign Here, John Hancock?* New York: Coward McCann.

——. 1977. *Can't You Make Them Behave, King George?* New York: Coward McCann.

——. 1980. *Where Do You Think You're Going, Christopher Columbus?* New York: Putnam.

——. 1983. *Shh! We're Writing the Constitution*. New York: Putnam.

——. 1994. *Around the World in 100 Years: From Henry the Navigator to Magellan*. New York: Putnam and Grosset.

Gallagher, Margaret C. 1986. Knowledge Acquisition in the Content Area Classroom: Exploring the Consequences of Instruction. Doctoral dissertation, University of Illinois. Dissertation Abstracts International Vol. 47 01A.

Gardner, Howard. 1991. *The Unschooled Mind: How Children Think and How Schools Should Teach*. New York: Basic Books.

Garland, Sherry. 1993. *The Lotus Seed*. San Diego: Harcourt Brace.

Gavelek, J., and T. E. Raphael. 1985. "Metacognition, Instruction and the Role of Questioning Activities." In *Metacognition, Cognition and Human Performance*, ed. D. L. Forrest-Pressley, G. E. MacKinnon, and T. G. Waller. New York: Academic Press.

Gershwin, Ira, George Gershwin, DuBose Heyward, and Dorothy Heyward. 1999. *Summertime from Porgy and Bess*. New York: Simon and Schuster.

Gherman, Beverly. 1992. *E. B. White: Some Writer*. New York: Atheneum.

Gibbons, Gail. 1995. *The Reasons for Seasons*. New York: Holiday House.

Gikow, L. 1993. *For Every Child a Better World*. Wave, WI: Golden Press.

Gilbar, Steve. 1990. *The Reader's Quotation Book*. New York: Barnes and Noble.

Goble, Paul. 1992. *Red Hawk's Account of Custer's Last Battle*. Lincoln: University of Nebraska Press.

Goldberg, Natalie. 1986. *Writing Down the Bones*. Boston: Shambhala.

Golenbock, Peter. 1990. *Teammates*. San Diego: Harcourt Brace Jovanovich.

Grace, Eric S. 1993. *Elephants*. San Francisco: Sierra Club.

Grafton, John, ed. 1991. *Abraham Lincoln: Great Speeches*. New York: Dover Publications.

Graham, Paula. 1999. *Speaking of Journals: Children's Book Writers Talk About Their Diaries, Notebooks, and Sketchbooks*. Honesdale, PA: Boyds Mills Press.

Graves, Donald. 1991. *Build a Literate Classroom*. Portsmouth, NH: Heinemann.

———. 1996. *Baseball, Snakes and Summer Squash: Poems About Growing Up*. Honesdale, PA: Boyds Mills Press.

Gray, Libba Moore. 1993. *Dear Willie Rudd*. New York: Simon and Schuster.

———. 1996. *Little Lil and the Swing-Singing Sax*. New York: Simon and Schuster.

Gray, Nigel, and Philippe Dupasquier. 1988. *A Country Far Away*. New York: Orchard Books.

Greenfield, Eloise. 1978. *Honey I Love*. New York: HarperCollins.

Greenfield, Eloise, and Lessie Jones Little. 1979. *Childtimes*. New York: HarperCollins.

Grindley, Sally. 1997. *Why Is the Sky Blue?* New York: Simon and Schuster.

Grutman, Jewel H., and Gay Matthai. 1994. *The Ledgerbook of Thomas Blue Eagle*. Charlottesville, VA: Thomasson-Grant.

Gutelle, Andre. 1989. *Baseball's Best: Five True Stories*. New York: Random House.

Hacker, Carlotta. 1998. *Explorers*. Women in Profile Series. New York: Crabtree.

Hagerty, Pat. 1992. *Reader's Workshop: Real Reading*. Ontario: Scholastic Canada.

Hakim, Joy. 1995. *A History of U.S.: The Story of America*. New York: Oxford University Press.

Hall, Susan. 1990. *Using Picture Storybooks to Teach Literary Devices*. Phoenix, AZ: Oryx Press.

Hamilton, John. 1998. Mission to Mars Series. Edina, MN: Abdo and Daughters.

Hansen, Jane. 1981. "The Effects of Inference Training and Practice on Young Childrens' Reading Comprehension." *Reading Research Quarterly* 16: 391–417.

Hansen, Joyce. 1997. *I Thought My Soul Would Rise and Fly: The Diary of Patsy, a Freed Girl*. New York: Scholastic.

Harper, Isabelle. 1995. *My Cats Nick and Nora*. New York: Scholastic.

Harrer, Heinrich. 1997. *Seven Years in Tibet*. New York: Putnam.

Harshman, Marc. 1993. *Uncle James*. New York: Cobblehill Books.

Harvey, Brett. 1988. *Cassie's Journey: Going West in the 1860s*. New York: Holiday House.

Harvey, Stephanie. 1998. *Nonfiction Matters: Reading, Writing, and Research in Grades 3–8*. York, ME: Stenhouse.

Harvey, Stephanie, Sheila McAuliffe, Laura Benson, Wendy Cameron, Sue Kempton, Pat Lusche, Debbie Miller, Joan Schroeder, and Julie Weaver. 1996. "Teacher Researchers Study the Process of Synthesizing in Six Primary Classrooms." *Language Arts* 73, 8.

Harwayne, Shelley. 1992. *Lasting Impressions: Weaving Literature into the Writing Workshop*. Portsmouth, NH: Heinemann.

———. 1999. *Going Public: Priorities and Practices at the Manhattan New School*. Portsmouth, NH: Heinemann.

Haskins, James. 1992. *The Day Martin Luther King, Jr. Was Shot: A Photo History of the Civil Rights Movement*. New York: Scholastic.

———. 1995. *Freedom Rides: Journey for Justice*. New York: Hyperion.

Haskins, James, and Kathleen Benson. 1999. *Bound for America: The Forced Migration of Africans to the New World*. New York: Lothrop, Lee and Shepard.

Hawking, Stephen. 1988. *A Brief History of Time*. New York: Bantam.

Hazell, Rebecca. 1996a. *Heroes: Great Men Through the Ages.* New York: Abbeville.
———. 1996b. *Heroines: Great Women Through the Ages.* New York: Abbeville.
Hazen, Barbara Shook. 1979. *Tight Times.* New York: Viking.
Heard, Georgia. 1992. *Creatures of the Earth, Sea, and Sky.* Honesdale, PA: Boyds Mills Press.
———. 1995. *Writing Toward Home.* Portsmouth, NH: Heinemann.
Hearne, Betsy. 1993. *The Known and the Unknown: An Exploration into Nonfiction by Jean Fritz.* The Zena Sutherland Lectures, 1983–1992. New York: Clarion.
———. 1997. *Seven Brave Women.* New York: Greenwillow.
Hehner, Barbara. 1999. *First on the Moon: What It Was Like When Man Landed on the Moon.* New York: Hyperion.
Heide, Florence Parry, and J. D. Gilliland. 1990. *The Day of Ahmed's Secret.* New York: Lothrop, Lee and Shepard.
———. 1992. *Sammy and the Time of Troubles.* New York: Clarion.
Henkes, Kevin. 1987. *Sheila Ray the Brave.* New York: Mulberry.
———. 1990. *Julius, the Baby of the World.* New York: Mulberry.
———. 1991. *Chrysanthemum.* New York: Mulberry.
———. 1993. *Owen.* New York: Greenwillow.
Hesse, Karen. 1999. *Out of the Dust.* New York: Scholastic.
Hest, Amy. 1995. *How to Get Famous in Brooklyn.* New York: Simon and Schuster.
———. 1997. *When Jessie Came Across the Sea.* Cambridge, MA: Candlewick Press.
Heyward, DuBose. 1939. *The Country Bunny and the Little Gold Shoes.* Boston: Houghton Mifflin.
Hindley, Joanne. 1996. *In the Company of Children.* York, ME: Stenhouse.
Hoestlandt, Jo. 1993. *Star of Fear, Star of Hope.* New York: Walker.
Hoffman, Mary. 1991. *Amazing Grace.* New York: Dial.
Hopkins, Lee Bennett. 1994. *Hand in Hand: An American History Through Poetry.* New York: Simon and Schuster.
Hopkinson, Deborah. 1993. *Sweet Clara and the Freedom Quilt.* New York: Knopf.
Houston, Gloria. 1992. *My Great-Aunt Arizona.* New York: HarperCollins.
Howard, Elizabeth Fitzgerald. 1991. *Aunt Flossie's Hats (and Crab Cakes Later).* New York: Clarion.
"Howling Again." 1999. *Wild Outdoor World* 3, January/February.
Hughes, Langston. 1994. *The Collected Poems of Langston Hughes,* ed. Arnold Rampersad. New York: Vintage Books.
Humphreys, W. A., and W. J. Humphreys. 1962. *Snow Crystals.* New York: Turtle Books.
Hunter, Sara. 1996. *The Unbreakable Code.* Flagstaff, AZ: Northland.
"In Sickness and in Health." 1999. *Kids Discover Magazine,* April.
Innocenti, Roberto. 1985. *Rose Blanche.* San Diego: Harcourt Brace.
Janeczko, Paul. 1988. *The Music of What Happens.* New York: Orchard Books.
———. 1990. *The Place My Words Are Looking For.* New York: Bradbury Press.
———. 1998. *The Sweet Diamond: Baseball Poems.* New York: Atheneum.
Jenkins, Steve. 1998. *Hottest, Coldest, Highest, Deepest.* Boston: Houghton Mifflin.
Jimenez, Francisco. 1997. *The Circuit: Stories from the Life of a Migrant Child.* Albuquerque: University of New Mexico Press.

————. 1998. *La Mariposa.* Boston: Houghton Mifflin.

Johnson, Dolores. 1993. *Now Let Me Fly: The Story of a Slave Family.* New York: Macmillan.

————. 1994. *Seminole Diary: Remembrances of a Slave.* New York: Macmillan.

Johnston, Tony. 1994. *Amber on the Mountain.* New York: Dial.

————. 1999. *The Wagon.* New York: Morrow.

Johnstone, Michael. 1997. *The History News: Explorers.* Cambridge, MA: Candlewick Press.

Jones, Charlotte Foltz. 1991. *Mistakes That Worked.* New York: Doubleday.

Jones, Thomas D., and June A. English. 1996. *Mission: Earth, Voyage to the Home Planet.* New York: Scholastic.

Joyce, William. 1999. *Baseball Bob.* New York: Harper Festival.

Kamensky, Jane. 1995. *Colonial Mosaic: American Women 1600–1760.* New York: Oxford University Press.

Kaplan, William, with Shelley Tanaka. 1998. *One More Border.* Toronto: Douglas and McIntyre.

Katz, William. 1995. *Black Women of the Old West.* New York: Simon and Schuster.

Keating, Kevin. 1998. "This Is Cruising." *Hemispheres Magazine.* March.

Keats, Ezra Jack. 1962. *The Snowy Day.* New York: Puffin.

Keene, Ellin L., and Susan Zimmermann. 1997. *Mosaic of Thought: Teaching Comprehension in a Reader's Workshop.* Portsmouth, NH: Heinemann.

Khalsa, Dayal Kaur. 1986. *Tales of a Gambling Grandma.* New York: Clarkson Potter.

King, Martin Luther, Jr. 1997. *I Have a Dream.* New York: Scholastic.

Kirkpatrick, Katherine. 1999. *Redcoats and Petticoats.* New York: Holiday House.

Kitamura, Satoshi. 1989. *UFO Diary.* New York: Farrar, Straus, Giroux.

Knight, Margy Burns. 1992. *Talking Walls.* Gardiner, ME: Tilbury House.

Knox, Bob. 1993. *The Great Art Adventure.* New York: Rizzoli.

Kobrin, Beverly. *The Kobrin Letter,* 732 Greer Road, Palo Alto, CA 94303.

Kodama, Tatsuharu. 1995. *Shin's Tricycle.* New York: Walker and Co.

Krakauer, Jon. 1997. *Into Thin Air.* New York: Villard Books.

Kramer, S. A. 1995. *Baseball's Greatest Hitters.* New York: Random House.

Kramer, Stephen. 1992a. *Avalanche.* Minneapolis: Carolrhoda.

————. 1992b. *Lightning.* Minneapolis: Carolrhoda.

————. 1992c. *Tornado.* Minneapolis: Carolrhoda.

————. 1997. *Eye of the Storm.* New York: Putnam.

Kroeger, Mary Kay, and Louise Borden. 1996. *Paperboy.* New York: Clarion.

Kroll, Steven. 1994. *Lewis and Clark: Explorers of the New American West.* New York: Holiday House.

————. 1998. *The Boston Tea Party.* New York: Holiday House.

Krulik, Nancy. 1991. *My Picture Book of the Planets.* New York: Scholastic.

Krull, Kathleen. 1992. *Lives of the Artists.* San Diego: Harcourt Brace.

————. 1993. *Lives of the Musicians.* San Diego: Harcourt Brace.

————. 1994. *Lives of the Writers.* San Diego: Harcourt Brace.

————. 1996. *Wilma Unlimited.* San Diego: Harcourt Brace.

Kuskin, Karla. 1975. *Near the Window Tree: Poems and Notes.* New York: Harper and Row.

Lamb, Brian. 1998. *Booknotes: America's Finest Authors on Reading, Writing, and the Power of Ideas*. New York: Random House.

Lamb, Charles, and Mary Lamb. 1996. *Illustrated Tales from Shakespeare*. North Dighton, MA: World Publications.

Lamb, Nancy. 1996. *One April Morning*. New York: Lothrop, Lee and Shepard.

Lamont, Anne. 1994. *Bird by Bird: Some Instructions on Writing and Life*. New York: Anchor Books.

Lasky, Kathyrn. 1993. *Monarchs*. San Diego: Harcourt Brace Jovanovich.

———. 1994a. *Day of the Dead*. New York: Hyperion.

———. 1994b. *The Librarian Who Measured the Earth*. Boston: Little, Brown.

———. 1995. *She's Wearing a Dead Bird on Her Head*. New York: Hyperion.

Lawlor, Laurie. 1994. *Shadow Catcher: The Life and Work of Edward S. Curtis*. New York: Walker.

Lawlor, Veronica. 1995. *I Was Dreaming to Come to America*. New York: Viking.

Lawrence, Jacob. 1993. *The Great Migration*. New York: HarperCollins.

Leedy, Loreen. 1992. *Postcards from Pluto*. New York: Scholastic.

Leon, Vicki. 1998. *Outrageous Women of Ancient Times*. New York: John Wiley and Sons.

Lesser, Carolyn. 1999. *Spots: Counting Creatures from Sky to Sea*. San Diego: Harcourt Brace.

Lester, Julius. 1998. *From Slave Ship to Freedom Road*. New York: Dial.

Le Tord, Bijou. 1995. *A Blue Butterfly: A Story of Claude Monet*. New York: Doubleday.

Levine, Ellen. 1989. *I Hate English*. New York: Scholastic.

Levstik, Linda. 1993. "I Wanted to Be There: The Impact of Narrative on Children's Historical Thinking." In *The Story of Ourselves*, ed. M. Tunnell and R. Ammon. Portsmouth, NH: Heinemann.

Lewis, Paul Owen. 1995. *Storm Boy*. Hillsboro, OR: Beyond Words Publishing.

Lewis, Thomas P. 1971. *Hill of Fire*. New York: Harper and Row.

Little, Jean. 1986. *Hey World, Here I Am!* New York: HarperCollins.

Littlechild, George. 1996. *We Are All Related*. Vancouver, BC: Polester.

Livingston, Myra, and Leonard Everett Fisher. 1998. *Space Songs*. New York: Holiday House.

Lobel, Arnold. 1970. *Frog and Toad Are Friends*. New York: Harper and Row.

———. 1971. *Frog and Toad Together*. New York: Harper and Row.

———. 1979. *Days with Frog and Toad*. New York: Harper and Row.

———. 1980. *Fables*. New York: Harper Trophy.

———. 1982. *Owl at Home*. New York: Harper Trophy.

———. 1984. *Frog and Toad All Year*. New York: Harper Trophy.

Locker, Thomas. 1985. *The Mare on the Hill*. New York: Dial.

———. 1990. *Snow Toward Evening*. New York: Penguin.

London, Jonathan. 1996. *Into This Night We Are Rising*. New York: Puffin.

———. 1998a. *Dream Weaver*. San Diego: Harcourt Brace.

———. 1998b. *At the Edge of the Forest*. Cambridge, MA: Candlewick.

———. 1998c. *Hurricane*. New York: Lothrop, Lee and Shepard.

———. 1998d. *Like Butter on Pancakes*. New York: Puffin.

———. 1999a. *Baby Whale's Journey*. San Francisco: Chronicle Books

————. 1999b. *The Condor's Egg*. San Francisco: Chronicle Books.

————. 1999c. *Puddles*. New York: Puffin.

Lopez, Barry. 1986. *Arctic Dreams*. New York: Charles Scribner.

Lord, Walter. 1997. *A Night to Remember*. New York: Bantam.

Lourie, Peter. 1991. *Amazon: A Young Reader's Look at the Last Frontier*. Honesdale, PA: Boyds Mills Press.

————. 1992a. *Hudson River: An Adventure from the Mountains to the Sea*. Honesdale, PA: Boyds Mills Press.

————. 1992b. *Yukon River: An Adventure to the Gold Fields of the Klondike*. Honesdale, PA: Boyds Mills Press.

————. 1997. *Erie Canal: Canoeing America's Great Waterway*. Honesdale, PA: Boyds Mills Press.

————. 1998. *Everglades: Buffalo Tiger and the River of Grass*. Honesdale, PA: Boyds Mills Press.

————. 1999. *Rio Grande: From the Rocky Mountains to the Gulf of Mexico*. Honesdale, PA: Boyds Mills Press.

Lucas, Eileen. 1997. *Cracking the Wall: The Struggles of the Little Rock Nine*. Minneapolis: Carolrhoda.

Lunn, Janet. 1998. *Charlotte*. Plattsburgh, NY: Tundra Books.

Lyon, George Ella. 1999. *Book*. New York: DK Publishing.

MacGill-Callahan, Sheila. 1991. *And Still the Turtle Watched*. New York: Dial.

MacLachlan, Patricia. 1994. *All the Places to Love*. New York: HarperCollins.

MacNeil, Robert. 1990. *Wordstruck: A Memoir*. New York: Penguin.

Madrigal, Antonio Hernandez. 1999. *Erandi's Braids*. New York: Putnam.

Maestro, Betsy, and Giulio Maestro. 1996. *The New Americans*. New York: Lothrop, Lee and Shepard.

Malone, Michael. 1996. *A Guatemalan Family*. Minneapolis: Lerner.

Mann, Elizabeth. 1996. *The Brooklyn Bridge*. New York: Mikaya Press.

Markun, Patricia Maloney. 1993. *The Little Painter of Sabana Grande*. New York: Simon and Schuster

Marshall, James. 1972. *George and Martha*. Boston: Houghton Mifflin.

————. 1973. *George and Martha Encore*. Boston: Houghton Mifflin.

————. 1976. *George and Martha Rise and Shine*. Boston: Houghton Mifflin.

Marshall, Rita. 1993. *I Hate to Read*. New York: Creative Company.

Martin, C. L. G. 1991. *Three Brave Women*. New York: Macmillan.

Martin, Jacqueline Briggs. 1995. *Washing the Willow Tree Loon*. New York: Simon and Schuster.

————. 1998. *Snowflake Bentley*. Boston: Houghton Mifflin.

Mason, Antony. 1994/95. Famous Artists Series. Hauppauge, NY: Barron's Educational Series.

Mathers, Petra. 1995. *Kisses from Rosa*. New York: Knopf.

McCullough, David. 1983. *The Great Bridge: The Epic Story of the Building of the Brooklyn Bridge*. New York: Simon and Schuster.

McCully, Emily Arnold. 1992. *Mirette on the High Wire*. New York: Putnam.

————. 1996a. *Ballot Box Battle*. New York: Knopf.

————. 1996b. *The Bobbin Girl*. New York: Dial.

McDonald, Megan. 1991. *The Potato Man*. New York: Orchard Books.

McGill, Alice. 1999. *Molly Bannaky*. Boston: Houghton Mifflin.

McKee, Tim, and Anne Blackshaw. 1998. *No More Strangers Now*. New York: DK Publishing.

McKenzie, Jamie. 1996. "Making Web Meaning." *Educational Leadership* 54 (3): 30–32.

McKissack, Patricia, and Fredrick McKissack. 1995. *Red-Tail Angels: The Story of the Tuskegee Airmen of World War II*. New York: Walker.

McPhail, David. 1993. *Santa's Book of Names*. Boston: Joy Street Books.

———. 1997. *Edward and the Pirates*. Boston: Little, Brown.

McPhee, John. 1966. *Oranges*. New York: Farrar, Straus, Giroux.

Mehler, Carl. 1998. *Satellite Atlas of the World*. Washington, DC: National Geographic Society.

Merk, Ann, and Jim Merk. 1994. Weather Report Series. Vero Beach, FL: Rourke.

Merrill Earth Science. 1993. Seventh-grade textbook. Westerville, OH: Macmillan/McGraw Hill.

Miller, Debbie, and Anne Goudvis. 1999. "Classroom Conversations: Young Children Discuss Fairness and Justice, Intolerance and Prejudice." In *Teaching for a Tolerant World*, ed. Judith Robertson. Urbana, IL: National Council of Teachers of English.

Miller, Sue. 1993. *For Love*. New York: HarperCollins.

Miller, William. 1994. *Zora Hurston and the Chinaberry Tree*. New York: Lee and Low.

———. 1995. *Frederick Douglass: The Last Day of Slavery*. New York: Lee and Low.

———. 1997. *Richard Wright and the Library Card*. New York: Lee and Low.

Mills, Lauren. 1991. *The Rag Coat*. Boston: Little, Brown.

Mitchell, Rita. 1993. *Hue Boy*. New York: Puffin.

Mochizuki, Ken. 1993. *Baseball Saved Us*. New York: Lee and Low.

———. 1997. *Passage to Freedom: The Sugihara Story*. New York: Lee and Low.

Moon, Nicola. 1995. *Lucy's Picture*. New York: Dial.

Mora, Pat. 1997. *Tomas and the Library Lady*. New York: Knopf.

Moss, Marissa. 1995. *Amelia's Notebook*. Singapore: Pleasant Company.

———. 1998. *Rachel's Journal*. San Diego: Harcourt Brace.

———. 1999a. *Emma's Journal*. San Diego: Harcourt Brace.

———. 1999b. *True Heart*. San Diego: Harcourt Brace.

Murphy, Claire Rudolf, and Jane Haigh. 1999. *Children of the Gold Rush*. Boulder, CO: Roberts Rinehart.

Murphy, Jim. 1990. *The Boys' War*. New York: Clarion.

———. 1995. *The Great Fire*. New York: Scholastic.

———. 1996. *A Young Patriot: The American Revolution as Experienced by One Boy*. New York: Clarion.

Murphy, Nora. 1997. *A Hmong Family*. Minneapolis: Lerner.

Murray, Peter. 1994. *The Space Shuttle*. Chicago: Child's World (Encyclopedia Britannica).

Myers, Walter Dean. 1998. *Angel to Angel*. New York: HarperCollins.

Navasky, Bruno, ed. 1993. *Festival in My Heart: Poems by Japanese Children*. New York: Harry N. Abrams.

Nivola, Claire. 1997. *Elisabeth*. New York: Farrar, Straus, Giroux.

Nofi, Albert. Comp. 1995. *A Civil War Journal*. New York: Galahad Books.

Nordstrum, Ursula. 1998. *Dear Genius: The Letters of Ursula Nordstrum*. New York: HarperCollins.

Norworth, Jack. 1999. *Take Me Out to the Ball Game*. New York: Aladdin.

Notorious Americans and Their Times Series. 1999. Woodbridge, CT: Blackbirch Press.

O'Brien, Tim. 1989. *The Things They Carried: A Work of Fiction*. New York: Broadway Books.

O'Connor, Karen. 1996. *A Kurdish Family*. Minneapolis: Lerner.

Ondaatje, Michael. 1992. *The English Patient*. New York: Vintage Books.

Oppenheim, Shulamith. 1992. *The Lily Cupboard*. New York: Harper and Row.

Orgill, Roxane. 1997. *If I Only Had a Horn*. Boston: Houghton Mifflin.

Osbourne, Mary Pope. 1998. *Standing in the Light: The Captive Diary of Catharine Carey Logan*. New York: Scholastic.

Palincsar, A. S., and A. L. Brown. 1984. "Reciprocal Teaching of Comprehension-Fostering and Monitoring Activities." *Cognition and Instruction* 1: 117–175.

Paris, S. G., M. Y. Lipson, and K. K. Wixon. 1983. "Becoming a Strategic Reader." *Contemporary Educational Psychology* 8: 293–316.

Parish, Peggy. 1995. *Play Ball, Amelia Bedelia*. New York: Harper Trophy.

Park, Frances, and Ginger Park. 1998. *My Freedom Trip: A Child's Escape from North Korea*. Honesdale, PA: Boyds Mills Press.

Parker, Nancy Winslow. 1998. *Locks, Crocs, and Skeeters: The Story of the Panama Canal*. New York: Philomel.

Partridge, Elizabeth. 1998. *Restless Spirit: The Life and Work of Dorothea Lange*. New York: Viking.

Paterson, Katherine. 1977. *Bridge to Terabithia*. New York: Crowell.

———. 1995. *A Sense of Wonder: On Reading and Writing Books for Children*. New York: Penguin.

Peacock, Louise. 1998. *Crossing the Delaware: A History in Many Voices*. New York: Simon and Schuster.

Pearson, P. David. 1995. Personal Interview.

Pearson, P. David, and M. C. Gallagher. 1983. "The Instruction of Reading Comprehension." *Contemporary Educational Psychology* 8: 317–344.

Pearson, P. David, J. A. Dole, G. G. Duffy, and L. R. Roehler. 1992. "Developing Expertise in Reading Comprehension: What Should Be Taught and How Should It Be Taught?" In *What Research Has to Say to the Teacher of Reading*, ed. J. Farstup and S. J. Samuels, 2nd ed. Newark, DE: International Reading Association.

Pennac, Daniel. 1999. *Better than Life*. York, ME: Stenhouse.

Perkins, David. 1992. *Smart Schools: Better Thinking and Learning for Every Child*. New York: Free Press.

Perspectives on History Series. 1991+. Carlisle, MA: Discovery Enterprises.

Peters, Russell M. 1992. *Clambake: A Wampanoag Tradition*. Minneapolis: Lerner.

Philip, Neil, ed. 1997. *In a Sacred Manner I Live: Native American Wisdom*. New York: Clarion.

Pinker, Steven. 1997. *How the Mind Works.* New York: W. W. Norton.

Pinkney, Andrea Davis. 1996. *Bill Pickett: Rodeo-Ridin' Cowboy.* San Diego: Harcourt Brace.

———. 1998. *Duke Ellington: The Piano Prince and His Orchestra.* New York: Hyperion.

Pinkney, Brian. 1994. *Dear Benjamin Banneker.* San Diego: Harcourt Brace Jovanovich.

Plimpton, George. 1988. *Writers at Work.* Eighth Series. New York: Penguin.

Polacco, Patricia. 1988. *The Keeping Quilt.* New York: Simon and Schuster.

———. 1991. *Some Birthday!* New York: Simon and Schuster.

———. 1992a. *Chicken Sunday.* New York: Putnam and Grosset.

———. 1992b. *Mrs. Katz and Tush.* New York: Bantam.

———. 1993. *The Bee Tree.* New York: Philomel.

———. 1994a. *My Rotten Red-Headed Older Brother.* New York: Simon and Schuster.

———. 1994b. *Pink and Say.* New York: Philomel.

———. 1996. *Aunt Chip and the Great Cripple Creek Dam Affair.* New York: Philomel.

———. 1998a. *Mrs Mack.* New York: Philomel.

———. 1998b. *Thank You, Mr. Falker.* New York: Philomel.

Pomerantz, Charlotte. 1989. *The Chalk Doll.* New York: Lippincott.

Proulx, E. Annie. 1993. *The Shipping News.* New York: Charles Scribner.

Quindlen, Anna. 1998. *How Reading Changed My Life.* New York: Ballantine Books.

Rabin, Straton. 1994. *Casey Over There.* San Diego: Harcourt Brace.

Rahaman, Vashanti. 1997. *Read for Me, Mama.* Honesdale, PA: Boyds Mills Press.

Raschka, Chris. 1992. *Charlie Parker Played Be Bop.* New York: Orchard Books.

Raven, Margot Theis. 1999. *Angels in the Dust.* New York: Troll.

Ray, Delia. 1991. *Behind the Blue and Gray: The Soldier's Life in the Civil War.* New York: Penguin.

Rief, Linda. 1992. *Seeking Diversity: Language Arts with Adolescents.* Portsmouth, NH: Heinemann.

Riggio, Anita. 1997. *Secret Signs.* Honesdale, PA: Boyds Mills Press.

Ringgold, Faith. 1992. *Aunt Harriet and the Underground Railroad in the Sky.* New York: Crown.

———. 1993. *Dinner at Aunt Connie's House.* New York: Hyperion.

Rochelle, Belinda. 1997. *Witnesses to Freedom.* New York: Puffin.

Rochman, Hazel, and Darlene McCampbell. 1997. *Leaving Home.* New York: HarperCollins.

Roessel, Monty. 1995. *Songs from the Loom.* Minneapolis: Lerner.

Rose, Deborah Lee. 1990. *The People Who Hugged the Trees.* Niwot, CO: Roberts Rinehart.

Rosen, Michael. 1992. *Home.* New York: HarperCollins.

Roy, Arundhati. 1997. *The God of Small Things.* New York: Random House.

Rudloe, Jack, and Anne Rudloe. 1994. "Sea Turtles in a Race for Survival." *National Geographic Magazine* 185: 94–121.

Rylant, Cynthia. 1982. *When I Was Young in the Mountains.* New York: Dutton.

———. 1984. *Waiting to Waltz: A Childhood.* New York: Simon and Schuster.

———. 1985a. *Every Living Thing.* New York: Aladdin Books.

———. 1985b. *The Relatives Came.* New York: Scholastic.

———. 1987. *Birthday Presents.* New York: Orchard Books.

———. 1988. *All I See.* New York: Orchard Books.

———. 1989. *Miss Maggie.* New York: Orchard Books.

———. 1992. *An Angel for Solomon Singer.* New York: Orchard Books.

———. 1994. *Something Permanent.* San Diego: Harcourt Brace.

———. 1995. *The Van Gogh Cafe.* San Diego: Harcourt Brace.

———. 1997. *The Blue Hill Meadows.* San Diego: Harcourt Brace.

San Souci, Robert. 1997. *A Weave of Words.* New York: Orchard Books.

Say, Allen. 1988. *A River Dream.* Boston: Houghton Mifflin.

———. 1993. *Grandfather's Journey.* Boston: Houghton Mifflin.

———. 1999. *Tea with Milk.* Boston: Houghton Mifflin.

Schaefer, Carol Lexa. 1996. *The Squiggle.* New York: Crown.

Schertle, Alice. 1999. *A Lucky Thing.* San Diego: Harcourt Brace.

Schmidt, Cynthia. 1984. *Colorado Grassroots.* Phoenix, AZ: Cloud Publishing.

Schroeder, Alan. 1996. *Minty: A Story of Young Harriet Tubman.* New York: Dial.

Seuss, Dr. 1954. *If I Ran the Zoo.* New York: Random House.

———. 1991. *The 500 Hats of Bartholomew Cubbins.* New York: Random House.

Sewell, Anna. 1941. *Black Beauty.* New York: Dodd, Mead.

Seymour, Isobel. 1997. *I Am Mexican American.* Our American Family Series. New York: Rosen.

Shaara, Michael. 1974. *The Killer Angels.* New York: Ballantine Books.

Shange, Ntozake. 1994. *I Live in Music.* New York: Welcome Enterprises.

Shea, Pegi Deitz. 1995. *The Whispering Cloth.* Honesdale, PA: Boyds Mills Press.

Shenk, David. 1997. *Data Smog: Surviving the Information Glut.* New York: Harper Edge.

"Should Cities Sue Gunmakers?" 1999. *Junior Scholastic* 101 (February 8): 5.

Simon, Seymour. 1985. *Saturn.* New York: Morrow.

———. 1986. *The Sun.* New York: Mulberry.

———. 1993. *Autumn Across America.* New York: Hyperion.

———. 1998. *Destination: Jupiter.* New York: Morrow.

Simon, Seymour, ed. 1995. *Star Walk.* New York: Morrow.

Sis, Peter. 1995. *Starry Messenger.* New York: Farrar, Straus, Giroux.

———. 1998. *Tibet: Through the Red Box.* New York: Farrar, Straus, Giroux.

Sisulu, Elinor Batezat. 1996. *The Day Gogo Went to Vote: South Africa, April 1994.* Boston: Little, Brown.

Sneve, Virgina Driving Hawk. 1989. *Dancing Teepees.* New York: Holiday House.

———. 1993. *The Navajos.* New York: Holiday House.

———. 1995a. *The Hopis.* New York: Holiday House.

———. 1995b. *The Iroquois.* New York: Holiday House.

———. 1996. *The Cherokees.* New York: Holiday House.

Sobel, Dava, and William J. H. Andrewes. 1998. *The Illustrated Longitude: The True Story of a Lone Genius Who Solved the Greatest Scientific Problem of His Time.* New York: Walker.

Sorenson, Henri. 1995. *New Hope.* New York: Lothrop, Lee and Shepard.

Soto, Gary. 1991. *A Summer Life.* New York: Dell.

———. 1992. *Neighborhood Odes.* San Diego: Harcourt Brace.

———. 1993. *Too Many Tamales*. New York: Putnam and Grosset.

Spivak, Dawnine. 1997. *Grass Sandals: The Travels of Basho*. New York: Atheneum.

Stadler, John. 1985. *Hooray for Snail*. New York: Harper Trophy.

Stamberg, Susan. 1993. *Talk: NPR's Susan Stamberg Considers All Things*. New York: Random House.

Stanley, Diane. 1983. *The Conversation Club*. New York: Aladdin Books.

———. 1990. *Good Queen Bess*. New York: Macmillan.

———. 1992. *The Bard of Avon*. New York: Morrow.

———. 1996. *Leonardo da Vinci*. New York: Morrow.

———. 1998. *Joan of Arc*. New York: Morrow.

Stanley, Jerry. 1992. *Children of the Dust Bowl*. New York: Crown.

Steig, William. 1969. *Sylvester and the Magic Pebble*. New York: Trumpet Club.

———. 1971. *Amos and Boris*. New York: Farrar, Straus, Giroux.

———. 1976. *The Amazing Bone*. New York: Farrar, Straus, Giroux.

———. 1980. *Gorky Rises*. New York: Farrar, Straus, Giroux.

———. 1982. *Doctor DeSoto*. New York: Scholastic.

———. 1985. *Solomon and the Rusty Nail*. New York: Farrar, Straus, Giroux.

———. 1986. *Brave Irene*. New York: Farrar, Straus, Giroux.

Stein, R. Conrad. 1993. *The Trail of Tears*. Chicago: Children's Press.

Stelson, Caren Barzelay. 1988. *Safari*. Minneapolis: Carolrhoda.

Stewart, Sarah. 1995. *The Library*. New York: Farrar, Straus, Giroux.

Strunk, William J., and E. B. White. 1999. *The Elements of Style*. 4th ed. New York: Allyn and Bacon.

Suskind, Ron. 1998. *A Hope in the Unseen: An American Odyssey from the Inner City to the Ivy League*. New York: Broadway Books.

Swanson, Diane. 1998. *Animals Eat the Weirdest Things*. Vancouver, BC: Whitecap Books.

Swinburn, Stephen. 1999. *Safe, Snug, and Warm*. San Diego: Gulliver Books.

Tanaka, Shelley. 1997. *The Buried City of Pompeii*. New York: Hyperion/Madison.

Thaher, Ernest Lawrence. 1995. *Casey at the Bat*. New York: Aladdin.

Thomas, Joyce Carol. 1993. *Brown Honey in Broomwheat Tea*. New York: HarperCollins.

Trelease, Jim. 1989. *The New Read Aloud Handbook*. New York: Viking Penguin.

Tsuchiya, Yukio. 1988. *Faithful Elephants: A True Story of Animals, People, and War*. Boston: Houghton Mifflin.

Tunnell, Michael O., and George W. Chilcoat. 1996. *The Children of Topaz: The Story of a Japanese-American Internment Camp*. New York: Holiday House.

Turbak, Gary. 1993. *Survivors in the Shadows*. Flagstaff, AZ: Northland.

Turner, Ann. 1987. *Nettie's Trip South*. New York: Aladdin Books.

———. 1992. *Katie's Trunk*. New York: Simon and Schuster.

———. 1999. *The Girl Who Chased Away Sorrow: The Diary of Sarah Nita, a Navajo Girl*. New York: Scholastic.

Uchida, Yoshiko. 1993. *The Bracelet*. New York: Philomel.

Ueland, Brenda. 1987. *If You Want to Write*. 2nd ed. Saint Paul: Graywolf Press.

The Unhuggables. 1988. Washington, DC: National Wildlife Federation.

Van Allsburg, Chris. 1979. *The Garden of Abdul Gasazi*. Boston: Houghton Mifflin.

———. 1983. *The Wreck of the Zephyr.* Boston: Houghton Mifflin.

———. 1984. *The Mysteries of Harris Burdick.* Boston: Houghton Mifflin.

———. 1985. *Jumanji.* Boston: Houghton Mifflin.

———. 1986. *The Stranger.* Boston: Houghton Mifflin.

———. 1991. *The Wretched Stone.* Boston: Houghton Mifflin.

Van der Rol, Ruud, and Rian Verhoeven. 1993. *Anne Frank: Beyond the Diary.* New York: Penguin.

Van Leeuwen, Jean. 1992. *Going West.* New York: Dial.

———. 1998. *Nothing Here But Trees.* New York: Dial.

Viorst, Judith. 1971. *The Tenth Good Thing About Barney.* New York: Aladdin Books.

———. 1972. *Alexander and the Terrible, Horrible, No Good, Very Bad Day.* New York: Scholastic.

———. 1974. *Rosie and Michael.* New York: Aladdin Books.

———. 1990. *Earrings.* New York: Trumpet Club.

Vogt, Gregory. 1999. Explore Space Series. Mankato, MN: Bridgestone Books.

Volavkova, Hana, ed. 1993. *I Never Saw Another Butterfly: Children's Drawings and Poems from Terezin Concentration Camp, 1942–1944.* 2nd ed. New York: Schocken Books.

Waber, Bernard. 1972. *Ira Sleeps Over.* Boston: Houghton Mifflin.

Ward, Geoffrey, Ken Burns, with Jim O'Connor. 1994. *Shadow Ball: The History of the Negro Leagues.* Baseball, the American Epic series. New York: Knopf.

Ward, Geoffrey, Ken Burns, with S. A. Kramer. 1994. *25 Great Moments.* Baseball, the American Epic series. New York: Knopf.

Ward, Geoffrey, Ken Burns, with Robert Walker. 1994. *Who Invented the Game?* Baseball, the American Epic series. New York: Knopf.

Warren, Andrea. 1996. *Orphan Train Rider: One Boy's True Story.* Boston: Houghton Mifflin.

Waters, Kate. 1989. *Sarah Morton's Day: A Day in the Life of a Pilgrim Girl.* New York: Scholastic.

———. 1991. *Tapenum's Day: A Wampanoag Indian Boy in Pilgrim Times.* New York: Scholastic.

———. 1993. *Samuel Eaton's Day: A Day in the Life of a Pilgrim Boy.* New York: Scholastic.

Watson, James D. 1991. *The Double Helix: A Personal Account of the Discovery of the Structure of DNA.* New York: New American Library.

Webster's New World Dictionary. 1991. New York: Simon and Schuster.

Weiss, George David, and Bob Thiele. 1995. *What a Wonderful World.* New York: Simon and Schuster.

Welty, Eudora. 1983. *One Writer's Beginnings.* Cambridge, MA: Harvard University Press.

Westridge Young Writers Workshop. 1997. *Kids Explore Kids Who Make a Difference.* Santa Fe, NM: John Muir Publications.

White, E. B. 1952. *Charlotte's Web.* New York: Harper and Row.

Whitman, Sylvia. 1993. *V Is for Victory: The American Home Front During World War II.* Minneapolis: Lerner.

Wick, Walter. 1997. *A Drop of Water: A Book of Science and Wonder.* New York: Scholastic.

Wiesel, Elie. 1982. *Night*. New York: Bantam.

Wiesner, David. 1988. *Free Fall*. New York: Lothrop, Lee and Shepard.

———. 1992. *June 29, 1999*. New York: Clarion.

Wilkes, Sybella. 1994. *One Day We Had to Run*. Brookfield, CT: Millbrook Press.

Williams, Terry Tempest. 1992. *Refuge: An Unnatural History of Family and Place*. New York: Vintage.

Wills, Garry. 1992. *Lincoln at Gettysburg: The Words That Remade America*. New York: Simon and Schuster.

———. 1994. *Certain Trumpets: The Call of Leaders*. New York: Simon and Schuster.

Winnick, Karen. 1997. *Mr. Lincoln's Whiskers*. Honesdale, PA: Boyds Mills Press.

Winter, Jeanette. 1988. *Follow the Drinking Gourd*. New York: Trumpet.

———. 1991. *Diego*. New York: Knopf.

———. 1996. *Josefina*. San Diego: Harcourt Brace.

———. 1998. *My Name Is Georgia*. San Diego: Harcourt Brace.

———. 1999. *Sebastian: A Book About Bach*. San Diego: Harcourt Brace.

Wollard, Kathy. 1993. *How Come?* New York: Workman.

Worth, Valerie. 1987. *All the Small Poems*. New York: Farrar, Straus, Giroux.

Wright, Alexandra. 1992. *Will We Miss Them?: Endangered Species*. Watertown, MA: Charlesbridge.

Wright, Courtni C. 1994. *Journey to Freedom: A Story of the Underground Railroad*. New York: Holiday House.

Wright-Frierson, Virginia. 1996. *A Desert Scrapbook: Dawn to Dusk in the Sonoran Desert*. New York: Simon and Schuster.

———. 1998. *An Island Scrapbook: Dawn to Dusk on a Barrier Reef*. New York: Simon and Schuster.

Yashima, Taro. 1983. *Crow Boy*. New York: Puffin.

Yildirim, Eljay. 1997. *Aunty Dot's Incredible Adventure Atlas*. Westport, CT: Reader's Digest.

Yolen, Jane. 1990. *The Devil's Arithmetic*. New York: Puffin.

———. 1991. *All the Secrets of the World*. Boston: Little, Brown.

———. 1992a. *Encounter*. San Diego: Harcourt Brace.

———. 1992b. *Letting Swift River Go*. Boston: Little, Brown.

———. 1994. *Granddad Bill's Song*. New York: Putnam and Grosset.

Yurkovic, Diane Short. 1998. *Meet Me at the Water Hole*. Denver, CO: Shortland Publications.

Zhensun, Zheng, and Alice Low. 1991. *A Young Painter: The Life and Paintings of Wang Yani*. New York: Scholastic.

Zinsser, William. 1976. *On Writing Well*. New York: HarperCollins.

Zolotow, Charlotte. 1972. *William's Doll*. New York: HarperCollins.

———. 1992. *The Seashore Book*. New York: HarperCollins.

———. 1993. *Snippets*. New York: HarperCollins.